The Imagination
of an Insurrection

Dublin, Easter 1916

A Study of an Ideological Movement

WILLIAM IRWIN THOMPSON

THE LINDISFARNE PRESS
West Stockbridge, Massachusetts

The author and publisher gratefully acknowledge
Mr. and Mrs. Amyas Ames
for their support and encouragement through the years,
and especially for their help in making this edition possible.

This book was originally published by Oxford University Press in 1967 and
is here reprinted by arrangement.

This edition published 1982 for The Lindisfarne Association by
The Lindisfarne Press, R.D. 2, West Stockbridge, Massachusetts 01266.

ISBN: 0-940262-02-9

By way of a dedication I would like to blame this book
on my mother (*Hibernis ipsis Hiberniores*)
and on Professor Robert Martin Adams who, at a
creaking wooden bridge, played billy goat to a few trolls.

PREFACE TO THE 1982 EDITION

To read a work in one's forties that one has written in one's twenties provides an interesting opportunity to consider one's life work at the halfway point. When I was at work on the manuscript of this book in 1965, the streets of Watts in Los Angeles were on fire with insurrection and national guard troops were machine-gunning civilians to protect the peace. When I was rereading this book to write this preface, Israeli jets were bombing civilians in Tyre, Sidon, and Beirut to smash the insurrections of the Palestinians. The plight of small, nationless peoples and the eruption of myth into history have not vanished into some storied past in our age of microchips and multinational corporations. The wisdom of A.E.'s *The Interpreters* still stands; in the *enantiodromias* of conflict we do become what we hate. What other nations were able to inflict upon the Jews, the Israelis are now able to inflict upon the Palestinians. The contradictions of our global technological civilization remain very much what they were when A.E. and Yeats worked to change the direction of the industrial British Empire.

Inspired by A.E. and Yeats in 1962, I had hoped to work to change the direction of scholarship. Appalled by the bureaucratic scholarship of the academic specialists, I wished to achieve a more integral vision of culture in the hope that this kind of intellectual activity could lead to new and more harmonious relationships between mind and spirit, society and art. If I had been simply an anthropologist, this book would have been only a study of a nativistic movement. If I had simply been an historian, this book would have been only a study of the insurrection and its socioeconomic causes. If I had been simply a literary critic, this book would have been only a study of the influence of Ferguson and O'Grady on the poetry of Yeats. Against the functionalism of the anthropologists, the economic-determinism of the historians, and the formalism of the New Critics, I wanted to put anthropology, history, and literary criticism together in a new form of cultural history. The book was meant to be a pilot study of the phenomenology of an ideological movement that was inseparably a nativistic movement, a political revolution, and a literary renaissance.

Obviously, only a young man in his twenties at work on his first book could be naive enough to think that the world of the modern university could be changed that quickly. In point of fact, the movements that I was seeking to counter have grown stronger and are now dominant. Literary criticism has moved from the formalism of the New Critics to the formalism of the post-structuralists, and, from the influence of linguistics, "Eng. Lit." is struggling to become a science. The shift from the humanities to behavioral science has been completed in departments of philosophy, history, and literature. The traditional humanities, with their Platonic concern for the Good, the True, and the Beautiful, have become like a tiny people caught in the path of technological development. The humanities, even as I knew them as an under-graduate in the early sixties, are dead. Holdout places like Lindisfarne cannot reverse this state, anymore than the first Lindisfarne could reverse the dominance of the Roman Imperial Church. Like the Ghost Dance of the American Indians against the railroads, small traditional groups can only become noble witnesses to their truth to join the long historical line of those who have always opposed the mechanization of the human spirit.

In spite of Charles Dickens and William Morris, or A.E. and Yeats, or E.F. Schumacher and Gregory Bateson, the mechanization of human culture has not been stopped. Humanity, through some strange and inscrutable inner compulsion, is hurtling itself with all its mass and momentum toward some huge technological climax. Let whatever records heaven keeps show that not all of humanity was of a piece before it went to pieces.

W.I.T.

Lindisfarne Mountain Retreat
June, 1982

PREFACE

When President Kennedy invited Robert Frost to read a poem at his inauguration, he was unconsciously following an ancient Irish tradition that demanded the presence of the poet at the coronation of the High King. Many were surprised at this untraditional and foreign gesture; some were pleased, and still others wondered who was doing the favor for whom. Poetry, we think in our American way, is fine in its place and, perhaps, useful in lending class to politics, but we are not fooled for all that. Nevertheless the invitations to poets continued, and the President came to joke about the White House that was becoming "a café for intellectuals." Robert Lowell received an invitation to one of those now vanished brilliant evenings, and after a night of elegance, discovered in the next morning's papers that during the night the Seventh Fleet had taken up a new position. "... you had the funny feeling of how unimportant the artist really was: that this was sort of window dressing and that the real government was somewhere else, and that something much closer to the Pentagon was really ruling the country. And maybe this is how it must be." [1] Very few Americans would think, even for a minute, that the artist had any *real* importance, and, therefore, they would be startled by the strange words of another country's aged poet, W. B. Yeats.

> All that I have said and done
> Now that I am old and ill
> Turns into a question till
> I lie awake night after night,
> And never get the answers right.
> Did that play of mine send out
> Certain men the English shot?

It is now over a hundred years since that Irish poet was born, and for the centenary celebration Dublin's Abbey Theatre put on "that play," that old museum piece, *Cathleen ni Houlihan*. One goes to such a thing with the common prejudice that, of course, the plays of Yeats are not really drama, and that Yeats's own question about the play is merely another example of his notorious self-dramatization. But the outbreak of a sudden and uneasy coughing from those old enough to remember or have heard, and an amazement at the power the play exerted on one who was too young and too American to be anything but superficially involved, answered Yeats's question. It did.

But how could it? What does a work of imagination counted out in syllables have to do with lives counted down by the leader of a firing squad? If the Irish patriot, Padraic Pearse, marched to revolution in the footsteps of the ancient legendary hero, Cuchulain:

> Who thought Cuchulain till it seemed
> He stood where they had stood?

We know from our literary histories that there was a movement called the Irish Literary Renaissance, and that Yeats was at its head. We know from our political histories that there is now a Republic of Ireland because of a nationalistic movement that,

[1] A. Alvarez, "A Talk with Robert Lowell," *Encounter*, XXIV (1965), 40.

militarily, began with the insurrection of Easter Week, 1916. But what do these two movements have to do with one another?

In attempting to study this encounter between literature and revolution, one is forced to wonder about the commonsense notions of historical reality, for unless the student is willing to reduce with glib facility one thing in favor of something else, he soon realizes that what he is studying is not merely a literary insurrection, but the role of imagination in history. Such a realization, to say the least, gives one pause. But if it is only a pause, and the student does again begin to move, it will be because he believes that he has found at least one possible direction for his own movement in the face of the impossible.

Because I came to history with literary eyes, I could not help seeing history in the terms and shapes of imaginative experience. Thus Movement, Myth, and Image came to be the way in which the nature of the insurrection appeared to me. This method of analyzing a historical event as if it were a work of art is not altogether as inappropriate as it might seem when the historical event happens to be a revolution. The Irish revolutionaries lived as if they were in a work of art, and this inability to tell the difference between sober reality and the realm of imagination is perhaps one very important characteristic of a revolutionary. The tragedy of actuality comes from the fact that when, in a revolution, history is made momentarily into a work of art, human beings become the material that must be ordered, molded, or twisted into shape. Therefore I feel that when one tries to come to terms with revolution, the terms are at hand in the familiar realm of literature. Of course when one is specifically concerned with the imagination of an event, he cannot avoid literary criticism; for it is not enough to invoke the supremacy of fact and catalogue the names of the men who were in each building and then dismiss "the poetic ambience" of the insurrection as mere legend based on the fact that three of the executed sixteen men happened to be poets. The reality of Easter Week spilled over the brimful minds of the patriots; we do not sense that fullness unless we re-achieve their sense of anticipation, of moment, of myth.

Over and over again one is struck by a sense of drama. Suddenly an individual awakens to his own moment in the longer movement of history. In the excitement of that moment History is seen to announce itself to the individual. Maud Gonne, writing her revolutionary memoirs in the genre of a girls' adventure novel, sees Cathleen ní Houlihan singling her out as one of the stones that will support her as she moves across the treacherous bog of time.[2] Such romantic nonsense can become terribly real, for in these imaginings, something happens to the personality, and a new coherence given to a formerly broken self allows the revolutionary to entertain the idea of death. If the revolutionary succeeds in seizing his moment, and does not let it slip by, he may, from an external point of view, achieve nothing more than a gesture, an image. Certainly the deaths of the poets before the firing squad were all gesture, all image. But the important point for any tough-minded view of history is that it is precisely this gesture that lingers as a social, cultural, and political reality. The consequences of an event take place in the mind, and the mind holds on best to images.

It is from this perspective that I see the Rising as a movement led by myth-possessed men who willingly perish into images, "that yet / Fresh images beget." In discussing the aftermath of the insurrection in the work of the Irish writers, I have considered only Yeats, A.E., and O'Casey because these three were most intimately involved with that moment of history, and, when taken together, these three express a full range of experience. A.E. (George William Russell, a mystic and poet) has the best sense of the mystique of the movement and its event; Yeats understands the more complicated tragic life of an image, and O'Casey sees best the actual nature of the ordinary human beings who make up the stuff of history. The list of writers could be lengthened, for I have in no way attempted to write a survey of all the literary images of the insurrection. I have not included James Stephens's rather standard

2 Maud Gonne, *A Servant of the Queen* (Dublin, 1950).

elegy or Liam O'Flaherty's or Iris Murdoch's novels: all are in increasing degrees artistic statements after the fact. I suppose that it is merely a matter of taste that I preferred a tightly articulated book to a loosely extended survey, but had I included one more than the major three, I felt that I would have to include them all, even Bernard Shaw's *Saint Joan*, for Padraic Pearse and the British Empire are symbolized in that conflict between nationalistic mysticism and Christendom. However the most compelling reason for staying with Yeats, A.E., and O'Casey is that the movement from *mystique* to tragedy to naturalism and its disappointment with myth seems to reflect the actual movement of Irish history before and after 1916.

This book is, therefore, not precisely a work of literary criticism, and not precisely a work of history, but a cultural study of the one ideological movement that contains the literature and the revolution, the images and the events.

WILLIAM I. THOMPSON

Cambridge, Massachusetts
February 1967

CONTENTS

PART ONE

THE MOVEMENT TOWARD THE EVENT

CHAPTER ONE

THE PAST RECAPTURED

Nothing ever begins where one thinks it should. The child learns that his father had a father, and then there's no stopping. Historical movements are no different: for every famous beginning there are a dozen other obscure beginnings that preceded it. Yeats is the prominent figure of the movement known as the Irish Literary Renaissance, but Yeats merely led the national movement into international recognition; he did not begin it. What was reborn in the Irish Renaissance was the Irish past, but if one looks for a beginning of that interest in the past, he will end up in the "dark backward and abysm of time."

Things do change, however. Gradually and almost unnoticeably they emerge into the more conspicuous existence that we call a beginning. The idea of a movement, with a start and finish, is an intellectual convenience we cannot do without, but like all convenient things, it is a great oversimplification. When we say that something began in such a year, we often mean that a greater number of people paid attention to it in that year than in the previous one. Clearly Ireland has always had a past, and there have always been Irishmen interested in it; but there have also been times when men have tried to forget the past, and have left it for their grandchildren to return in peace to what they themselves left in pain.

There was Elizabethan England. The men of that time wished to forget the Wars of the Roses, the crude, vulgar days of baronial strife. The story of Elizabethan England is one of zest for the present, for the new Italian clothes, the new refinement, the new literature, and the New World. The land was coming to consciousness of itself in a city; civilization and elegance were the exciting values of the time. But excitements cannot endure forever, and even civilizations are subject to boredom and changes of interest. A century and a half would make any nation bored with civilization and elegance. By the middle of the eighteenth century a gentleman seated in a rococo drawing room might look out of the window at some wild and rugged prospect and think of the country as a place holding some values the city had overlooked. In a quiet mood, he might dream fondly of the good old days. He would dream, not of civilization, but of a simple community; not of elegance, but of energy; not of the city, but of the moor or glen. In Tudor days the country folk were moving into the city and doing their best to become refined. The country held no romance for them, but painful memories of drudgery. The myth of the pastoral landscape where the shepherd sweetly pipes to his innocent lass is the dream of a busy man of city affairs. To an eighteenth-century London gentleman, the descriptive poetry of primitive places, the meditations among ruins, the Norse and bardic odes of Gray, and most sensationally of all, the lays of Ossian by James Macpherson, offered a new mode of consciousness. We have since named this mode romanticism, and the Irish Literary Renaissance has its beginnings in this larger movement.

The first scholar to reach into the Celtic past was James Macpherson, but by a quirk of Celtic contrariness this scholar's Scottish appropriation of Irish materials was published in Dublin.[1]

1 James Macpherson, *Temora, An Ancient Epic Poem* (Dublin, 1763).

Macpherson had published fragments of Highland poetry in 1760, but in his publications of 1762 and 1763 he tried to convince the guardians of neoclassical taste that epic poems had been written in Scotland in the third century. Dr. Johnson, who made a journey to the western islands of Scotland, was not convinced, but the more romantic Goethe was only too willing to believe in an ancient and heroic Northern literature; and in translating the poems, Goethe created an enthusiasm among students of the time for literature that bore a closer ancestral relation to the Germans than did the famous works of the Romans and Greeks. In the nineteenth century these students, turned philologists, were to take the lead in the study of the Celtic past. The Irish, however, did not wait a century to respond to Macpherson's insulting remarks.

While some doubt the authenticity of the composition of Ossian, others strenuously endeavour to appropriate them to the Irish nation.[2]

Scottish scholars like the Reverend Hugh Blair or David Hume were apt to dismiss the Irish claim to a history older than Christendom, for the Irish were generally regarded as a savage and rebellious people who knew nothing of civilization until they were conquered by the Normans.[3] Hume's sentence on the case was considered final.

The Irish, from the beginning of time, had been buried in the most profound barbarism and ignorance; and as they were never conquered or even invaded by the Romans, from whom all the western world derived its civility, they continued still in the most rude state of society, and were distinguished only by those vices, to which human nature, not tamed by education nor restrained by laws, is for ever subject.[4]

Readers in Great Britain were, of course, only too eager to believe this, and the Irish were not in a position to argue. And so when the Irish claimed Ossian for themselves, the British saw only further evidence of their thievish instincts. But unkind as Macpher-

2 Ibid. p. xxviii.
3 Rev. Hugh Blair, *A Critical Dissertation on the Poems of Ossian* (Dublin, 1765).
4 David Hume, *History of Great Britain*, I (London, 1767), p. 454.

son was, the Irish are in his debt, for his embellished version of the detritus of Irish sagas that he encountered in the Highlands started the gradual landslide of Celtic materials. Soon after the poem's publication, newly founded Ossianic societies rediscovered the imaginary island of Finn, Oisin, and Cuchulain.

That the insult of Macpherson stirred the Irish into looking into their own past is clearly seen in the career of Sylvester O'Halloran. Even while he was working on a history, O'Halloran took time out to issue a shorter plea for the establishment of a foundation devoted to the preservation of the ancient Irish annals. The tone of his plea reveals the incentive behind his scholarship.

Even in these modern days of erudition and curiosity, we have seen such monstrous accounts of this country and people, as are truly astounding.... Since then we have had further attempts on our History and Annals in Macpherson's famous poems.[5]

O'Halloran was angered by the scholarship of the Scots, but he was himself no mere provincial Irishman incensed by the slurs of rival Celts. Though a physician in Limerick, he had studied medicine on the Continent, and in his medical career published treatises on glaucoma and gangrene, and helped found the Royal College of Surgeons. A gentleman of the Enlightenment, O'Halloran was impressed with the effect learned societies could have in the advancement of knowledge. With this effect in mind, he campaigned for the establishment of an academy devoted to the study and preservation of Irish antiquities, and to this study he contributed by publishing Irish histories of his own in 1772 and 1778. In the earlier history, O'Halloran included an appendix devoted to a refutation of Macpherson's claims.[6] The doctor's work was successful, for in 1785 the Royal Irish Academy was founded to further the study of science, polite literature, and antiquities, and the doctor now became Sylvester O'Halloran, M.R.I.A.

In the following year one of the charter members of the Acad-

5 Sylvester O'Halloran, *Insula Sacra* (Limerick, 1770), p. ii.
6 Sylvester O'Halloran, *An Introduction to the Study of the History and Antiquities of Ireland* (Dublin, 1772).

emy, Charles Vallancey, published his *Vindication of the Ancient History of Ireland.* General Vallancey, like Dr. O'Halloran, was a gentleman, but unlike the man of science, the general was a man of the world; therefore, his interests were more apt to drift toward the exotic and dilettantish. Vallancey was interested in comparing Irish, Phoenician, and Hindustani words, and, on the basis of early Christian monuments, he elaborated a theory about Ireland in a Buddhist, pre-Christian era. Even in its early days the Academy was showing that learned societies can move in two directions in the advancement of knowledge. The British cult of the amateur had made its appearance in Irish scholarship, and for a hundred years to come it would continue to infuriate the Irish into redoubling their own efforts. Whether minuet or jig, the pace of Irish scholarship continued to quicken, and in 1789 Charlotte Brooke, with somewhat effusive apologies for leaving her pianoforte and needlepoint to take up the pen, published her very important *Reliques of Irish Poetry.* This volume was indeed a milestone, for here was a bilingual edition of the poems concerning the figures that were about to become legend once again: Cuchulain, and Deirdre, and Finn. Significantly, it was O'Halloran who wrote an introduction for the young lady's work.

When General Vallancey attempted to establish some relationship between Irish and Hindustani, he was, of course, groping in the dark toward the Indo-European hypothesis that was to be articulated in the later and more famous work of Jakob Grimm. The General was mistaken not in his hunch, but in his method and in his efforts to hinder more prosaic scholars in pursuing theories that were not sweeping embraces of universal history. Nevertheless much good can often come from crank notions and irresponsible methods; historically, a few proud sciences have had such humble origins. The Scots and the Irish had had their say, and now it was time for the Welsh to come forth. In 1831 a Welshman, James Prichard, published a work devoted to the study of the relationship between the Celts and the Eastern peoples, but this volume was dedicated to the German philologist, Grimm. Prichard's work

showed that the Welsh were as eager as the Irish to defend themselves from the attacks of the English. Prichard quotes a Mr.
Pinkerton as revealing the general attitude of the time concerning
the Celts.

The real Celtic is as remote from the Greek as the Hottentot from the
Lapponic.... The mythology of the Celtae resembled, in all probability,
that of the Hottentots, or others of the rudest savages, as the Celtae
anciently were, and are little better at present, being incapable of any
progress in society.[7]

This new tone of English vexation, so different from the Royal
patronage that had founded the Royal Irish Academy, was apparent, no doubt, because in 1798 the Irish had again rebelled against
the Crown and, what was far worse in the minds of the terror-
stricken British Establishment, had sought the aid of Revolutionary France. For a brief period it had seemed that Irish history and
poetry could be a matter of *belles-lettres,* but with a new rising to
prove the incorrigibility of the Irish, Irish history and poetry again
became a political matter. This did not hurt the Welsh, however,
and six years later, in 1837, another woman did for the Welsh
what Charlotte Brooke had done for the Irish, for in that year
Lady Charlotte Guest published the Welsh legends in the *Mabinogion.* It was to go through many editions and was influential in
creating the neo-medievalism of Tennyson and Morris.

Precisely because Irish literature had fallen from scholarship
into politics, the next advances in the study came from the Continent. In 1837 Adolphe Pictet published his *De l'affinité des lan-
gues celtiques avec le sanscrit,* and in 1838 Franz Bopp published
his *Über die celtischen Sprachen vom Gesichtspunkte der verglei-
chenden Sprachforschung.* This work was part of the great movement of Continental philology, for Bopp had published early
studies in 1816, which were followed by the more famous work
of Rasmus Rask in 1818 and Jakob Grimm in 1819. Whereas Vallancey had made rather unsystematic comparisons of Irish words
with similar words in Phoenician and Hindustani, the Germans

[7] James Prichard, *The Eastern Origin of the Celtic Nations* (Oxford, 1831), p. 21.

argued that systems rather than words should be compared. Irish
scholarship received an even more secure footing when Johann
Kaspar Zeuss began a study of the Celtic place names in his native
Bavaria and ended up writing the definitive *Grammatica Celtica*
in 1853.[8] If all this sounds like incredibly heavy Germanic scholarship, one should not be deceived into thinking it was all a dry
business.[9] The Germans were passionately interested in discovering the *Urmythologie* of the ancestral *Volk*. The ancient form of
a word was not merely a lexical unit; it was a relic of a time when
the heart ruled a body that lived outdoors, a relic of that exalted
time when the mind knew no French and the body was free of
silks. In Goethe's Ossian the Germans had a living incarnation of
the world view they were looking for.

The Germans were not alone in their romantic enthusiasms.
What had begun in the work of Macpherson and the bardic odes
of Gray became a general fashion in literary taste. The Scottish
poetry of Burns and Sir Walter Scott flowed upon the crest of a
new sensibility. Thomas Moore was becoming rich by singing his
Irish Melodies in the drawing rooms of ladies of fashion, and Lady
Morgan, authoress of the best seller, *The Wild Irish Girl*, was creating a sensation by appearing at parties in the imaginary native
dress of her characters. It was a time for effusions of sensitivity in
countless meditations among ruins, graveyard poems, and lays of
minstrels of forgotten kingdoms. Lady Morgan was quick to sense
the possibilities of the graveyard and ruin genre, and taking advantage of the instinctive desire of the wealthy to be accused, she
attempted to show the English that if they must weep over ruins,
they might weep over the ruins they had created.

I sat down on the tomb of the royal O'Connor, and plucked the weed
or blew away the thistle that waved there its lonely head. The sun was
setting in gloomy splendour, and the lofty angles of the Abbey-tower

8 See Francis Shaw, S.J., "The Background to the *Grammatica Celtica*," *Celtica*
III, Zeuss Memorial Volume, ed. Myles Dillon (Dublin, 1956).
9 Rudolph Thurneysen, "Why Do Germans Study Celtic Philology," *Studies:
An Irish Quarterly Review*, XIX (March 1930), 21-32.

alone caught the reflection of his dying beams, from the summits of the mountains where they still lingered.[10]

When the romantic's eye had tired of viewing the ruins of time, it might wander to take in the eternal hut of the peasant, to see that there in spite of the ravages of wars, the ancient, and therefore sacred, way of life was still preserved. And who could be certain that in a humble peasant the blood of a vanished king did not flow? The romantics were in the habit of climbing mountains and meditating upon the prospect, but the movement up for them always involved a movement down for someone else. As divinity no longer hedged a prince, it began to gather about the peasant, and the romantic might dream in apocalyptic reverie of a time when every valley would be exalted, and every hill made low. It was perhaps in this general spirit of the time that the Third Estate in France discovered its own nobility.

The French were told by no less a person than Siéyès that all their troubles came from the usurpation of the Franks over a thousand years ago. French noblemen in 1789 were descendants of barbarous Germans, while French commoners were descendants of civilized Gauls and Romans.[11]

The peasant was coming into his own, and in the future the usurpation of the Gall would be righted by the Gael, but in the early half of the nineteenth century the image of the peasant was not so fixed and hard and sharp. He could at one moment be a symbol of tears and grief, and in the next a figure of laughter with his comic face of loutish expression. William Carleton had begun his *Traits and Stories of the Irish Peasantry* (1830) as a commission to express the evils of popery, but he went far beyond that to describe the primitive mode of life where grotesque humor and sudden violence are part of the day-to-day matters of experience. As true an artist as Carleton was (and Synge credits him with being

---

10 As quoted in Thomas Flanagan, *The Irish Novelists* (New York, 1959), p. 188.
11 Crane Brinton, *The Anatomy of Revolution* (New York, 1956), p. 51.

the father of modern Irish literature),[12] it was only too easy for
the Tory Englishman to mock the Liberal's pathetic, long-suffer-
ing Irish peasant with the image of the violent, *shillelagh*-wielding
Paddy of Carleton's stories, who became, through frequent journalistic use, the simian-featured Irishman of the London illustrated papers.

Writers of the first half of the nineteenth century like Lady
Morgan, Thomas Moore, and William Carleton had created a
superficial fashion for things Irish, but their success in this was
based more upon their ability to exploit an already existing market
for the ethnic and exotic than on their ability to create an understanding and appreciation of Irish culture. Their work had its importance in placing a romanticized image of the Irish past before
the public eye, but the public mind was freighted with other
images so that Ireland's tended to blur out of focus. As late as
1853 the founders of the Ossianic Society could still complain of
Ireland's mistreatment.

Though Ossianic lore has been almost neglected by most writers, nevertheless, it is but fair to record a few honourable and praiseworthy
exceptions. The first is C. Wilson, who published a small quarto volume
of Ossianic poetry in 1780, and next Miss Brooke, who published in
1786 [sic] a large volume which has been reprinted by the patriotic
and enterprising Christie of Dublin, in 1816. The Ossianic poems after-
wards remained unnoticed until the late Edward O'Reilley and the Rev.
D. Drummond wrote their prize essays on their authenticity, and in
refutation of Macpherson's false assertions....[13]

One of the members present at the founding of the Ossianic Society
was John O'Donovan, and with O'Donovan, George Petrie, and
Eugene O'Curry, Irish scholarship takes on a more professional
character. The previous generation of gentlemen-scholars were, at
their best, men of the Enlightenment; at their worst, they were
dilettantes who wished to do more than ride to hounds. O'Dono-

---

12 J. M. Synge, *The Aran Islands and Other Writings*, ed. R. Tracy (New York,
1962), p. 361.
13 *Transactions of the Ossianic Society*, ed. Nicholas O'Kearney (Dublin, 1853),
I, p. 10.

van and O'Curry, however, were men without an independent
income; they worked, and the work did not pay well at all. In
1833 O'Donovan went to work, for shilling wages, mapping the
antiquities of Ireland for the Historical Department of the Ordnance Survey. His superior in this position was George Petrie, an
artist and scholar who had visited the Aran Islands in 1820 to
collect music and make sketches. Petrie's most famous works were
to be his studies of the round towers in particular and ecclesias-
tical architecture in general, and all this was done to disprove the
common notion that Ireland had had no civilization before the
Norman Conquest. Together with Petrie and O'Donovan, Eugene
O'Curry formed a triumvirate that gained European attention.
Petrie's task was to administer the survey, O'Donovan's was to do
the field work, and O'Curry's was to do the manuscript research.
In over a decade of ascetic conditions in the field, O'Donovan managed to produce one hundred and fifty volumes of descriptive
letters on Irish monuments. These letters, however, are not merely
archaeological catalogues; they are also romantic meditations
among ruins.

I was moved by various emotions upon viewing the graveyard which
encloses the ashes of Prince Eoghan, the first Christian convert in
Inishowen, and of fifty generations of his descendants, and these emotions were heightened by viewing the princely figure of MacLaughlin,
the eldest branch of his descendants, who is now the actual possessor of
the old graveyard and of the field in which the celebrated Uisige Chaoin
or Clarifont flows.[14]

The romantic style of O'Donovan's prose indicates that history for
this Irish scholar was not merely a matter of facts, but even more
than that, the passage illustrates the particular *idea* of Irish history
that was beginning to emerge in Irish archaeology. The past is perceived to be a realm of value that gives meaning and directives to
the present, and the survivor of this past, the peasant, is seen to be
a noble creature whose veins contain the blood of a lost kingdom,

14 As quoted in P. M. MacSweeney, *A Group of Nation Builders: Petrie,
O'Donovan, and O'Curry* (Dublin, 1913), p. 16.

of a kingdom older and more noble than Great Britain. Not surprisingly, the English were not oblivious to the nationalistic power of such historical scholarship; as the facts began to gather around the hypothesis that there was a civilization in Ireland long before the English could boast of one, the government stopped its subsidy for the Survey in 1840. But since these men received little in the way of salary, the suspension of the subsidy did not stop their work. They carried on their research in the newly founded Irish Archaeological Society, and from there moved into the Royal Irish Academy. Once in the more prestigious Academy, these professional scholars encountered the gentlemen-dilettantes. Sir William Betham, the president of the Academy at the time, had a polite knowledge of philology that he exercised in free associations of Celtic with Etruscan. When other members of the Academy insisted on recognizing Petrie's considerable achievements by presenting him with a gold medal, Betham resigned. Petrie was also responsible for the discovery of the poet James Clarence Mangan, and it was Petrie who had given the poet a position on the Ordnance Survey, where Mangan could turn into verse the literal translations provided him by O'Donovan and O'Curry.

Mangan was a legendary figure of the Dublin of the 1830's. He published his poems in the *Dublin University Magazine,* where the tales of William Carleton were also appearing. With the labors of the scholars and the imaginations of the writers, Dublin was beginning to have a literary existence. The *Dublin University Magazine* is, admittedly, not as historically important as Scotland's *Edinburgh Review,* and the movement that gathered about the Trinity College journal was tiny in comparison with the later Dublin movement of the early twentieth century. Mangan was not Yeats, and Carleton was not Joyce, yet both Yeats and Joyce paid tribute to these writers of the early movement. Mangan is now chiefly remembered for his poem, "Dark Rosaleen," and it is hard to make sense of the esteem Yeats and Joyce bestowed upon him. But as legend and not artist he makes some sense. The figure in broad-brimmed hat and flowing cloak, the figure lost in meditation upon a high ladder in the long hall of the Trinity College Library, the tortured soul who consumed liquor and opium and died at forty-six: all add up to the Edgar Allan Poe variation on a theme from Byron. As common as such a figure might be in the French artists' war against the complacent piety and greed of the bourgeoisie, it was something new for provincial Dublin. In Ireland the breach between poet and society was not so extreme—if the voice of the poet was raised in the cause of the downtrodden Irish nation. Mangan was on the right side, so his personal mannerisms were overlooked. Mangan did not restrict himself to publishing in the intellectual *Dublin University Magazine,* for he also published in the more popular *The Nation.* This magazine was the journal of the younger generation of mid-nineteenth-century Ireland; its editor, Thomas Davis, was a graduate of Trinity College who had become dissatisfied with the garrison mentality of his fellow Anglo-Irishmen and wanted to catch Ireland up in the romantic nationalism that was rising in Germany and Italy. Davis and his associate Gavan Duffy tried to create a Celtic national identity by fostering a literature of patriotism. Impatient with the parliamentary politics of Daniel O'Connell, these members of Young Ireland celebrated the glory of Ireland's heroic past. Through countless battle poems the new ideology of physical force galloped anapestically until an entire generation knew *The Nation* by heart. Unfortunately for Yeats, who would later have to fight his way free of this mnemonic literature, it was *The Nation,* and not the *Dublin University Magazine,* that was to pass on a standard of taste to the end of the nineteenth century.

But while the broadsides and ballads circulated among the politically awakening masses, Petrie, O'Donovan, and O'Curry continued their slow work of translating the immense number of manuscripts that were untouched in the libraries of Trinity College and the Royal Irish Academy. O'Donovan's works were his *Irish Grammar* and his edition of the *Annals of the Four Masters.* For these works he was, with the help of Jakob Grimm, elected in 1856 to a corresponding membership in the Royal Academy of

Berlin. O'Curry's great achievements were his translations and his detailed descriptive catalogue of the Irish manuscripts in the libraries of Ireland and England. Petrie, O'Donovan, and O'Curry all died in the 1860's, but in that decade the work of O'Curry was noticed and praised by Matthew Arnold, and it was this English poet who made the next significant contribution to the Literary Renaissance.

In 1867 Matthew Arnold published his Oxford Lectures *On the Study of Celtic Literature.* These lectures are not the best of Arnold, for they are dated by his facile notions of race and national temperament, but at the time they were a welcome advocacy of the Irish cause. As Professor Kelleher has said:

When Matthew Arnold set out to describe the characteristics of Celtic literature and to analyze its effects, he paid the Celtic world the first valuable compliment it had received from an English source in several hundred years.[15]

Arnold was quick to attack the willful misconception that there was not a great quantity of Irish literature by quoting O'Curry's estimate that there were thousands of manuscripts (so many, in fact, that O'Curry could not even complete the task of cataloguing them). Arnold as an Englishman had something other than a patriot's interest in eliminating anti-Celtic prejudice. He saw Celtic literature as a useful antidote for the poisons of philistinism and materialism that corroded the society of industrial England. With this purpose in mind it is not surprising that Arnold saw only sweetness and light, mist and faery magic in the literature of the Celt. Overlooking the hard, sharp, and often fierce qualities, Arnold saw precisely what he was looking for. In spite of all his writings on culture, Arnold was not an anthropologist interested in reconstructing a primitive world view, and his ethnocentric perceptions became the official Victorian view. This Victorian Celt of Arnold proved to be as long-lived as his grandfather, the Georgian Celt of Macpherson, for even Lady Gregory, who knew modern Irish, came

15 John V. Kelleher, "Matthew Arnold and the Celtic Revival," in *Perspectives of Criticism,* ed. Harry Levin (Cambridge, 1950), p. 197.

to see Cuchulain through Arnold's mist. Yeats, Lady Gregory's collaborator in folklore, never learned more than a few words of
Irish, so Arnold's antinomies were perhaps irresistibly attractive.
Arnold contrasted the yeomanly sense of form of the Saxon with
the magical qualities of the Celt, and thought that English literature was in need of the spirituality of the Celt. The Professor of
Poetry at Oxford was, of course, not primarily interested in Celtic
literature, for it was scarcely available to him; instead he was interested in the Celtic element in English literature. He believed
that it had made a significant contribution to the poetry of the
past, and concluded that modern England had an even greater
need of it.

Now, then, is the moment for the greater delicacy and spirituality of the
Celtic peoples who are blended with us, if it be but wisely directed, to
make itself prized and honoured.[16]

Arnold was not parochially interested in the preservation of Welsh
and Irish as spoken languages; he wanted to see the Celtic element
take part in the immense future he foresaw for English poetry. In
this, he was a good prophet. In the work of Tennyson and Morris,
the Arthuriad and the *Mabinogion* had shown their possibilities
for contemporary poetry; therefore it seemed reasonable to think
that the Irish legends as well could be put to such high use.

One Irish poet attempted to do just that. Sir Samuel Ferguson
was in the center of the Irish literary activity of his time, for as
a member and president of the Royal Irish Academy, he was
familiar with O'Donovan and O'Curry, and as an editor of the
Dublin University Magazine, he was well acquainted with Mangan
and Carleton. But Ferguson was also a man whose Irish sensibility was prudently modified by an extensive knowledge of English poetry and a late nineteenth-century taste. That this opposition between England and Ireland caused him divided loyalties is
seen clearly in the preface to his epic poem, for there he says of
the Irish sagas:

[16] Matthew Arnold, *On the Study of Celtic Literature* (London, 1867), p. 27.

They seemed to possess, to a remarkable degree, that largeness of purpose, unity, and continuity of action which are the principal elements of Epic poetry, and solicited me irresistibly to the endeavour to render them into some compatible form of English verse. After some time, however, I found the inherent repugnancies too obstinate for reconcilement, and, with some regret, abandoned that attempt.[17]

The pagan light of ancient Irish poetry did not pass through Pre-Raphaelite stained glass, and the Christian conventions of the poet laureate completely blacked out the force of a battle poetry that was not chivalric. Ferguson could not hope to re-create either the compression of the Irish line or the cascades of epithets and kennings. Following Tennyson, Ferguson's approach was to seize upon the lyric moment that was framed by the entire tragedy. The approach was naturally more congenial to short poems than "epics," and in his lyrics Ferguson directly influenced Yeats. In his lyric on the abdication of King Fergus, he does not tell the entire story of King Fergus and the boy Conchubor, but concentrates on the moment of abdication. (Cf. Yeats's "Fergus and the Druid.") Ferguson's poetic career extended over five decades, and though he never achieved fame as a poet, he was an important influence. In him the continuity of Irish poetry is maintained, for he connects the literary movement of Dublin in the 'forties with the later revival of the 'nineties. As early as 1834 his "Versions from the Irish" began appearing in the *Dublin University Magazine* and eventually were published in book form as the *Hibernian Nights' Entertainment* in 1857. His production kept up its slow but steady pace and he published books of poetry taken from the Irish in 1864, 1872, and 1880. This poetry seems now exactly what it is: part of the literary history of the mid-nineteenth century in Ireland; but what appealed to Ferguson appealed to others, so he has his place in the line of men and women who created an audience for the Irish past. Yeats, in his first venture in literary criticism, tried to make a case that the only reason Ferguson turned from poetry to antiquities and the presidency of the Royal Irish Academy was

17 Sir Samuel Ferguson, *Congal, A Poem* (Dublin, 1872), p. ii.

because he did not have, in Ireland, an audience sensitive to poetry. There were more obvious reasons for Ferguson's failure as a poet, but Yeats was not entirely overstating the situation. Because of the wretched educational system, the reading public in Ireland was pitifully small. From the beginning the Irish artist was placed in that psychologically painful situation which the American Negro writer now encounters: the audience for his art is not with his own downtrodden people but with the educated classes in power, and success in that art lifts him out of the togetherness of propaganda into the aloneness of poetry. But for the uneducated members of his former world, the movement into art always seems like a betrayal, and that is why only a genius can stand the aloneness, for he has his genius to fill up the space once owned by the crowd. The others return to the shouting. But the young writer can avoid the problem and postpone a decision until the years of mastery. The young Yeats was not yet troubled with such problems; he wished to create an audience for poetry among his countrymen and hoped, with the example of the neglected Ferguson, to shame the Irish into making up their losses with him. He was not yet accusing the Irish of debasing literature into political cant; quite the opposite, he was yoking the ethereal Pegasus of the quiet scholar's poetry to the bandwagon of Irish nationalism.

Of all the many things the past bequeaths to the future, the greatest are great legends; they are the mother of nations. I hold it the duty of every Irish reader to study those of his own country till they are familiar as his own hands, for in them is the Celtic heart.

If you will do this you will perhaps be saved in their high companionship from that leprosy of the modern—tepid emotions and many aims.

. . . I appeal . . . to those young men clustered here and there throughout our land, whom the emotion of patriotism has lifted into that world of selfless passion in which heroic deeds are possible and heroic poetry credible.[18]

The essay was printed in Trinity College's successor to the former *Dublin University Magazine*, the new *Dublin University Review*,

18 W. B. Yeats, "The Poetry of Sir Samuel Ferguson," *Dublin University Review*, II (1886), 941.

and the appearance of a sermon on Irish nationalism that took
the work of a past president of the Royal Irish Academy as its text
did not fail to startle and annoy the very pro-British community
of Trinity College. Ferguson never made his poetry a war-cry for
independence, but he had helped to find an Irish past that was to
dominate the future.

Although the work of Sir Samuel Ferguson is artistically not
very interesting, his synchronic structures of history do arouse an
intellectual curiosity. In his early *Hibernian Nights' Entertainment,* Ferguson superimposes Irish history on Irish legend. Here
the story of the fall of the kingdom of Emain Macha and the death
of Deirdre and the sons of Usnach is told through an interesting
technique. The book opens with a sentinel keeping his watch, and
because, from the Table of Contents, one is expecting to hear the
story of Deirdre, the sentinel's speech immediately recalls the
opening of the *Oresteia;* but the sentinel is not of the time of
Deirdre, but of the sixteenth century, and the story he tells is of
Red Hugh's captivity; it is in the dungeon that a companion of
the Irish prince tells the story of the fall of Emain Macha to pass
away the hours of imprisonment. For the reader, this is a double
past: he goes back to the sixteenth century only to find within the
frame of this picture another and more ancient past. The fall of
the ancient kingdom of Ulster is thus juxtaposed with the fall of
Ireland to the English, for "Hugh was to be the last of the old
Gaelic kings." [19] But even beyond this double-time, the literary
echo of the sentinel's speech suggests a comparison of Deirdre with
Helen of Troy, and another thousand years is added to the horizon.
All this is, of course, implicit, but it is arresting to see that the
early Irish writers, even in the act of recapturing the past, were
reaching for the synchronic structures that were to become so fully
realized in the late poetry of Yeats and the last work of Joyce.
Yeats acknowledged his debt to Ferguson, made a prophecy, and
lived to fulfill the terms of the prophecy himself: "Whatever the

[19] Edmund Curtis, *A History of Ireland* (London, 1964), p. 208.

future may bring forth in the way of a truly great and national
literature . . . will find its morning in these three volumes." [20]

By 1880 well over a century had been devoted to the study of
early Irish literary remains. And that was the chief difficulty: the ancient writings were literary remains and not living legends. Neither
the work of literary archaeologists nor the polite literature of academy presidents could affect the public lack of interest. The Irish,
from a popular point of view, simply had failed to put forth anything to compete with the Scottish *Ossian* or the Welsh *Mabinogion*. From the beginning the Irish response to Macpherson had
been scholarly, and ultimately this response was very important to
the general fund of knowledge, but the knowledge remained in
the libraries. Even among the educated classes, Irish history was
an arcane subject. The historian who changed this, Standish James
O'Grady, described the situation as follows.

At school and in Trinity College I was an industrious lad and worked
through curriculums with abundant energy and some success; yet in the
curriculums never read one word about Irish history and legend, nor
even heard one word about these things from my pastors and masters.
When I was twenty-three years of age, had anyone told me—as later on
a professor of Dublin University actually did—that Brian Boromh was
a mythical character, I would have believed him. I knew absolutely
nothing about our past, not through my own fault, for I was willing
enough to learn anything set before me, but owing to the stupid educational system of the country. I knew Sir Samuel Ferguson and was often
his guest, but knew him only as a kind, courteous and hospitable gentleman; no one ever told me that he was a great Irish poet.[21]

The paradox of Irish studies at the time was that the more educated a man was, the more likely he was to know absolutely nothing about Irish history. It was a simple matter of geography that
when a member of the ruling Anglo-Irish Ascendancy directed his
gaze toward London, he turned his back on Ireland. The Catholic
middle classes kept memories of Catholic Ireland alive, but even

20 W. B. Yeats, *Dublin University Review*, loc. cit.
21 *Standish O'Grady: Selected Essays and Passages*, ed. Ernest Boyd (Dublin,
1918), p. 3.

they knew little or nothing of pagan Ireland. Other than the
scholars, only the Irish-speaking peasants of the very primitive
west had any knowledge of the ancient days, for they still told the
stories of the Fianna, but even the peasants had forgotten Cuchulain.[22] O'Grady might never have discovered the past if it had not
been for an accident. Once when this young landlord and barrister
was a house-guest in the country, the rain prevented him from following the usual round of upper-class diversions. Wandering into
the library, the young man happened to come upon a copy of
O'Halloran's history. What followed must have been something
like a conversion experience, for this enthusiast of Carlyle stumbled upon heroes and histories he had never even dreamed of.
What Odin was for Carlyle, Cuchulain became for O'Grady. The
shock of encounter must have been explosive, for judging by the
history he was to write, the Georgian front of Dublin was lifted
out of sight like a stage-prop and a cosmic drama began to unfold
itself beyond the bounds of little time or local space. The young
man hurried off to the Royal Irish Academy to find the books that
no one read, but not even knowing where to begin and what
sources to trust, he wandered into the blind alley of Vallancey.
Fortunately, the librarian came to his aid and set him on the track
of O'Donovan and O'Curry. Interested as O'Grady was, he was
not fascinated by what he found, and this, he thought, was a serious problem. Dissatisfied, he set out to right the situation himself.

In history, there must be sympathy, imagination, creation. The sorry
remnants discussed by the antiquarian do not themselves supply a picture.... Until this mass of information is popularized, and by being
popularized, secured and appropriated, it is unlikely that any new
surge of antiquarian enthusiasm will again ruffle the tranquil mind of
the intellectual classes of Ireland.[23]

O'Grady lacked the intellectual metabolism of the scholar. Modern
Irish was difficult; ancient Irish, extremely difficult; consequently

---

[22] See Robin Flower, *The Irish Tradition* (Oxford, 1948), p. 104.
[23] Standish James O'Grady, *History of Ireland: Heroic Period*, I. (London,
1878), p. v.

he chose not to go over the same ground with the philologists. O'Grady chose instead "the reconstruction by imaginative processes of the life led by our ancestors in this country." [24] This imaginative reconstruction was not intended as merely another book to put away on a shelf in the Academy. "I desire to make this heroic period once again a portion of the imagination of the country, and its chief characters as familiar in the minds of our people as they once were." [25]

O'Grady's approach was to take the Cuchulain legends from the Ulster Cycle and place them in a context of a cosmic drama, for his vision extended even beyond the life of the ancestors. His history practically begins in the brooding anticipation of the silent instant before Creation. What unfolds is not Eden again, but a visionary Darwinism in which huge monsters, the as yet clumsy laborings of some inchoate passion yearning for expression, lumber across the stage of Pleistocene Ireland. Across the frozen island that awaits its destiny pass Gods, Fomorians, Firbolgs, and, finally, the high Milesian race that is brought to consummate expression in its Hero, Cuchulain. The work is fascinating in its imaginative conception and narration, and for such a thoroughly a-Christian and immense vision of history, one would have to go to Wagner's *Ring* for a comparison. And it was precisely a Wagnerian excitement that the work was most likely to generate. The later writer, A.E., said that in reading O'Grady, "It was the memory of race which rose up within me, and I felt exalted as one who learns he is among the children of kings." [26] O'Grady's history is, therefore, not simply a retelling of past events, but a conjuration that overwhelms the present, and, further, gives the present its full meaning. In imaginatively handling such an idea of the past, O'Grady uses an *entrelacement* whereby the reader moves from the past to a more ancient past and back again. In relating the story of the flight of Lara to Slieve Mish, he introduces a chapter

24 Ibid.
25 Ibid.
26 Hugh Art O'Grady, *Standish James O'Grady, The Man and Writer* (Dublin, 1929), p. 64.

that tells the ancient tale of the Milesian invasion of Ireland. It seems that the Tuatha de Danan goddess, Bamba, was awaiting the predestined moment. She appears to the leader, Heber, and blesses him and his descendants, and tells him that this is the last time that she will be seen by the Gael, for she will live, unseen by men, in the fairy mound of Slieve Mish. The chapter is sufficiently long that the reader is allowed time to forget Lara, but upon turning to the next chapter, he is brought forward in time again.

This then, Slieve Mish, of the Shiel Heber, was the territory, and this the city to which the exiles of Dinn Rie came flying from the unjust king.[27]

A sequence of events, the present, is set off with its own day-to-day consciousness, then suddenly it intersects with another sequence of events, the past, with a consciousness that understands it even though the present had no knowledge of the other's existence. In juxtaposing past and present, O'Grady re-created the structure of his own conversion experience on that rainy day. As an Anglo-Irish gentleman, O'Grady was involved in the life of the definite and circumscribed values of the British Empire; suddenly he encountered a world in which the horizon expanded to infinity, but yet, and most importantly, it was a world that had a place for him. This is the messianism of the elect and it is a motif that was to linger on in Irish affairs, for from such imaginings of the past it was only natural to reason that the future contained a destiny befitting such an exalted heritage.

In ancient days the memory of the past exerted a conservative force on society: the models of the ancestors served to keep the young in harmony with the social order. It is then not as surprising as it would seem to note that O'Grady was a conservative Unionist and not a Liberal Home-Ruler or a radical Nationalist. For O'Grady, Cuchulain was the model of aristocratic virtue; he was appreciated because he was a far cry from the vulgar, commercial, and ignoble man of the modern industrial world. O'Grady

[27] S. J. O'Grady, *History of Ireland: Heroic Period,* I, p. 78.

did not want to awaken a nationalistic consciousness in the mob,
but he did want to awaken the moribund class of Irish landlords
to a sense of nobility and duty. For O'Grady the agricultural tur-
moil of the Land Campaign came about because the landlords
were apeing the penurious small-mindedness of shopkeepers.
O'Grady tried to fight the coercion and boycotting of Michael
Davitt's Land League, but his brand of benevolent despotism
whereby the state attempted to guarantee the employment of the
working classes did not open up the treasure-chest of the Tory's
heart. Michael Davitt scoffed at O'Grady's futile stance, and the
landlord class continued on its way to extinction.[28] The man who
could not find a publisher for his history of Ireland and had to pay
for its publication himself did not succeed in finding a political
audience either. It was not until ten years later when the scandal
of Parnell and the collapse of his Home-Rule movement had
turned people away from politics that O'Grady found an audience in the young men of a generation with new interests. It was
as editor of the warm and personally engaging *All-Ireland Review*
that Standish O'Grady became respected as "the father of the Irish
Literary Renaissance." [29] From time to time O'Grady would scold
Yeats for his affected manners and his letters to the *Review* that
read as if they were intended for the London *Times,* but when
Yeats in his own aristocratic old age looked back, he looked back
with respect.

All round us people talked or wrote for victory's sake, and were hated
for their victories—but here was a man whose rage was a swan song
over all that he held most dear, and to whom for that reason every
imaginative writer owed a portion of his soul. In his unfinished *History
of Ireland* he made the old Irish heroes, Fion, and Oisin, and Cuchul-
lan, alive again, taking them, for I think he knew no Gaelic, from the
dry pages of O'Curry and his school, and condensing and arranging,
as he thought Homer would have arranged and condensed. Lady

28 See "Irish Conservatism and Its Outlooks," first O'Grady's in *Dublin University Review,* August 1885, p. 4; then Michael Davitt's reply, September 1885,
p. 105.
29 Ernest Boyd, *Ireland's Literary Renaissance* (London, 1922), p. 7.

Gregory has told the same tales, but keeping closer to the Gaelic text, and with greater powers of arrangement and more original style, but O'Grady was the first, and we had read him in our teens.[30]

If O'Grady started the imaginings of a literary movement, he also shared in the beginnings of other imaginings, for in the Cuchulain of this Irish Unionist, one revolutionary nationalist saw the supreme glorification of violence when sanctified by a noble cause. This revolutionary, Padraic Pearse, as a schoolmaster had a mural painted at the entrance to his school: there the boys could see the boy Cuchulain taking arms from the Druid, and there they could read the Irish motto, "I care not if my life have only the span of a night and day if my deeds be spoken of by the men of Ireland." [31] O'Grady achieved his goal, and certainly and ironically more than was ever his goal. But the Ireland of revolution was not O'Grady's Ireland and "He did not know what his own work meant to Padraic Pearse." [32] O'Grady wrote many books, newer Cuchulain versions, short stories, historical novels, even a critical history in answer to the objections of scholarship to his romantic history; he tried newspapers, publishing, and political schemes from benevolent despotism to socialistic communities, but his masterpiece remained the *History of Ireland: Heroic Period* that he had published in 1878. By 1916 O'Grady had retired from public life into the absolute silence of advanced old age.

While O'Grady was at work bringing the translations of the scholars to a wider public, the philological movement was itself gaining momentum. Whitley Stokes, a young man who had accompanied Petrie, O'Donovan, O'Curry, and Ferguson on a visit to the Aran Islands in 1857, now collaborated with the German philologist, Ernst Windisch, in publishing the *Irische Texte* (1880) in Leipzig. The production of scholarly translations was, perhaps, accelerated beyond the usual academic rate because there arose an almost militant competition between Windisch in Leipzig and

[30] W. B. Yeats, *Autobiographies* (London, 1961), p. 220.
[31] Desmond Ryan, *A Man Called Pearse,* in *Collected Works of Padraic Pearse* (Dublin, 1924), p. 157.
[32] A.E., *The Living Torch,* ed. Monk Gibbon (London, 1938), p. 145.

Heinrich Zimmer (the elder), Professor of Sanskrit and Celtic, in Berlin.[33] This competition was not restricted to the Germans, for in 1899 the Irish Text Society began its publications with the hope that it could do for Irish literature what the Early English Text Society had done for the study of medieval English literature. The competitive spirit even touched family relations, for Standish James O'Grady's cousin, Standish Hayes O'Grady, published a large two-volume collection of translations in 1892. Unfortunately the prose style of Hayes's *Silva Gadelica* shows that he provided no literary competition at all for his cousin; his work was purely scholarly.

Scholarship and literature had been combined in the work of Standish James O'Grady, but the combination made his *History of Ireland* a thing apart from either pure scholarship or pure literature. The relationship between scholarship and art was not always so ambiguous. John Synge had a sensibility that was more alive to the ironies and contradictions of human nature than to the historical conflations of Teutonic messianism. In his plays he was to make the most original and authentic portrayals of Irish peasant life. Perhaps Synge's originality was helped by the fact that he came to the Aran Islands by way of a detour through Europe. In 1893 Synge was in Paris living the usual life of starvation in a garret while at work on translations of Rabelais, Ronsard, and Petrarch. But Synge was not an expatriate; he was also in touch with the philological movement, for he was attending de Jubainville's lectures on Celtic mythology at the Sorbonne.

The relationship between literature and scholarship was equally distinct in the work of the philologist, Kuno Meyer. As a schoolboy Meyer had spent two years in Scotland; as a student his interest in Celtic matters was stimulated by the lectures of Ernst Windisch. But Meyer was not merely a man of academic interests. As consulting philologist to the writers of the literary revival, he earned his place in George Moore's gossip-novel *Hail and Farewell*. Meyer was often on hand for the cultural activities

33 Rudolph Thurneysen, op. cit.

in Dublin, for as Professor of Romance Languages in Queens College, Liverpool, it was a simple matter to cross over and maintain a double life, teaching in Liverpool and doing research in Dublin. Meyer was able to keep visionary schemes and Celtic mist out of his philology; he was, however, unable to keep out of politics. In the First World War the Professor remarked on the strong ties that bound Ireland and Germany. Becoming something of a recruiting sergeant, he suggested that captured Irish soldiers should form an Irish Brigade to fight against England. Not surprisingly, the Professor lost his Chair at Liverpool while he was making banquet speeches in America.[34]

If all the German professors did not make their presence felt in such dramatic ways, the high seriousness of mind that was the natural tone of Germanic scholarship helped in convincing the Irish that they possessed a tradition to be proud of. Together the German and the French scholars were winning an international audience for ancient Irish literature, but the Anglo-Irish professors at Trinity College refused to alter their opinions. Professors Dowden and Mahaffy were rather vocal on the aboriginal crudity, if not outright obscenity, of the Irish sagas. Expelled from the university, the Irish movement had to find a home elsewhere; fortunately for the revolution that was to come, the movement found a home in the lower classes.

By the twentieth century, a hundred and fifty years of scholarship had given Irish writers a substantial tradition. O'Grady had popularized the scholars' work for readers at home, and now Yeats, Synge, and Lady Gregory extended the campaign to the entire English-speaking world. With the appearance in 1902 of Lady Gregory's *Cuchulain of Muirthemne* the legend reached its widest audience: President Theodore Roosevelt kept a copy to pass away the time on his long political train-journeys.[35] Now the people of the great cities of England and America could read the story of Cuchulain told in the charming dialect of the peasants of Kiltar-

[34] As reported in the *Cork Examiner*, January 7, 1915, p. 4.
[35] Herbert Howarth, *The Irish Writers* (London, 1958), p. 97.

tan. Yeats thought it one of the best books to come out of Ireland. Lady Gregory was not Synge's patron, so he felt free to be a little more critical. Synge was grateful enough for Lady Gregory's experiments in dialect, but he prefered to take his Irish straight.

For readers who take more than literary interest in these stories a word of warning may be needed. Lady Gregory has omitted certain barbarous features, such as the descriptions of the fury of Cuchulain, and, in consequence, some of her versions have a much less archaic aspect than the original texts. Students of mythology will read this book with interest, yet for their severer studies they must still turn to the works of the German scholars and others, who translate without hesitation all that has come down to us in the MSS.[36]

The important point, however, was that the reader now had a choice he never had before, and the range of choice from Lady Gregory to Ernst Windisch was a genuine one indeed.[37]

Now in twentieth-century Dublin began the literary movement that was to prove far more successful than the earlier one that had centered on *The Nation* and the *Dublin University Magazine*. The earlier movement had ended in delusion, frustration, failure, and silence; for the curtain that fell upon its act was really a shroud: the million deaths of the famine, the typhus-infested "coffin ships" of the mass emigration, and the utter failures of the rebellions of 1848 and 1867 had exhausted the energy of the nation. But even of their own accord the earlier efforts would probably have come to a halt. Here the judgment of this movement's best historian is necessary.

If we were to judge it by its bulk alone, we would be tempted to say that nineteenth century Irish fiction was devoted primarily to the production of historical novels, sumptuously bound in green and lavishly decorated with gilt shamrocks. For the most part they have fallen into a merciful oblivion. It could be argued that their lack of literary worth reflects invidiously upon the shallow and constrictive nationalism to which Davis committed his contemporaries and his successors. It was

36 J. M. Synge, *The Aran Islands and Other Writings,* ed. Robert Tracy (New York, 1962), p. 371.
37 Ernst Windisch, *Tain Bo Cualigne* (Leipzig, 1905).

upon this charge that Davis would be arraigned by a later generation of Irish writers. But in fact Davis's larger error lay in his failure to see that the Irish mind had always been influenced, to the point of obsession, "by the deeds and passions of the past." And when, at his bidding, Irish writers turned directly to national history for material, they brought with them the old, sullen grudges and the old, delusive lies. He had asked for a school of historical fiction which transcended hatred, accusation, and guilt. He had forgotten that these were the very forces which had shaped and determined the history of Ireland.[38]

The past that the earlier writers had used for their work hurt too much for art and was still too painfully present. Another past was needed, a past not owned by hatred. Unlike the writers, the scholars were motivated by patriotism, but not possessed by it. It was this deeper past that stood before history that Yeats and Synge inherited.

[38] Thomas Flanagan, *The Irish Novelists* (New York, 1959), p. 188.

CHAPTER TWO

THE INTERPRETATION OF THE PAST

In the nineteenth century there arose in Europe two ideological movements based upon primitive mythology and peasant culture that profoundly changed the body and mind of Western civilization: the movement in Ireland signaled the disintegration of the British Empire; the movement in Germany climaxed in history's largest war. In both cases movements of political violence developed out of seemingly nonpolitical cultural enthusiasms, and, again in both cases, these cultural enthusiasms were a response to intense political disappointment and frustration.

Germany's prolonged quest for national unity had the effect of turning her best minds toward problems of national destiny. This unity could have come about at the Congress of Vienna after the fall of Napoleon, but instead a loose German Confederation emerged which left the individual German states to pursue their independent ways. As a result, those Germans who wanted unity looked increasingly to the formation of a cultural cohesion among their people rather than to a political unity which seemed far distant. They conceived this cultural unity in terms of national roots and of opposition to the foreigner.[1]

In Ireland the cultural phase followed upon the highly dramatic fall of Parnell and the sudden ruin of what had been a brilliant decade of Irish politics. Like the Germans before them, the best Irish minds turned away in disappointment and disgust and began to think on national destiny in the realm of imagination. In the search for a distinctly national identity, the Germans had to free themselves of the overwhelming intimidation of French civilization; they had to free themselves of the cultural self-abnegation that had embarrassed Frederick the Great and Leibniz into speaking and writing French. When the Germans turned their backs on the neoclassicism of the French, they were joined by the Irish who were also struggling to free themselves of the inferiority they felt before English civilization. Responding to Macpherson, Irish and German scholars collaborated in the attempt to recapture the Aryan past. The result of this work was that readers who had been educated to think that the classical epic was one of the crowning achievements of the intellect of man, had to make room for romantic pretenders to the throne in the case of the *Edda,* the *Niebelungenlied,* and *Tain Bo Cualigne.* But as long as the nations were intensely preoccupied in a political campaign there was little chance that the work of philologists would be noticed. Once the political situation had been quieted, the voices of the scholars had a chance against the shouting of the crowds. The past was brought to the attention of the public, and the existence of a great past indicted the present, for the present had betrayed that past by taking on the ways of the foreigner. A new situation was created whereby "the best" elements of society were the most guilty, for they were best in the cultured ways of the foreigner. It was the peasants who now became the collective representation of national identity. In the geography of the mind, the situation was reversed,

[1] George L. Mosse, *The Crisis of German Ideology* (New York, 1964), p. 2. See also Peter Viereck, *Metapolitics: The Roots of the Nazi Mind* (New York, 1961).

for now when a man directed his gaze toward the Aran Islands, he turned his back on London. Thus there arose in Ireland a folk movement at a time when the Volkish Ideology was already highly developed in Germany. The two movements were, of course, part of the general European movement of romanticism that encouraged regional literature, folklore, and fairy tales. Untouched by the Renaissance, Ireland was used to its isolation from the life of the Continent, but for once, in the Romantic Movement, it was linked with the rest of Europe, and, on the basis of its own resources, it could dream of becoming a cultural leader. But the Great Famine and the mass emigration finished the movement in Ireland after it had scarcely begun. The literary movement simply had to wait until 1890 when Parnell fell from power.

As much as the fall of Parnell damaged Irish political ambition, it could not entirely nullify two generations of significant and effective political organization. Before the existence of Parnell's Irish Party, Davitt's Land League and O'Connell's Catholic Association had helped sublimate terrorism into parliamentary pressure. For centuries Irish resistance to England consisted in rather hopeless miitary defeats, and when the Irish realized that they could not beat England in the field, they took to individualistic acts of violence in small clandestine societies. The persistent Irish failure to resort to due process of law for a just redress of grievances was not due to perversity, for under the Penal Laws there was no recourse to law for the vast Catholic multitude. Law, in the abstract sense, did not exist for the Irishman, and it was no joke that the judge's gavel was replaced by the *shillelagh*.[2] Unfortunately these terroristic acts fostered by English law only convinced the English of the inveterate lawlessness of the Irish and their utter inability to rule themselves. The lessons of history, as written by David Hume, pointed out the fact that if it had not been for the Norman Conquest, the Irish would never have known

2 For a different picture of the *shillelagh*-wielding Paddy of St. Patrick's Day cards, see William Carleton's story, "The Party Fight and the Funeral," in *The Courtship of Phelim O'Toole: Six Irish Tales*, ed. Anthony Cronin (London, 1962).

the slightest amenities of civilization. This political impasse is again familiar to us in America, and much as the American-Irish of Boston, New York, and Chicago would not like to face it, the point is obvious: the Irish were the Negroes of nineteenth-century Great Britain, and the political conflict on both sides was intensely racist. The Irishman of the London illustrated magazines had the features of a monkey, crossed a puddle of urine to enter his cottage where he lived with his pig and slept with his wife and children in the family bed. Except for the simian features, the picture was altogether too true of peasant Ireland in the nineteenth century. African savages lived on a higher level than the ancestors of the American-Irish racists.[3] The lawless Celts were thought to be racially inferior to the Anglo-Saxons who had given to the modern world the Magna Carta and the Bill of Rights. It is, therefore, one of the ironies of history that the American Negroes are now fighting for their rights with the political techniques that were discovered by the Irish in their fight against England. Because violence only increased both anti-Irish prejudice and the size of the British garrison (a garrison already larger than the one needed to hold all India), another strategy was required, and the political genius who discovered the modern technique of nonviolent mass demonstration was Daniel O'Connell.

The intimate relationship between art and history is clearly seen in the career of Daniel O'Connell. The political event that made him a nationalist was the Act of Union of 1801, by which Ireland lost her native Parliament, but in thinking over this political catastrophe, his mind perceived reality in the forms of art. O'Connell's meditation upon Ireland took the romantic form of a meditation among ruins.

The year of the Union I was traveling through the Mountain district from Killarney to Kildare. My heart was heavy at the loss Ireland had sustained, and the day was wild and gloomy.... My soul felt dreary,

[3] For a description of the level of urbanization achieved in precolonial West Africa, see William Bascom, "Urbanization Among the Yoruba," in *Cultures and Societies of Africa*, ed. Simon and Phoebe Ottenberg (New York, 1960).

and I had many wild and Ossianic inspirations as I traversed the bleak
solitudes. It was the Union that first stirred me up to come forward in
politics.[4]

O'Connell's contribution to Irish politics was to replace the secret
societies of terror with an organization of such overwhelming size
and perfect discipline that it would once and for all silence the
conviction that the Irish could not rule themselves by presenting
the English with what amounted to a *de facto* government. The
peasants paid a small rent to O'Connell's Catholic Association,
and these *de facto* taxes were used to set up a local association in
every parish to adjudicate wrongs brought to its attention by the
peasantry, to apply pressure to the local magistrates to act in the
interest of justice and not of the landlord, to give grants to education, and to build the schools that the *de jure* government would
not. The British government recognized its threat and suppressed
the organization by Act of Parliament, but O'Connell immediately
reformed the organization as the "New" Catholic Association in
1825. Attacked by Parliament, it was now the Association's move
to intimidate Westminster. In 1828 "O'Connell determined to use
the strength of the Catholic Association to show once and for all
that political control of the peasant had passed from the landlord
to the priest." [5] O'Connell stood for Parliament in the election
at County Clare, and his defeat of a popular landlord, Vesey-
FitzGerald, who was himself in favor of Catholic Emancipation,
demonstrated the power of the new organization. O'Connell won;
Catholics realized their voting power and refused to vote for the
Protestant candidates put up by their landlords. Catholics could
vote, but they could not yet take a seat in Parliament. When
O'Connell was elected the government knew that it was faced with
the terrifying prospect of civil war and, therefore, passed Catholic
Emancipation. With one hand the British government opened the
door to Parliament for O'Connell, but with the other slammed it

[4] As quoted in P. S. O'Hegarty, *A History of Ireland under the Union* (London,
1952), p. 23.
[5] G. M. Trevelyan, *British History in the Nineteenth Century and After:
1782-1919* (New York, 1966), p. 220.

in the face of the electorate that had given him his seat, for the government raised the franchise qualification from forty shillings to ten pounds.

The Duke of Wellington detested the thought of civil war, but the Prime Minister had little to fear from O'Connell on that account, for the Irish leader had an even deeper abhorrence of violence. The rising of 1798 convinced O'Connell that the best way for the Irish to secure the repeal of the Act of Union was to obey the law with overwhelming force. O'Connell's particular strategy was to call meetings of upwards of 200,000 people and to call on Britain to observe a demonstration of perfectly controlled obedience to law. These "monster meetings" were peaceful and disciplined, but the discipline of 200,000 people in the field was not a tranquilizing sight to the government. The British were prepared in 1829 to free the Catholics, but they were not prepared to free Ireland and thereby dismember the Empire. By 1843 they had lived with O'Connell for some time, and they began to believe that he was sincere in his nonviolent program. Having eliminated the threat of an electorate of 100,000 forty-shilling freeholders, they now addressed themselves to the problem of mass demonstrations. O'Connell called for a monster meeting that was to be the largest of them all. Previously, the largest meeting had been held at the ancient seat of the Irish kings, the hill of Tara; the next meeting was to be held at Clontarf, where King Brian Boru had defeated the Danes. This time the government decided to call O'Connell's bluff; it proscribed the meeting, called up the troops, and trained artillery guns on the hill. O'Connell gave in and called off the meeting. Clontarf ended his political effectiveness, for although the peasants did not desert The Liberator, the younger generation did. The Young Ireland Party of Thomas Davis, Gavan Duffy, Fintan Lalor, and John Mitchel was in favor of independence secured through physical force. Through the many ballads that Davis and Duffy printed in *The Nation* they sought to revive the glory and heroism of the warriors of the past. But the strategies of both Davis and O'Connell ended inconclusively. After Clontarf, O'Connell's health began to fail, and he died in 1847. Davis, not yet thirty years old, died in September of 1845, the very month in which the potato blight first appeared. With the Famine everything came to a dead stop. When the Irish could again think of improving their abject condition, agricultural reform was uppermost in their minds.

With the collapse of O'Connell's movement effective political organization had to wait a generation. The proponents of physical force made an effort to seize power, but in 1848 people had enough to worry about in keeping alive. The pathetic insurrection of 1848 was put down by a garrison of police, and the leaders of the Young Ireland Party were transported. Those who were out in 1848 tried again in the Fenian rising of 1867, but once again quixotic revolts against the British Empire ended in mere farce.

There were no plans save to capture police barracks, there were no arms save pikes, there was no co-ordination in the various districts. Thousands of men in dozens of places marched out to agreed places of rendezvous, found themselves without arms and in many cases without leaders, and were either dispersed by police or military or disbanded themselves and returned home.[6]

Though Fenianism failed in the field, it did not cease to be a force of importance, for one of the men imprisoned for his part in 1867 was Michael Davitt, and it was with Michael Davitt and Charles Stewart Parnell that a New Departure in Irish politics began. The contribution of Fenianism to separatist politics was that it made revolt an international issue, for funds collected in America could now be used to support campaigns in Ireland. When Davitt was released from prison he attempted to use the existing international Fenian organization to support a Land Campaign at home. In 1879 the Irish National Land League was formed, and the chairman of the Irish Party, Parnell, became its first president. Peasants now joined together in boycotts and rent-strikes; if one of their members was dispossessed, no new tenant

[6] P. S. O'Hegarty, *Ireland Under the Act of Union* (London, 1952), p. 446.

was permitted to take his land. Effective political organization again helped to sublimate sporadic, individualistic acts of violence, as it had in the time of O'Connell, but it could not hope to efface the effect of centuries. Though Parnell could take the Land Campaign into Parliament, the fight was fierce and tenants were evicted with the help of troops. Often enough the hedges contained armed tenants lying in wait for the landlord.

The harvest of 1879 was the worst since the Great Famine, in 1880 there were 2590 agrarian outrages and between 1874 and 1881 some ten thousand evictions. The peasant's "wild justice of revenge" displayed itself in the shooting of many landlords and their agents. "Captain Moonlight" was the phrase for the secret terror, and in towns secret societies were pledged to obtain Ireland's independence by methods of assassination.[7]

Against such a background of peasant unrest, the aristocratic land-lord Parnell tried on the one hand to use the violence that existed to convince Parliament of the necessity for legislation, and on the other to convince the violent Irish of the necessity for political agitation. This tactic (still at work in our own Civil Rights Movement) was brilliant, but volatile. The New Departure's union of agrarian reform and parliamentary tactics was enormously powerful: "Nothing less than the strongest native revolt for over two hundred years, it sought to disrupt the bases of the Cromwellian settlement and of British rule."[8] But this union required a balance that was almost impossible to maintain. Upon the success of Gladstone's Act of 1881, which reduced rents by 20 per cent and gave the tenant a right in his land, Parnell had to contend with the threat to his English support contained in the Phoenix Park assassination of Lord Frederick Cavendish, Chief-Secretary for Ireland, and his Under-Secretary, Mr. Burke. His leadership was again undermined by the dynamiting campaign supported by the extremist wing of the American-Irish Clan-na-Gael. To the

[7] Edmund Curtis, *A History of Ireland* (London, 1961), p. 379.
[8] J. L. Garvin, as quoted in Conor Cruise O'Brien, *Parnell and His Party* (Oxford, 1957), p. 6.

Tories, Irish politics in the 'eighties had the look of one single, highly organized conspiracy directed by Parnell and aided and abetted by the bleeding-heart Liberals of Gladstone's party. Too willingly the London *Times* accepted a forged letter that implicated Parnell in the Phoenix Park murders. But Parnell cleared his name with brilliant success and managed, throughout all these enormous difficulties, to come out ahead. With the Irish party behind him as a single voting bloc, in 1885 neither Liberals nor Tories could form an administration without coming to terms with Parnell. Suddenly Ireland stood in the midst of the politics of the British Empire, and, for the Irish, Parnell became "the uncrowned king of Ireland." It seemed, therefore, nothing less than the tragic fall of a prince when Parnell was named co-respondent in a divorce suit. His megalomania would not permit him to stand down, and over the interests of his party, his Catholic constituents, and the equally pious Low-Church constituents of Gladstone's party, he decided to take the fight to the country. His fierce pride helped make him legend after his death, but while he was alive it gave the Catholic bishops and Ireland a most difficult problem, and some months passed before they could decide how to handle the situation.[9] The theme of adultery and divorce stirred up religious passions so much that, at a meeting, lime was cast in Parnell's eyes. Two years after the divorce petition, on October 6, 1891, Parnell died. The Irish Party broke into Parnellite and anti-Parnellite factions, and the next decade was spent in futility and invective. But as often happens in history, the structure of an existing ideology can be used for the dissemination of a new utopia; Christian missionaries followed the roads that Roman engineers had built. The peasant of Davitt's Land League, who was always a rather dangerous sort, now became the peasant of Douglas Hyde's Gaelic League, the most lovable type of human being imaginable.

When the constitutional techniques of securing parliamentary concessions disgusted the Young Ireland Party, they turned to the

9 See Emmet Larkin, "The Roman Catholic Hierarchy and the Fall of Parnell," *Victorian Studies*, IV (June 1961), 315-36.

celebration of the Irish warriors. And once again when the parliamentary tactics failed with Parnell as they had with O'Connell, the Irish brought out the old battle songs and warrior ballads. The school of Thomas Davis, the Irish poet who died young, underwent a revival. To be sure no one thought of putting an army in the field, and an Irishman singing "A Nation Once Again" was no more dangerous than a Welshman singing "Men of Harlech." The Irish did not attack in body, but in mind, for going back to the pages of *The Nation* they revived its irresistible claims.

The gay, bold, joyous Irishman has no tendency to the darker vices. His animal spirits and his love of fun supply him with abundant materials for enjoyment. If you give him the plodding habits of the Briton, he will have his vices along with them.[10]

One pretty ideologue of the 'nineties, Maud Gonne, simplified the struggle into the style of the Catechism: "What is the origin of Evil?" The answer: "England." [11] The first and most durable characteristic of the ideological movement had appeared: the Irishman's dismissal of evil from his consciousness of Ireland. If England was the origin of evil, then it followed that to speak the language of the devil was not the road to salvation. Disgusted with Westminster, the Irish were only too willing to turn their backs on London to gaze toward Aran and Connemara. Thus began the making of pilgrimages to the Gaeltacht, until a fisherman of Aran could remark: "Believe me there are few rich men now in the world who are not studying the Gaelic." [12] It was not enough, however, merely to make the journey to the Irish-speaking regions of the west. Action on the part of the entire nation had to be taken, for by the end of the nineteenth century it looked as if the Irish-speaking peasant was just about ready to disappear from the face of the earth.

---

10 *The Voice of the Nation, A Manual of Nationality,* ed. Charles Gavan Duffy (Dublin, 1844), p. 18.
11 As quoted in Joseph Hone, *W. B. Yeats 1865-1939* (London, 1962), p. 173.
12 J. M. Synge, *The Aran Islands and Other Writings,* ed. Robert Tracy (New York, 1962), p. 21.

This time of crisis found its champion in Douglas Hyde. Hyde, like Thomas Davis, was a graduate of that English fortress, Trinity College, but unlike Davis, Hyde was not content to have the people singing the old songs in translation. He wanted the entire Irish nation to speak its own language once again. That Irish was a peasant language hardly adequate for expressing the complexities of contemporary life was no deterrent to Hyde, for these complexities were the commercial and industrial vulgarities that all romantics despised. Matthew Arnold had seen the Celt as a savior from Saxon philistinism; Hyde picked up the Sword of Light to begin a crusade. And for the simple rhetoric that crusades require, Hyde was not above invoking the facile antinomies of *The Nation.*

... what I advocate brings with it no substantial or material advantages at all. It will neither make money nor help to make money; but I hope this confession will not put us out of court with an Irish audience, as I know it would with an Anglo-Saxon one.[13]

In 1893 Douglas Hyde founded the Gaelic League to achieve the high purpose of making Ireland a well of Gaelic pure and undefiled, but in that year he also published his *Love Songs of Connacht,* which in its use of a fine Anglo-Irish idiom (as opposed to the traditional *begorras* of stage-Irishman cant) paradoxically frustrated his primary goal, for it furnished Synge, Lady Gregory, and Yeats with an idiom that was to make an Irish literature written in English seem all the more possible. But whether Hyde served Ireland or the world, he and his Gaelic League spread the enthusiasm for folk literature and the Irish language beyond the confines of the intelligentsia to the entire populace. Now in drawing rooms and pubs, the revival of Irish was the topic of conversation.

Of course one instinctively suspects people who meet in drawing rooms to praise the peasant over tea and cakes. Clearly the intelligentsia had an ulterior motive and were not thinking of a

---

13 Douglas Hyde, "A Plea for the Irish Language," *Dublin University Review* (August 1886), 666.

peasantry that reeked of cow-dung. Centuries of polite literature
had taught the upper classes to think of the peasant as a good sort
who composes verses to his Rosalind. If the pastorals of Sidney
were remote, the peasants of Wordsworth could provide an immediate model. The Irish writers of the Protestant Ascendancy, writers
like Hyde, Yeats, Synge, and Lady Gregory, were people of good
family who had stumbled upon difficult times; in the eighteenth
century the Anglo-Irish upper classes had known an era of brilliance and prosperity, but with the Act of Union and the Industrial Revolution, feudal Ireland went into eclipse, and Dublin became a provincial city. Born into a world that favored the machine,
commerce, and the growth of cities, slums, and empires, a person of
imaginative capacity recoiled from a setting that offered no role
for his abilities. The peasant, therefore, recalled the good old days
of the integral community, when, as Yeats put it; there was no mob
of shopkeepers to come between the big house and the hut; when
literature was a tale told by a warm fire, and not a sixpenny novel;
when a dwelling was a thatched cottage, and business was a personal and concrete form of barter for the peasant, and an understanding among gentlemen for the aristocrat. An artist in Yeats's
time was like an actor trained to think in terms of soldier, lover,
wise-man, and fool, but cast into a crowd-scene where he was asked
only to raise a cheer or stamp a ballot. Men like Yeats and other
members of the Anglo-Irish Ascendancy longed for the integral
community of the old manorial days. Ironically, just as feudalism
was about to vanish as an economic reality in Ireland, it discovered
its fullest artistic expression. What these writers and intellectuals
wanted was, in fact, the elimination of civilization with all its discontents. And this is the second characteristic of the ideology: the
rejection of industrial civilization. In the first characteristic of the
dismissal of evil from their own national identity the Irish had presented, against the reality of man's inwardly divided self, an image
of absolute innocence, simplicity, and unity. The next natural step
was to move out from the individual to society, and to present,
against the fragmented collective of Ireland's vestigial feudalism

and primitive capitalism, an image of the beautiful community of moor and glen.

If the sweet vision of the peasant community sounds like a mere wishful dream, it was nevertheless based upon a genuine sense of terror, upon that disorientation and formless anxiety that is the terror of complexity. A few months before the Gaelic League was formed, Douglas Hyde addressed the Irish National Literary Society on "The Necessity for De-Anglicising Ireland." [14] Without losing the sense of balance required for such a social occasion, Hyde succeeded in conveying sufficient horror to make it seem that if something were not done immediately the Ireland of monuments and cottages would be inundated by a flood of black spuming factories, traveling salesmen, and cockney corner-boys. After his speech, things began to move. And once under way, the new movement spilled its energies into many fields, clubs, societies, newspapers, magazines, and anything that was not British and could float on the lifting tide of enthusiastic nationalism. Hyde had addressed the National Literary Society; its president was George Sigerson, a respected scholar who as far back as 1860 had published *Poets and Poetry of Munster*. When it was his turn to speak, Sigerson could impress his audience by describing the continuity of Irish poetry over a thousand years. His *Bards of the Gael and Gall* of 1897 was another step in revealing the independence of the Irish tradition, for in his full discussion of Irish metrics he presented a system that had little to do with the weighted quantities of Tennyson. If Sigerson's National Literary Society was not enough, there was the Irish Literary Society in London, which Yeats and T. W. Rolleston had founded, but which came to be presided over by the elderly Sir Charles Gavan Duffy (newly returned from a political career in Australia) of Young Ireland days. With the appearance of the elderly survivor of the time of the idolized Thomas Davis, the amorphous good will of the movement became more definite, because different ideas of its purpose came

14 Douglas Hyde, *The Revival of Irish Literature and Other Addresses,* ed. Sir Charles Gavan Duffy (London, 1894).

into the open. The movement in Dublin of the 'nineties now attempted to determine its distinctness from the literary movement of the 'forties. And the distinct man in the act of definition was W. B. Yeats.

In 1888 Yeats, with others, published *Poems and Ballads of Young Ireland*. Yeats, however, did not come to an appreciation of the school of Davis through a lonely perusal of its yellowing pages. Yeats had been caught up by the romantic figure of the old Fenian, John O'Leary, who had returned to Dublin after five years' penal servitude and fifteen years of exile in Paris.

> It was through the old Fenian leader John O'Leary I found my theme. His long imprisonment, his longer banishment, his magnificent head, his scholarship, his pride, his integrity, all that aristocratic dream nourished amid little shops and little farms, had drawn around him a group of young men; I was but eighteen or nineteen and had already, under the influence of *The Faerie Queene* and The Sad Shepherd, written a pastoral play, and under that of Shelley's *Prometheus Unbound* two plays, one staged somewhere in the Caucasus, the other in a crater of the moon; and I knew myself to be vague and incoherent.[15]

In the Young Ireland poetry that O'Leary gave him, with full admission of its limitations as poetry, Yeats found the public voice of the poet very attractive, for there he saw the individual expressing the generations in the act of expressing himself. In Irish history and national poetry, Yeats hoped to find a culture closer than the abstractions of the Caucasus, a medium through which he could relate himself to his fellow man, and in the gestures and images of that relation, find a unity of self beyond mere vagueness and incoherence. It was the gestures and images of O'Leary's noble head that Yeats wanted, and since the poetry of Davis had been the beginning for O'Leary, Yeats hoped this poetry would serve for himself. It was in such a spirit of eager discovery that Yeats had written his challenge to Anglo-Irish culture in the essay on Ferguson (quoted in Chapter One). With Fer-

---

[15] W. B. Yeats, "A General Introduction to My Work," in *Essays and Introductions* (New York, 1961), p. 510.

guson and O'Grady, Yeats found a deeper past that had not been available to the Young Ireland poets who only exploited the bardic poetry. In 1889 Yeats published *The Wanderings of Oisin*. With this poem the Irish Literary Renaissance began, and it was John O'Leary who gathered enough subscriptions to convince the publishers to print it. Yeats began to have great hopes that a literary movement of more than local merit could come to Ireland. With a movement of politics and one of scholarship behind him Yeats felt certain of his hour, and made arrangements to begin a publishing program of works of literary interest. It was at this moment that Sir Charles Gavan Duffy came to London and, hearing from Rolleston of Yeats's idea, embarked on a plan to publish more books of scholarship and Young Ireland poetry. Yeats was livid at the theft of his idea. Now no longer in sympathy with Young Ireland, he found himself in a position where he could not side with the belletristic school of Professor Dowden at Trinity College, or with the propagandistic and sentimental art of the middle classes. Thus began his crusade for a literature that was art first and Irish second; and thus began the inevitable conflicts and controversies that were to exasperate and exalt him into becoming Ireland's greatest poet.

Yeats's early crusade had three goals: the creation of a new form of literature, a new philosophy, and a new Irish nationalism.[16] But since he saw "many aims" as the curse of the modern, Yeats labored to hammer these diverse thoughts into unity. Most contemporary critics regard this unity as the achievement of a separate "late Yeats," but as early as the 'nineties Yeats's three goals had a unity. Irish nationalism contributed material and an idiom for a new form of literature, and Irish folklore (as Yeats read it) expressed a philosophy that was similar to the thought of Swedenborg, Blake, and the theosophists.

An impulse toward what is definite and sensuous, and an indifference toward the abstract and general, are the lineaments, as I understand the

16 W. B. Yeats, "If I Were Four and Twenty," *Explorations* (New York, 1962), p. 263.

word, of all that comes not from the learned, but out of common antiquity, out of the "folk" as we say, and in certain languages, Irish for instance—and these languages are all poetry—it is not possible to speak an abstract thought. This impulse went out of Swedenborg when he turned from vision. It was inseparable from this primitive faculty, but was not a part of his daily bread, whereas Blake carried it to a passion and made it the foundation of his thought.[17]

Yeats was never content to promote the study of Irish folklore simply because it was Irish; he saw the peasant as the preserver of an ancient and mystical world view, a world view that had since been obliterated as life had become more deliberate, abstract, and complex. In this folklore he saw a way of bringing together his three passions for the national, the pastoral, and the mystical. To use Yeats on Yeats, we could say that the peasant expressed his opposite, for the peasant seemed simple, sensuous, and animally unified; whereas Yeats was complex, intellectual, and fragmented. As a poet, Yeats had eaten of the fruit of knowledge and had been cast out of this peasant Eden where the supernatural still existed in the common life of man. Yeats's first attempt at unity was, there-fore, a desire for ecstasy, not through a dialectical resolution of innocence and experience, but through an annihilation of experi-ence. The ideal realm was the Happy Islands of the West that the mythic Oisin had visited, or, in the title of Yeats's play that ex-pressed this flight from and rejection of civilization, *The Land of Heart's Desire*. This realm is free of conflict simply because the self has destroyed everything that is other to the self. In the phe-nomenology of the early Yeats, will and responsibility are impos-sible; since pain does not exist, no toil or passionate tragedy can raise the self into a heightened consciousness where the divisions of the self fuse into a newer unity. Early Yeats and late Yeats knew unity, but what the early unity lacked is what Yeats himself would call the Vision of Evil. In his collection of fairy tales and in his *Celtic Twilight*, Yeats, as much as Hyde, was involved in the ideological dismissal of civilization. But beyond the merely lin-

17 W. B. Yeats, "Swedenborg, Mediums, Desolate Places," *Explorations*, p. 43.

guistic atavism of the gentlemanly Hyde, Yeats's was a total atavism
that rejected the world for the land of faery. The dreamy art of
this period was one of fantasy and wish-fulfillment; the lament of
Yeats's shepherd was: "Of old the world on dreaming fed; / Grey
truth is now her painted toy." But Yeats was an intensely self-
analytical young man as well as a good critic of his own work.
When eighteen he knew himself to be vague and incoherent; when
twenty-two, he knew even more about himself.

> I have noticed something about my poetry I did not know before, in
> this process of correction; for instance, that it is almost all a flight into
> fairyland from the real world, and a summons to that flight. The Chorus
> to the "Stolen Child" sums it up—that it is not the poetry of insight
> and knowledge, but of longing and complaint—the cry of the heart
> against necessity. I hope some day to alter that and write poetry of in-
> sight and knowledge.[18]

Yeats's answer to this situation was to thrust himself into the midst
of experience. He moved from attending literary societies and banquets to riding the bandwagon with Maud Gonne and helping
direct the celebrations for the centenary of the rising of 1798.
In 1900 he worked on the assembly protesting Queen Victoria's
Boer War recruiting visit to Ireland: on the day of the assembly
in Drumcondra, he tagged along and watched the furious republican, Maud Gonne, swear a multitude of children to the undying
hatred of England.[19] But all this was not exactly an artist's work,
and Yeats soon realized that he had succumbed to the chief temptation of the artist, "creation without toil."

Seeing in the past a society that appealed to him, Yeats labored
to bring the middle classes back into line with the passionate
aristocrats and the storied folk, but the middle classes were not
co-operative. For a man of Yeats's sensibility, such resistance only
sharpened his image of a cultured aristocracy. Culture became a
group of the select, a secret society based upon the mysteries of

[18] *The Letters of W. B. Yeats,* ed. Allan Wade (London, 1954), p. 63.
[19] Edward Malins, "Yeats and the Easter Rising," Dolmen Press Yeats Centenary
Paper (Dublin, 1965), p. 6.

the Near East. Yeats belonged to the Theosophical Society, the National Literary Society, the Rhymers Club, the Irish Republican Brotherhood, the Gaelic League, the Cumman na Gaedheal, because he was looking for a Fianna, Seventy Disciples, or, at least, a Mermaid Tavern (read Cheshire Cheese). Forever in a court in his imagination, Yeats had a grand way of turning his friends into knights for the crusade. In London he sent George Moore back to work in Ireland for the Irish Literary Theatre; in Paris, he sent Synge to the Aran Islands, thinking at the time that he had found merely the makings of a good scholar; in Galway, he set Lady Gregory to the toil of gathering tales that he would put style upon and furnish with philosophical notes. Used to such co-operation, Yeats was rather taken aback when a young unknown named James Joyce returned the ticket and said that it was a shame that Yeats was too old to be influenced by him.[20] But Yeats had good reason in undertaking all this literary entrepreneurship, for he sensed that the self could not achieve unity of being in a fragmented collective; therefore, he labored to create a new community.

If we would create a great community—and what other game is so worth the labour?—we must re-create the old foundations of life, not as they existed in that splendid misunderstanding of the eighteenth century, but as they must always exist when the finest minds and Ned the beggar and Sean the fool think about the same thing, although they may not think the same thought about it.[21]

Yeats instinctively felt what the sociologist has observed, that "The individual has as many different social egos as there are different social groups and strata with which he is connected." [22] A pluralistic society breaks up the self; its many institutions hold out conflicting and contradictory roles, and when an individual who must play separate roles as he moves from institution to institution encounters a contradiction between the instructions for one role

---

20 See Joyce's version of the encounter in *Finnegans Wake* (New York, Compass Edition, 1959), p. 37.
21 W. B. Yeats, *Explorations*, p. 28. Note that Yeats envisions beggars in his Great Community.
22 Pitrim Sorokin, *Society, Culture, and Personality* (New York, 1962), p. 345.

and another, he experiences the disorientation anxiety or *anomie* that leads to the rejection of civilization and all its conflicting institutions. The romantic clears the landscape with an impatient sweep of the hand. The early Yeats made the impatient gesture, but as he gained experience in playing, and playing with, different roles in all the dozens of societies to which he belonged, Yeats began to pause and think more seriously about the idea of the role and about society as a drama of conflict. Significantly, after the saber-rattling exercises of the celebrations of 1898, Yeats's next attempt to create a great community was the founding of a theater. Sensing that personality could not really come to consciousness in a void, that it needed a culture, a community, or what he would later call a Body of Fate, Yeats hoped to create a theater where the best minds and the rest of the community would be separated by nothing more than the curtain of a stage. With genius on one side, and applause on the other, everything would be fine. A theater would provide a meeting place, a coming together of classes, a consensus of nationality. Since Yeats felt that Ireland, through him, was reaching its hour, Ireland must have the theater that Greece, England, Spain, and France had had in theirs. Even when this dream failed, or let us say when the Irish failed Yeats, he continued to follow historical precedent and merely exchanged the public Athenian theater of Dionysus for the gathering of the elect at Eleusis.

In all these efforts and activities, Yeats was moving out toward complexity and away from any simple nationalism. In his search, he was looking toward the examples of European art. When Yeats came to the work of Thomas Davis he had been reading Spenser and Shelley, but in the society and societies in which he moved, he was often to meet people who had read Davis and Mangan, but not Spenser and Shelley. Yeats managed to get along in this company because for much of his time he was vocal in print against the Anglo-Irish denial of the worth of native literature. One of these controversies was waged in the columns of Dublin's Unionist *Daily Express*. There Yeats, John Eglinton the essayist, and A.E.

argued with one another about the significance of the Irish legends and the new literary ideals. Eglinton, more a man of circumspection than enthusiasm, was more interested in the future than the past, more in a slow process of cultural enlightenment than in any sudden millennium. In all, he was doubtful that Celtic myth provided the answer for the problems of civilization. His picture of Ireland at this point in history is, in contrast to Yeats's, a much more measured one.

If, also, as seems likely, the approaching ages on the Continent are to be filled with great social and political questions and events which can hardly have immediate results in literature, it is quite conceivable that literature, as it did once before, would migrate to a quiet country like Ireland, where there is no great tradition to be upset or much social sediment to be stirred up, and where the spectacle of such changes might afford a purely intellectual impulse.[23]

Although the calm and rational Eglinton did not shudder with chiliastic anticipations, he expressed, if not an artistic, a moral messianism. If Ireland was denied the opportunity to become a political or social force, she yet might find her role as a source of moral regeneration.

What Renan says, in speaking of the Jews, that "a nation whose mission it is to revolve in its bosom spiritual truths is often weak politically," may be used with regard to Ireland as an argument that at least nothing stands in its way in this direction.[24]

In this statement by Renan, a French scholar of literature and comparative religion—and, in fact, a Breton Celt—the Irish had an appealing rationalization for the defeat of Home Rule, for in defining Celtic Messianism in the Welsh, Renan had said that the belief in a future avenger who was to restore Cambria was the manner in which "little people dowered with imagination avenge themselves on their conquerors." [25] The parallels between tiny Is-

23 John Eglinton, *Literary Ideals in Ireland* (Dublin, 1899), p. 10.
24 Ibid.
25 Ernest Renan, *The Poetry of the Celtic Races and Other Essays* (London, 1896), p. 10.

rael lost in the immensity of the Egyptian Empire, tiny Judea lost
in the immensity of the Roman Empire, and tiny Ireland lost in
the immensity of the British Empire were very attractive. The
Irishman of Young Ireland days was merely pictured as "gay, bold,
and joyous" with a good sense of fun; evil was dismissed as something entirely alien to the Celtic spirit, though not to the Saxon.
The new movement was going even beyond that to picture the
Irish as the instrument of the Lord for His work in history. Although Eglinton was not caught up in the enthusiasms of Gaelic
League or the new literature, his quotation from Renan was over-
whelmingly attractive, and once he had placed it in the newspapers,
it was destined to move from the circumspect thought of Mr.
Eglinton to the context of the streets. Men who lacked the patience
to read volumes of O'Grady could seize a sentence, and for the
religious Irishman, such a sentence would speak volumes. It is,
of course, true that the average Irishman did not read the Unionist
Daily Express, and even if he did, he might be inclined to pass up
a collection of literary letters to the editor; but it is more than
likely that Dublin's famous orator of the time, John F. Taylor,
would follow the opinions of his opponents in Dublin's literary
societies. And it was John F. Taylor who put the messianism of
the elect into the mind of every Irishman in the street. Coming
to the defense of the revival of the Irish language, which had again
been criticized by Trinity College members of an educational commission as "a return to the Dark Ages," Taylor rose and said in an
extemporaneous speech: "If Moses had listened to the counsels of
that learned professor he would never have come down from the
mountain, his face glowing as a star, and bearing the Tables of
the Law written in the language of the outlaw." [26] The speech
was reported in the Home Rule newspaper, *The Freeman's Journal,* was reprinted as a pamphlet and spread all over Dublin, and
was finally immortalized in *Ulysses.* What Eglinton had proposed

[26] The speech was given on October 24, 1901; the pamphlet, undated, is in
the National Library of Ireland's collection of historical pamphlets. Joyce's
slightly improved version is on page 141 of the Modern Library edition.

as a goal and an ideal for the Irish suddenly became a statement of fact. The Irish were the chosen people of the modern world.

Yeats's part in the *Daily Express* debates was not to promulgate a moral messianism, but an artistic one. What is, of course, lacking in all this messianism is a messiah. Israel had Moses, and Judea had Christ, but what of Ireland? Since Yeats saw art as the new religion, he probably saw himself as its prophet. In this kind of artistic religion based upon primitive myth, Yeats had Wagner as a precursor, and Yeats was quick to invoke Wagner in defending the Irish legends on his side of the controversy. Yeats spoke of "the influence both words and music are beginning to have upon the intellect of Germany and of Europe," and said that many were coming "to see the German soul in them." [27] All of which was rather hypocritical, since Yeats was tone deaf and disliked music; no doubt his friend and collaborator in the Irish Literary Theatre, Edward Martyn, drew the parallel between Siegfried and Cuchulain, for Martyn was a devoted Wagnerian. But this new faith of the aesthete was a little too much to ask of a Catholic country. Yeats was out on a limb, and its luxuriant European foliage did not make it more attractive in the eyes of his fellow Dubliners.

A.E. came to the defense of Yeats and tried to reconcile the argument between the skeptical Eglinton and the devout Yeats, for both of them were his friends. A.E. smoothed over Yeats's aesthetic-symbolist tendencies by claiming that Yeats was trying to ennoble literature by making it more religious. A.E., however, was only seeing in Yeats what he wanted to see; A.E. was a mystic first and a poet second. When his fellow members of the theosophical lodge asked him for a contribution to their journal, he asked whether they would prefer prose or verse. Since theosophical verse was a new wrinkle that even Madame Blavatsky could countenance, they asked for verse and received the poems that eventually became his book, *Homeward: Songs by the Way*. For a man of A.E.'s religious sensibility, Yeats's flowing tie, tousled hair, his numerous trips to London and Paris where he kept the notoriously

[27] John Eglinton, *Literary Ideals in Ireland*, p. 31.

bad company of the critic Arthur Symons, were a little disquieting. A.E. wanted none of the "Decadence" in Ireland, and therefore he went on to express his own deep conviction concerning the controversy.

... the country which preserves its individuality does so with the pro-found conviction that its peculiar ideal is nobler than that which the cosmopolitan spirit suggests—that this ideal is so precious to it that its loss would be as the loss of the soul, and that it could not be realized without an aloofness from, if not an actual indifference to, the ideals which are spreading so rapidly over Europe.[28]

The irony of A.E.'s point is that the ideals which at that time were spreading so rapidly over Europe were precisely the anti-cosmopol-itan ideals he favored. Both Ireland and Germany were shudder-ing with horror at the cosmopolitan spirit of the latter-day Sodom and Gomorrah, London and Paris. And, interestingly enough in the history of ideas, both the German and the Irish nativistic move-ments shared not only folklore and pagan myth, but theosophy as well; and both countries created the messianism of the elect out of feelings of national inferiority.[29] But in the language of theoso-phy, the messiah is known as the avatar, and for every *magnus annus,* every cycle of two thousand years, there appears a new avatar. As history was turning into the twentieth century, mystics felt that the hour was approaching. A.E. had good reason for not seeing art as the new religion and Yeats as its prophet, for in June of 1896 A.E. had had a vision of the avatar.[30]

In a letter telling Yeats of his vision, A.E. asked him to return to Ireland so that they could discuss the implications of this im-portant event. Yeats returned to Ireland that summer, and in the castle of his Wagnerian friend, Edward Martyn, Yeats had a vision too. Herbert Howarth has much to say of this vision that seemed to grow and change in Yeats's mind with each new recollection.

[28] Ibid. p. 82.
[29] George L. Mosse, *The Crisis of German Ideology,* p. 41. For a comparative study of nativistic movements, see Vittorio Lanternari, *The Religions of the Oppressed: A Study of Modern Messianic Cults* (New York, 1965).
[30] See *Letters from A.E.,* ed. Alan Denson (London, 1961), p. 17.

A.E.'s vision was of wild drumming, a beautiful woman holding a babe, and, in a sudden change of scene, the figure of an infirm queen that "let fall the scepter from its fingers." [31] Yeats's vision, as described first in a letter to William Sharp, was of a beautiful woman shooting an arrow to the stars.[32] In his poem, "The Seven Woods," the archer seems to be a man, and in "The Trembling of a Veil," and its "Notes" in *Autobiographies,* the archer is a woman of incredible beauty, and a galloping centaur has been added, which is a decided improvement.[33] Finally, in the vision's ultimate expression in the late poem, "Parnell's Funeral," Yeats adds the archetypal images that a man, "learned in Near-Eastern antiquities," had given him to the context of the comet that Standish O'Grady and others had seen on the day of Parnell's funeral. Now mystic visions as everyone knows do not change like this; they come, once and forever themselves, out of the timeless into time, and never do they undergo the permutations of the world of flux. Profound dreams and reveries of the preconscious imagination are, of course, another matter. One awakes, remembering only pieces, and as experience provides sudden reminders, the total image slowly emerges. In Yeats's theory of visions, a large vision is broken into smaller images, and these images are perceived by people separated in space, if not time. If the people are able to come together and discuss their dreams, then the total, greater vision emerges. For this reason, Yeats was interested in William Sharp's experiences, as well as the experiences of others who spent the night of Yeats's vision in Tulira Castle. Strangely enough, Yeats says absolutely nothing about A.E.'s vision of the avatar, even though he was later to write the play, *The Resurrection,* in which the *magnus annus* is ushered in by wild drumming, and in the shock of Incarnation, the Roman Empire drops the reins of peace and war. Perhaps Yeats was offended that anything as momentous as a vision of the avatar was not first granted to him, for after all,

---

[31] A.E., *The Candle of Vision* (London, 1918), p. 99.
[32] *Letters of W. B. Yeats,* ed. Allan Wade (London, 1954), p. 266.
[33] W. B. Yeats, *Autobiographies* (London, 1961), p. 372; see also Herbert Howarth, *The Irish Writers* (London, 1958), *passim.*

it was his movement. Both A.E. and Yeats were theosophically inclined and were fellow-conspirers in apocalypse, so it matters little
in the long run which was first with the truer vision. If Yeats stole
his vision from A.E., we must concede from the poems he wrote
with it that he was able to make it his own in a deeply personal
way. On a much more mundane historical plane, these visions are
important, for they show that the messianic ideology of the poets
and dreamers is beginning to have military implications.

What Yeats would undoubtedly have discussed with A.E. upon
his return to Ireland in the summer of 1896 was the prophecy of
another theosophical friend, MacGregor Mathers. "He began to
foresee changes in the world, announcing in 1893 or 1894 the im-
minence of immense wars." [34] In Yeats's 1899 book of poetry, *The
Wind Among the Reeds*, he begins to move away from dreamy
lamentation to give the reader the shape of things to come. One
poem is worth looking at in its entirety, for it shows how theosophy, poetry, and ancient Irish myth, through the alchemy of imagination, are being fused into the alloy that will later be made into
bullets.

THE VALLEY OF THE BLACK PIG

> The dew drops slowly and dreams gather: unknown spears
> Suddenly hurtle before my dream awakened eyes,
> And then the clash of fallen horsemen and the cries
> Of unknown perishing armies beat about my ears.
> We who still labour by the cromlech on the shore,
> The grey cairn on the hill, when day sinks drowned in dew,
> Being weary of the world's empires, bow down to you,
> Master of the still stars and of the flaming door.

The title of the poem comes from an Irish legend which has it that
the Fenians will return, and in a great battle fought in this valley,
drive out the foreigners. Yeats, gazing at twilight on Maeve's cairn
as it stands on top of the mountain of Knocknarea, sees and hears
the ancient armies of pagan Connacht, and knows of their return.

[34] W. B. Yeats, *Autobiographies*, p. 336.

But all this violent activity is, in theosophical terms, on the *astral plane,* in that fluid solution that, working on the film of the material world, fixes the images of things to come. Yeats labors apart in the real world, but being weary of that world and its British Empire, he would rather bow down to the glory of the exalted Irish past. The past opens like a golden door; destiny awaits. In terms of the actual physical images of the poem, the sunset over Yeats's native Rosses Point would indeed make Maeve's cairn stand out golden in the long evenings of an Irish summer. The sun which is master of the still stars thus turns Maeve's cairn from unpromising gray to gold; the past and the future come into line, for when the planets drop into the sun, there is the star of Bethlehem and the coming of the avatar.

If the messianism of Yeats was occult and astrological in the extreme, the messianism of the Irish peasant was much simpler to grasp. Douglas Hyde also wrote about the legend of the return of the ancient Fianna, and Hyde too was weary of the British Empire. In his essay, "The Coming of the Fenians," he describes the great black cloud that is sweeping over Ireland as the English mind. Exhorting his fellow Irishmen to dispel this darkness with the Sword of Light, he makes his plea for the revival of Irish.[35] Hyde's writing is highly metaphoric and literary, and he quotes an Irish poem that, for him, describes the great wonders that will happen when the Irish speak their own tongue.

> There is a change coming, a big change!
> And riches and store will be worth nothing;
> He will rise up that was small enough,
> And he that was big will fall down.[36]

Hyde was not a revolutionary nationalist and he strove to keep the Gaelic League a cultural and not a militant organization, but his good nature often got the best of him, for he thought that his

[35] *The Sword of Light,* or *An Claidheamh Soluis,* was the journal of the Gaelic League.
[36] John Eglinton, *Ideals in Ireland,* ed. Lady Gregory (London, 1901), p. 65.

fellow countrymen would take these metaphors in a literary, but not literal, way. The return of the Fenians, the overturning of classes: these metaphors proved to be something much larger than advertisements for O'Growney's Irish Grammar.

If, in the early phase of the ideological movement, Hyde was encouraging the Irish to re-create their national identity along grammatical lines, A.E. was preaching that Irish identity should be achieved by nothing less than an immersion in the collective racial consciousness. For A.E., national identity was not in speaking, but in being.

> The idea of the national being emerged at no recognisable point in our history. It is older than any name we know. It is not earth born, but the synthesis of many heroic and beautiful moments, and these, it must be remembered, are divine in their origin. Every heroic deed is an act of the spirit, and every perception of beauty is vision with the divine eye, and not with mortal sense. The spirit was subtly intermingled with the shining of old romance, and it was no mere phantasy which shows Ireland at its dawn in a misty light thronged with divine figures, and beneath and nearer to us, demigods and heroes fading into recognisable men.[37]

The shining of old romance that A.E. is talking about is, of course, the old romance of O'Grady's history, and, in fact, A.E. admitted that whatever was Irish in him, O'Grady had kindled to life.[38] But A.E. took O'Grady's history farther than the romantic historian himself would have wished. A.E. read theosophy into the ancient myths and made O'Grady's history into sacred scripture. Standing on a sea-wall at Bray, A.E. preached to a crowd about the return of the pagan Irish gods, about the radiations of astral light that came from the sacred mountains of the land. O'Grady, by coincidence, was in the crowd and was more than slightly amazed to see what could happen to his work when it became part of the imagination of others. Later, as the Irish gods and heroes became

37 Ibid. p. 15.
38 Hugh Art O'Grady, *Standish James O'Grady, The Man and Writer* (Dublin, 1929), p. 72.

part of the traffic on the public stage, he protested against what was in fact the continuation of a process he had begun.[39]

Since the fall of Parnell, the nationalists had spent a decade in the new enthusiasms; but small meetings, literary banquets, and a lonely reading of books were not enough. The intellectuals longed to address themselves to a multitude; they were in flight from "The Decadence" and the solipsism of the Aesthetic Movement of the 'nineties in England and France; and the people longed to give their individual excitements a collective intensity. At the turn of the century, visionary men like A.E. and Yeats might, like Kubla Khan, hear "ancestral voices prophesying war," but even men who were as quiet, rational, and ironic as John Synge sensed that a drama was being played in Ireland on the other side of the stage. One of the new plays based upon the ancient Irish legends was the Irish Literary Theatre's production of Yeats and George Moore's *Diarmuid and Grania* which, along with Douglas Hyde's Gaelic version of Yeats's story, *The Twisting of the Rope (Casadh an tSugain)*, was presented on the night of October 21, 1901. Of the performance, Synge commented:

It was the first time that a play in Irish had ever been acted in a theatre, and the enthusiastic members of the Gaelic League stormed the cheaper seats. In spite of the importance of the League, when it organizes a demonstration one always senses (as in all deep-seated popular movements) the ridiculous rubbing shoulders with feelings of profound emotion. Thus, at the beginning of the play one could not help but smile at seeing all around the room the beautiful girls of the Gaelic League, who were chattering away in very bad Irish with palely enthusiastic young clerks. But during an intermission of *Diarmuid and Grania* it happened that the people in the galleries began to sing, as is the custom in this theatre. They sang the old songs of the people. Until then I had never heard these songs sung in the ancient Irish tongue by so many voices. The auditorium shook. In these lingering notes, of incomparable sadness, there was something like the death rattle of a nation. I saw one head bend down behind a program, and then another. People were weeping.

Then the curtain rose and the play was resumed in the midst of

---

39 See John Eglinton, *A Memoir of A.E.* (London, 1937), p. 41.

lively emotion. One sensed that the spirit of a nation had hovered for an instant in the room.[40]

Synge saw in the emotion of the crowd a death rattle, but since Synge was dying of lymphatic sarcoma and was obsessed with death and the images of death, it is not surprising that he saw the ashes and not the phoenix. Another Irish writer who was present, Padraic Colum, felt the situation in a more positive way.

Why did the occasion seem so vibrant? Why was there such unison in the crowd of young people in the sixpenny seats of the gallery? Looking back on it one who was present recognizes that a *mystique* was being given expression, a *mystique* that was arising from new sources....The play in English was over, and there on the stage was the leader of the Gaelic movement in the part of a poet, Douglas Hyde, whom they greeted by his Gaelic name "An Craoibhin Aoibhinn." [41]

Six months later the plays that O'Grady criticized, A.E.'s *Deirdre* and Yeats's *Cathleen ni Houlihan*, were presented in St. Teresa's Hall.[42] There in the title role of Yeats's play was the beautiful Maud Gonne playing the aged woman of Ireland, the Shan Van Vocht. There through the mask of age the beautiful woman asked for young men to help throw the strangers out of her house and restore her four green fields, her Ulster, Leinster, Munster, and Connacht. And in A.E.'s play a thrill went through the audience as the name of the ancient warrior, Cuchulain, was pronounced upon a stage for the first time.[43]

This was the ethos of Dublin at the beginning of the twentieth century. For a decade since the death of Parnell, the writers and journalists had elaborated a new ideology with its new values expressed as antitheses: past vs. present, agricultural community vs. industrial collective, small moral nation vs. decadent empire, intuition vs. reason, Gaelic vs. English. But for the unsophisticated

---

40 J. M. Synge, *The Aran Islands and Other Writings*, p. 364.
41 Padraic Colum, *Arthur Griffith* (Dublin, 1959), p. 57. The American edition is entitled *Ourselves Alone* and contains an introduction by Crane Brinton.
42 O'Grady's editorial in his *All-Ireland Review* (April 19, 1902), 100.
43 Padraic Colum, *Arthur Griffith*, p. 69.

mind of the man in the street, it meant simply Ireland vs. England. This was the ethos of enthusiasm and romanticism, or, more simply, nativism. But for all that Yeats, Hyde, and A.E. would have it so, Ireland was not a community, and there were men present in Dublin whose minds favored deliberation, common sense, and the high art of Europe over the folk tales of Eirú. John Eglinton possessed the cosmopolitan mind (his name was a *nom de plume* for the more provincial William Kirkpatrick Magee) and suspected the folk movement and its grandiose claims. In a review of Yeats's *Ideas of Good and Evil*, Eglinton showed that to decline to join the movement was not simply to enroll among the ignorant who could not follow the argument in Yeats's Swedenborgian reading of folklore. With the perception that one would expect from a man who had devoted a career to the study of such things,[44] Eglinton goes directly to the heart of the matter. Speaking of the peasant, he says:

The supernatural effects in his tales are a confusion of planes. He views the landscape of the world of his imagination as if it were on a flat surface. The stars are hung up in the trees.[45]

Joyce and Yeats liked to think of themselves as the only minds in Dublin, and though they were indeed its greatest geniuses, there were others with some degree of intelligence. Eglinton, although his literary powers did not extend beyond the essay, had a subtle and intelligent mind, and, often, an expressive if elaborate prose style.

Among the stalwart farmers who made Rome or the burgesses of early London, whom William Morris loved to imagine on the wharves of an uncontaminated Thames, we hear little of seances, hypnotism and the like; it is in imperial Rome, in Nineveh and Babylon, in modern London and Paris, in the vast urban populations of India and China, that we hear of such things, and if our towns increase so as to suck up all the

[44] See, for example, Jean Piaget's theory of the transformation of the child's view of reality in *The Child's Conception of Physical Causality* (Paterson, 1960), p. 237.
[45] See John Eglinton, "Philosophy of the Celtic Movement," in *Anglo-Irish Essays* (Dublin, 1917), p. 44.

remains of peasant life it may be expected that this product of city life may increase proportionally.[46]

Another young critic, James Joyce, attacked the gentler half of the Yeats-Lady Gregory school of Irish folklore. Certain that only a mind in its dotage could prefer the incoherent sentimentalities of Connacht to the masterpieces of Europe, Joyce did not let shallow patriotism or respect for a possible patron interfere with his discrimination.

In fine, her book, wherever it treats of the "folk," sets forth in the fulness of its senility a class of mind which Mr. Yeats has set forth with such delicate scepticism in his happiest book, "The Celtic Twilight." [47]

And if the disciples of the Gaelic League screamed with delight at the Irish Literary Theatre's production of their master's play, Joyce shuddered in disgust. Joyce, an admirer of Ibsen, had been expecting the theater to live up to its promise to present Continental drama in translation. When, instead, a Gaelic League production was announced, Joyce felt that the artists had given in to the mob. So strongly did he feel about this matter that when his review of the production was rejected by the authorities of his university magazine, he went to the trouble and cost of printing it at his own expense. In this pamphlet Joyce made a good case for his views by pointing out a simple, if unpatriotic, fact of literary history: "A nation which never advanced so far as a miracle play affords no literary model to the artist, and he must look abroad." [48] Joyce was disappointed and concerned for the future of art in Ireland. Since he had already begun his career with a published essay on Ibsen, he had hoped to follow up by offering the Irish Literary Theatre a translation of his own.[49] As he saw it the theater "by

---

46 Ibid. p. 46.
47 Joyce's review of Lady Gregory's *Poets and Dreamers*, Dublin *Daily Express*, March 26, 1903.
48 James Joyce, "The Day of the Rabblement," *Two Essays: Francis Sheehy-Skeffington and James Joyce* (Dublin, 1901).
49 See Richard Ellmann, *James Joyce* (New York, 1958), p. 94.

its surrender to the trolls has cut itself adrift from the line of advancement." If A.E. saw turn-of-the-century Dublin as a tumulus in which the pagan gods were awakening, Joyce saw it as a mind affected by "paralysis."

Another cosmopolitan, George Moore, allowed himself to be swept up in the enthusiasm of the popular movement, but since Moore avoided the effort of learning Irish, it is most likely that he was merely gathering material for his gossip-novel on the literary revival, *Hail and Farewell.* One can never tell when Moore is being serious and when snide, for he is master of the technique in which the author makes light of himself so that he is free to ridicule the enthusiasm of others: Moore heard a voice telling him to return to Ireland on the road to Sussex, but when the Irish would not take him in as the new avatar, he sent off a letter to the *Irish Times* announcing his apostasy from Catholicism to the Church of Ireland. The great, original, and profound vision that led Moore to this conversion was that Catholic dogma destroys literature and that the works the Irish Catholics esteemed were absolute drivel. Moore appears devoted to literature, and in the banquet scene in *Ave* he seems full of excitement for the occasion in which all the leading literary figures of Dublin gather to celebrate the passing of the intellectual torch from Europe to Ireland. Characteristically, the great banquet is followed by a pilgrimage to Bayreuth in the company of Edward Martyn, and though on the surface this may seem to support the comparison between Cuchulain and Siegfried, in reality the journey only squashes the pretensions of the banquet and its few neo-Celtic lyrics with the immense weight of *The Ring* and the colossus of Continental art in general. Moore and Joyce both show an ironic mode of perception that saves them from enthusiasm and its attendant follies and rescues their identities from a commitment to anything larger than themselves. Moore has a playful and enjoyable time with the banquet, but he never seems to have noticed a moment that Yeats could never forget:

> Standish O'Grady supporting himself between the tables
> Speaking to a drunken audience high nonsensical words.

For on that night in 1899 Standish James O'Grady made a prophecy: "We have now a literary movement, it is not very important;
it will be followed by a political movement, that will not be very
important; then must come a military movement, that will be important indeed." [50]

[50] W. B. Yeats, *Autobiographies*, p. 424. The lines about O'Grady are from
Yeats's poem, "Beautiful Lofty Things."

CHAPTER THREE

THE REALIZATION OF THE PAST

In the early days of nationalistic enthusiasm a friend of Ireland was a friend of all, for in the passion for Ireland's language a humble peasant of the west might find himself sharing a podium and a crystal pitcher of water with doctors, lawyers, and clergymen. But the peasant of the city found himself where he had always been: in the slums. For those who could make it into the lower middle class, or for those willing to range out beyond class lines, there was a chance for broader associations in all the countless clubs and societies. Yet the new companionship in things Irish remained the bond of a generation. While their parents argued about the fall of Parnell, haggled in the shop, and paid the taxes, a new generation dreamed and talked about the future. With parliamentarianism in splinters, it was only natural that the dreams should turn again to revolution. Yeats's *Cathleen ní Houlihan* had been inspired by the centenary celebrations of the 1798 rising, and it was the young who had not yet come into power in society who were fired by this thinly disguised call to arms. Society as a whole hoped for the best and rationalized its disappointment with the benefits

of the Tory policy of "killing Home Rule with kindness." The
Balfour Acts of 1891 and 1896 enabled the tenants to buy their
lands from the landlords, and the Irish Land Purchase Act of 1903
encouraged the landlords to sell by offering them bonuses. The
peasants had won their Land War; feudalism was dying in Ireland.
And the middle classes, always aware of how much they stand to
lose, went on in their law-abiding way. Revolution, as it often
seems to be, was a dream of those insecurely placed people at the
bottom of the top and the top of the bottom. It is only when the
subjunctive sigh, "If only we" changes its mood into the interrogative "What if?" that the intellectuals are startled to find their literary speeches being cheered by the semi-literate working classes.
When the idea of revolution passes from general dreams to particular programs, or when, in Standish O'Grady's terms, the literary
movement is succeeded by the political, a new body-politic is
created in which labor and the intelligentsia become the left and
right hands of revolution. In the early days and dreams of the
movement, the hands were not yet swinging fists, but were clasped
in a handshake that seemed to cross over class divisions. Of the
many nationalistic societies that strove to maintain a unity of all
Irishmen against the common Saxon menace, the Gaelic League
was the strongest and most popular for the simple sociological reason that its celebration of folklore appealed to the intellectuals
while its moralistic rejection of civilization, decadence, and empire
appealed to the Catholic lower-middle class. D. P. Moran's weekly,
The Leader, was another attempt to keep the Irish united against
the common enemy, but Moran's particular aim was to bring the
upper-middle class of civil servants, professional people, and other
white-collar workers into line with nationalism. Traditionally, the
shabby-genteel, the white-collar and lace-curtain Irish were apt to
be the strongest imitators of their English betters; it was to combat
the snobbery of these people that Moran invented his term of
derision, "West Briton." [1] By attacking their apeings of the Eng-

---

[1] This is the taunt that Miss Ivors whispers in the ear of Gabriel Conroy in
James Joyce's short story, "The Dead."

lish, Moran hoped to bring a large section of the urban populace back into Gaeldom.[2] But for all that people were thinking of the pure Irishman, the peasant, and what he had to offer in the way of a national identity to other classes, few yet were thinking about the peasant of industrial society, the slum-dweller. In many ways the evolution of the ideological movement from 1902 to 1916 is seen in the manner in which the Dublin slum-dweller comes to distract our attention from the Connacht peasant. As the ideological movement passed into the twentieth century, the fluid and shifting state of nationalist enthusiasm began to crystallize into fixed, hard, and definite programs. Cultural leaders like Douglas Hyde and W. B. Yeats began to be displaced by men with particular programs like Padraic Pearse and Arthur Griffith. This development can perhaps best be seen in a new nationalist organization that was formed out of a dozen smaller ones in 1899.

The *Cumman na nGaedheal* had been suggested by the editor of the nationalist newspaper *The United Irishman,* Arthur Griffith, but it was presided over by the more venerable John O'Leary. With the hero of the Fenian movement as president, the *Cumman* could hope to attract many—Arthur Griffith was, at this time, known only to a small circle. Griffith had begun his career as a printer's apprentice and had worked until he was able to start a paper of his own.[3] While he was waiting for the day when he could campaign for Ireland in his own newspaper, he devoted his energies to organizing one small nationalist club after another. Together with his best friend, William Rooney (to whom Yeats dedicated *Cathleen ni Houlihan*), Griffith worked in the Leinster Literary Society. The quality of literary nationalism without Yeats is described in the youthful careers of these two men: Rooney wrote poetry in the manner of Thomas Davis and Griffith wrote graveyard meditations in the manner of Lady Morgan and John O'Donovan. Together the young men collaborated on a series of

2 See D. P. Moran, in *Ideals in Ireland,* ed. Lady Gregory (London, 1901).
3 The biography is Padraic Colum's *Arthur Griffith* (Dublin, 1959). The reader should be warned, however, that what Lady Gregory did to Cuchulain, Colum does to Griffith.

articles for the *Evening Herald* entitled "Notable Graves in and around Dublin." A few years later William Rooney formed the Celtic Literary Society, and here Griffith was able to expand the circle of his acquaintances to include Yeats, Maud Gonne, and the labor agitator James Connolly. As the movement developed, all these people came into conflict with one another, but in the early days they shared the common bond of Ireland, and at the time that was enough. The Celtic Literary Society shared the same fate as the Leinster: it underwent a transformation and became the *Cumman na nGaedheal*, yet more was changed than the name, for at the third annual convention of the *Cumman* in October 1902, Arthur Griffith presented the members with a political program. Using the career of the Hungarian patriot, Francis Deak, as a model, Griffith urged that the Irish members of Parliament refuse to sit in Westminster, demand the reinstitution of their Irish Parliament of 1782, and pledge allegiance to the king as the king of Ireland, not of England. The restitution of the Irish Parliament had been a political aim since the days of O'Connell, and O'Connell had toyed with the idea of a unilateral declaration, but he did not force the issue.[4] Griffith's program again proposed a strategy of passive resistance. In contrast to the civilized behavior of sitting in Parliament or the singing of battle-hymns at election time, the program attempted to bring the strategy of O'Connell up to date by turning the Irish M.P.'s into a *de facto* constitutional convention. Many thought that there was not enough solidarity among the Irish to support such a scheme, but one young intellectual of the parliamentary persuasion, T. M. Kettle, paid it a compliment by calling it the "largest idea contributed to Irish politics for a generation."[5] Under the title of the *Resurrection of Hungary* the program was serialized in Griffith's *United Irishman* and later published and distributed widely in pamphlet form.

A literary society had become the place for the announcement of a new political policy, and this shift of emphasis describes the

---

[4] P. S. O'Hegarty, *A History of Ireland Under the Union* (London, 1952), p. 130.
[5] Padraic Colum, *Arthur Griffith*, p. 77.

general development in the new twentieth-century Dublin. The patriots with literary genius were growing into greater consciousness of their art; inevitably this meant a growing away from naïve patriotism and the simple-minded rhetoric of nationalist societies. Yeats was drifting away from clubs to devote all his energies to his theater, and his theater was Anglo-Irish and not Gaelic. Synge, who knew Gaelic and knew more about the revered peasant than the Dubliners who declaimed their views about him in demotic Irish, stood aloof and watched his early prediction about the fate of the Gaelic League come true: the League was contaminating Gaeltacht Irish with the journalistic cant of Dublin.[6] He contemplated a play in Irish, but continued to write in English. With the appearance of Lady Gregory's comedies on the national stage, the Irish theater began to have a suspiciously Protestant, and therefore Ascendancy, tone.[7]

The popular ideological movement was beginning to split away from the intellectual and literary movement. The first phase of the ideological movement, the literary phase, had two very marked characteristics: the dismissal of evil from the national identity, and the rejection of civilization. The marked characteristic of the second phase of the movement, the political phase, was the alienation of the literary geniuses and the displacement of the nonpolitical cultural leaders. This second phase was a continuation and an intensification of the first, for in both phases the general tendency was toward the romantic simplification of complexity. The dismissal of evil, civilization, and genius amounts to a progressive simplification of consciousness in which ideas were turned into slogans, and the slogans turned into occasions for action. In the movement from national identity to political action, the genius's profound consciousness of tragic complexity was simply knocked aside as an obstruction to national ambition. Inevitably, and most painfully for the artists involved, the political simplifiers saw the

---

[6] See J. M. Synge, "The Old and the New Ireland," *The Aran Islands and Other Writings*, ed. Robert Tracy (New York, 1962), p. 381.
[7] See Sean O'Casey, *Autobiographies*, I (London, 1963), p. 516.

protests of genius as an apology for the status quo. There is no better indication of this shift in ideology than in the row over Synge's play, *The Playboy of the Western World.*

As one looks back on the riots, it seems unbelievably absurd to find an audience rioting because of the supposedly indecent use of the word "shift"; but the text of the play was only a pretext to express a deeper resentment. Yeats called his theater the Irish National Theatre, and that is precisely what Dubliners wanted: more stirring propaganda pieces in the manner of his *Cathleen ní Houlihan.* Yeats, obstinate in his own Irish way, was intent on giving them art, and for the Irish, Yeats's art had the distinct smell of Europe. The reviewer for *The Leader* diagnosed Mr. Yeats's difficulties in the following manner:

Should Mr. Yeats desire to conduct a further campaign in favour of his doctrine of the sacrifice of mere temporal things to the true ideal of the good and the beautiful, a very high doctrine in itself, seeing that his special vice is indefiniteness, he would be better advised to give our early heroes a rest, and make modern life the vehicle of his expression. The same ideas can be expressed, with the only difference that they are likely to be understood.[8]

Even before the *Playboy* row Dubliners were tired of the Abbey Theatre's artiness. The new tone of twentieth-century Dublin life was moving away from the vague romanticism of the Celtic Twilight; ironically, the play that was far closer to a twentieth-century view of things proved to be even more infuriating. When Synge's *Playboy* was presented, many saw the chance they were waiting for, and that is why crowds came to shout down the play they had not even heard. Speaking of *The Playboy, The Leader* continued its attack on Yeats's theater: "They claim that their works are unsuited for the common air; they are precious plants, and need the neurotic atmosphere of the Abbey in which to thrive." [9] The rigid minds of the orthodox lacked the mental confidence and flexibility to see the humor of the ridiculous; they saw the play as praising patricide

8 "The Spirit of the Abbey," *The Leader,* January 19, 1907.
9 "The Playboy in the Abbey," *The Leader,* February 9, 1907.

and sexual lust. They considered it a slander on both Irish nationalism and its hero, the peasant, and also a slander against the noted
purity of Irish womanhood. The play did not fail to receive condemnation on both points, and Arthur Griffith was one of the most
vigorous and outspoken of those who attacked it. Once a friend of
Yeats, but since estranged by Yeats's interest in his theater to the
detriment of his own idea of nationalism, Griffith was thorough in
his review, and certainly not modest in his claims to authority as a
literary critic:

> Mr. Synge's play as a play is one of the worst constructed we have wit-
> nessed. As a presentation on the public stage it is a vile and inhuman
> story told in the foulest language we have ever listened to from a public
> platform.[10]

For Griffith the age was advancing with all its pressing necessities
and he was most impatient with anything that threatened to distract
public attention from its proper fixation on his campaign for Irish
independence. He had been impatient with his old friend, James
Connolly, because Connolly's war against Irish capital on behalf
of Irish labor was a distraction; he was now impatient with Yeats,
for the art of Yeats and his circle had become a distraction. After
Ireland had its freedom, then something could be done about the
nation's literature and its internal problems.

Internal self-reliance was the platform of Griffith's party, *Sinn
Fein* (Ourselves Alone). Part of this program was never to recognize
or use the services or forces of the enemy, and here Yeats had
sinned most grievously, for he had called in the police on the mob
that rioted at the Abbey. An Irish playwright had sought the help
of the English forces at Dublin Castle in maintaining order within
the theater and thus had given strength to the enemy by recognizing and using his forces of occupation. As Griffith put it: "On
Tuesday this story of unnatural murder and unnatural lust, told
in foul language, was told under the protection of a body of police
and concluded to the strains of "God Save the King." This future

[10] Arthur Griffith, *Sinn Fein*, February 2, 1907.

head of the Irish Free State was a talented political propagandist, for in this single sentence he was able to exploit anti-Protestant prejudice in a deft, rapid association of obscenity, the English Crown, and its lackeys, the Protestant playwrights. When Yeats brought in a claque of Trinity College boys, when Yeats declaimed about the better sort in the stalls who had better taste than the mob in the pit, when Yeats lectured about the freedom of Art while ordering in the police, he put an end to his career as a popular Irish nationalist. Mr. Griffith's verdict was clear.

As to his country, Mr. Yeats claimed on Monday night that he had served it, and the claim is just. He served it unselfishly in the past. He has ceased to serve it now—to our regret. It is not the nation that has changed towards Mr. Yeats—it is Mr. Yeats who has changed towards the nation.[11]

Griffith announced his pleasure that the Gaelic League and other patriotic societies were going to form a theater that would be truly national. He declared that the Abbey would be left to serve the same function for Ireland that the sewers do for Dublin. This type of denunciation strikes a new note not heard before in the movement, and Yeats was most astonished at it and thought long about its shrillness.[12] Yeats began to wonder about the quality of a movement impelled by hatred, for, in many ways, *The Leader* was right: Yeats, if not exactly indefinite, lacked the capacity to lock the will in a single-minded fixation upon one thing. Griffith had enormous will power in this respect, for when his friend and fellow leader of *Sinn Fein,* Edward Martyn, gave ten thousand pounds to establish a Palestrina choir in the Dublin Pro-Cathedral, Griffith objected and felt that the money could have been better spent on "a newspaper that would advance the Irish cause." [13] But this single-mindedness, and its resultant petrification of the heart, was not a fault restricted to Arthur Griffith; it was becoming the lineaments of the mask of the revolutionary.

11 Arthur Griffith, *Sinn Fein,* loc. cit.
12 See W. B. Yeats, *Autobiographies* (London, 1961), p. 486.
13 Padraic Colum, *Arthur Griffith,* p. 86.

Padraic Pearse, then editor of another Dublin newspaper, the Gaelic League's *An Claidheamh Soluis,* reviewed *The Playboy of the Western World* in a lower, quieter, but equally intense tone.

The "Playboy of the Western World" was not a play to be howled down by a little mob. It was a play to be left severely alone by all who did not care to listen to it ... The Anglo-Irish dramatic movement has now been in existence for ten years. Its net result has been the spoiling of a noble poet in Mr. Yeats, and the generation of a sort of Evil Spirit in the shape of Mr. J. M. Synge. "By their fruits ye shall know them." [14]

Arthur Griffith's literary criticism had been political; Padriac Pearse's criticism added religion, for many would recognize the biblical quotation that Pearse took for his text: "Every tree that bringeth not forth good fruit is hewn down, and cast into the fire. Wherefore by their fruits ye shall know them." [15]

Pearse came to be deeply sorry and ashamed for his part in the *Playboy* row,[16] and later he tried to remedy matters, but only after the death of Synge.

When a man like Synge, a man in whose sad heart there glowed a true love of Ireland, one of the two or three men who have in our time made Ireland considerable in the eyes of the world, uses strange symbols which we do not understand, we cry out that he has blasphemed and we proceed to crucify him.[17]

But even in his retraction, Pearse was mindful of Scripture, and this association of art and religion is an extremely important feature of the popular ideological movement. Any kind of naturalism, or even realism, was rejected by the pietistic aesthetic of the time. Pearse was a poet, and art for him as for many of his countrymen was a meditation on what was noble in human character and transcendental in nature. A deeply divided man, Pearse was horrified

[14] Padraic Pearse, *An Claidheamh Soluis,* February 9, 1907.
[15] Matthew 7:19.
[16] See Pearse's friend's pamphlet on the 1916 Rising, "Memories of the Dead," Martin Daly [Stephen MacKenna] (Dublin, n.d.), p. 19. Pamphlet in the National Library of Ireland.
[17] Padraic Pearse, *Collected Works: Political Writings and Speeches* (Dublin, 1924), p. 145.

at Synge's ironic perceptions about the divided, conflicting, and contradictory nature of human experience. Pearse was an intensely serious idealist and temperamentally lacked the imaginative flexibility to laugh at himself or Holy Ireland. This lack was not idiosyncratic, but national, for Irish Catholicism tends to be a rather severe form of Christianity. For the Irish Catholic aesthetic of the time, to be conscious of evil was to be morbid, neurotic, and evil oneself. There was simply no other way of coming to terms with the Vision of Evil except through dismissal and repression. The patriots thought that art *must* uplift the people; it must convince them of their goodness, their innocence, and their justness in the face of their oppressors.[18] Action demands an undivided consciousness, for people who are aware of complexity are not the most efficient men for politics. Irish evil was therefore literally unthinkable. But as Freud has since taught us, the devil kicked out the front door always finds a window or a door in back. The Dismissal of Evil in the popular ideology resulted in a national loss of compassion that proved deadly enough in the Civil War to come, but it also found immediate expression in the hypocrisy of the attack on Synge.

As I stood there watching, knowing well that I saw the dissolution of a school of patriotism that held sway over my youth, Synge came and stood beside me, and said, "A young doctor has just told me that he can hardly keep himself from jumping on to a seat, and pointing out in that howling mob those whom he is treating for venereal disease." [19]

Even after the horror of the Civil War, when the dismissers of evil became its fiercest agents, the pious rioted at another play and exhibited the same contradictory nature. The following dialogue

18 The Dismissal of Evil is probably a necessary feature of all militant ideologies; at the time of this writing SNCC's Stokely Carmichael said in Greenwood, Mississippi: "The only way we gonna stop them white men from whuppin' us is to take over. We been sayin 'freedom' for six years and we ain't got nothin'. What we gonna start sayin' now is 'black power'! ... Ain't nothin' wrong with anything all black, cause I'm all black and I'm all good." As reported in *Newsweek*, June 27, 1966, p. 36.
19 W. B. Yeats, "Synge and the Ireland of His Time," *Essays and Introductions* (New York, 1961), p. 312.

is not taken from an O'Casey play; it is taken from Lady Gregory's *Journal* and records an incident that occurred in the hallway of the Abbey while O'Casey's *Plough and the Stars* was on the stage.

> Donaghy met Holloway in the hall, in a state of fury—"An abominable play."
> D.: "I see nothing abominable in it."
> H.: "Then you have a dirty mind."
> D.: "No, I haven't."
> H.: "Well, you have a filthy mind. There are no streetwalkers in Dublin."
> D.: "I was accosted by one only last night."
> H.: "There were none in Dublin till the Tommies brought them over." [20]

One row is much like another, but the moral principle is always the same, whether it is a row over a play, a film, or a book: there is no evil in Ireland except that which is introduced by the English or Americans.

The particular row over Synge's play, however, is a crucial indication of the development of Irish nationalism in 1907. The sanctified parochialism had been present in the literary movement since Young Ireland days, but the parochialism of the literary movement of the 'nineties was not so fervent and hysterical: probably because the hysteria was saved for the Parnell controversy. The riots over the *Playboy* introduce a note of desperation and intensity; the complex issues of the literary movement are being simplified into the slogans needed for action in the political movement. And in Standish O'Grady's prophecy, the political movement is one very large step closer to the military movement. No more appropriate indication of this change in ideology exists than the ironic circumstance that one of the men Yeats testified against at the trial following the riots in January 1907 was Piaras Beaslai (Pierce Beasley), the future I.R.A. officer and intimate associate and biographer of the military mastermind of that army, Michael Collins. Mr. Beaslai was fined, but Yeats's popularity suffered because of his new association with the police.

[20] *The Journal of Lady Gregory,* ed. Lennox Robinson (London, 1964), p. 99.

Yeats was later to lament the bitter qualities that possessed his nationalist friends. In perhaps his most famous lines he characterized the age and its overmastering hatred as one in which "The best lack all conviction, while the worst / Are full of passionate intensity." This passionate intensity was becoming the *mask* of the revolutionary. The young men who dreamed and formed committees were growing up and growing apart. Each was accepting a different role. To play the role of a publicist for independence, one sacrifices the sensibility of a poet to achieve the simplified energy of the propagandist. For years Yeats had tried to have it both ways; he succumbed to what he called the chief temptation of the artist, "creation without toil," by seeking influence and power in public affairs. None of the shouting was really his business, and that is why, Yeats said, he could not keep out of it. When Yeats, disappointed in his love for Maud Gonne, had grown tired of riding the bandwagons with that furious republican, when he had grown tired of the artificial enthusiasm of programs and slogans, he turned aside and dreamed of a new role: not a man upon a platform facing multitudes, but an aged, white-haired man whose secret wisdom and passionate rage influenced society from the stone hermitage of a lonely tower.

The poet-patriots of the Easter Rising moved in the opposite direction: failing to achieve a personal apotheosis in the role of sage or poet, they left personal self-confrontation and, accepting the role of rebel, attempted to lead a multitude toward some overwhelming event. Each moved remorselessly into his role and accepted the friends and enemies attendant to that role. Holding to the image of the rebel, they projected onto the screen of history the mythic action the image required. The image of the self is dreamed of in private, but the myth of the self comes from the difficult encounter of that image with society. At another moment of history, the poet-rebels might have been popular heroes who led the nation on to success, but they came at a time when their own self-images encountered the ridicule and indifference of the majority. Out of that ridicule and indifference they fashioned the myth of martyrdom. The rebels are in many ways characters of tragedy, characters whose tragedy is as fully realized in history as it could be in art. They are figures whose exaggerated passions are irrelevant to the business of society, and in the failure of society to accommodate them in any other way but a famous death, one recognizes the tragic sense of waste. From this perspective, the rebels are heroes who achieve a nobility that is denied to those men of secure, gray, common sense who always prosper. These are the rebels when seen in the darkness of one's imagination, but when they are brought into the light and perceived with historical objectivity, they become incompetent, irrational, pretentious, and ridiculous. The *Playboy* row is absurd at a distance, simply because distance is required for laughter at the absurd. But those in the midst of an action lack that distance; they cannot take a comic perspective on their own activities; instead they gravely persist and follow their own ridiculous convictions into tragedy.

No revolutionary took himself more seriously than Padraic Pearse. Because his father was a gravestone cutter, it would seem that from the beginning Pearse was surrounded by death and the heroic monuments to death. His English father was sufficiently anti-imperialist to name his son Patrick Henry, and although Pearse fulfilled the older patriot's famous challenge, his military hero was not the American revolutionary but the ancient Irish warrior, Cuchulain. So impressed was he with the ancient hero's deeds that when he was ten he went down upon his knees and vowed to devote the rest of his life to the freeing of Ireland. The unusual thing about the vow was that Pearse never forgot it; instead he made the fervent idealism of boyhood the governing value of his adult life. As a university student he continued in this boyish idealism and addressed his fellow countrymen on the ideals of national destiny.

The Gael is not like other men; the spade, and the loom, and the sword are not for him. But a destiny more glorious than that of Rome, more glorious than that of Britain awaits him: to become the saviour of idealism in modern intellectual and social life, the regenerator and re-

juvenator of the literature of the world, the instructor of nations, the
preacher of the gospel of nature-worship, hero-worship, God-worship—
such, Mr. Chairman, is the destiny of the Gael.[21]

With other members of his *fin de siècle* generation, Pearse felt that
the decadent industrial world could be purified with the help of
the language, literature, and ideals of the peasant. With this aim
in mind, he was active in the Gaelic League, edited its journal,
and wrote poems and short stories in the Irish language. But
Pearse's major effort in the restoration of idealism was his school,
St. Enda's. The school was a development of his Gaelic League
activities, for it was bilingual, but even more than that it was an
attempt to see that the high ideals natural to boyhood would survive into later life. Pearse looked on the educational system of his
time with utter contempt; he saw it as a "murder machine" in
which the spirit was deadened by an inhuman discipline and a
diet of the useless facts that were required to pass an examination
for the civil service. He went to Belgium to model his school on
that nation's bilingual curriculum, but more than teaching boys
to speak Irish, he wanted to teach them the courage, heroism, and
nobility of Cuchulain. The first thing a boy would see upon enter-
ing St. Enda's was a mural of the boy Cuchulain taking arms. The
moral was obvious, even for a boy. Pearse's friend, Stephen Mac-
Kenna (the renowned translator of Plotinus), has spoken of his
educational motives.

Pearse found in the stately and often tender figure of Cuchulain a hero
to inspire the noblest devotion. His stories and poems, and all his work
and speech for that matter, show him to have been profoundly a
Christian, a Catholic, intensely under the spell of the beauty of Irish
Christianity: but taking this, once for all, as a fundamental fact of his
intellectual complex, we might rightly add, to his praise, that he was
also a splendid pagan and lived under the inspiration of the Irish
ideals of the pre-Christian time. He hoped no less than to see Ireland
teeming with Cuchulains; he conceived education, apart from its essential Reading, Writing and Arithmetic, as the art of giving Cuchulains

21 Padraic Pearse, *Collected Works: Political Writings and Speeches*, p. 221.

to the country; his ideal Irishman, whom he thought might be a living reality in our day, was a Cuchulain baptized.[22]

A country teeming with Cuchulains! The idea threatens to become comic at any moment, but Pearse was not given to laughter. Like Griffith, Pearse had the capacity to lock his mind on a single thought. He had vowed to free Ireland and he took every opportunity that came to him, first in the Gaelic League and its journal, then in St. Enda's, and finally in the Irish Republican Brotherhood. But as the Irish Revival dragged on year after year without ever coming to a point, Pearse began to despair: he would never be given his chance, and still another generation would pass into old age without having taken arms against the British. As Pearse moved into middle age, he became more desperate and violent. The tone of his earlier writings is meditative, lyrical, and human in his concern for education; but the tone of his later writing is not personal at all. The human voice is replaced by the shrill screech of crowd rhetoric. The imagery shows an almost pathological lust for violence. The desperation reveals just how much was at stake for Pearse psychologically, for if he slipped into old age without having taken arms, then his whole life, from his boyhood vow to the founding of his school, became meaningless and absurd. In the face of that threat, even action that failed would be a welcome relief from futility.

The years before the outbreak of World War I were the years of agony and self-doubt for the nationalists. Revolution seemed far off, fifty years off in the chronology of a play by Pearse's friend and helper Thomas MacDonagh. Reality had turned the enthusiasts into the disappointed ones. Pearse, always dogged by a sense of failure, was encountering financial difficulties with his school. MacDonagh despaired over the failure of the Gaelic League and the increasing vulgarization of Irish.[23] Griffith failed in his efforts to put out a daily *Sinn Fein,* for there simply was not a sufficiently

22 Martin Daly [Stephen MacKenna], "Memories of the Dead" (Dublin, n.d.) p. 17. Pamphlet in the National Library of Ireland.
23 See W. B. Yeats, *Autobiographies,* p. 488.

large audience in Ireland for a daily nationalist newspaper. History was moving in other shapes outside the personal imaginations of the disappointed nationalists, but soon the international march of events was to give them an escape from the social futility of their own position. Poems, plays, and magazines had given a new voice to the Irish movement that had followed in the wake of Parnell, but in 1910 the voice of the movement returned to the newspaper cries of the street.

What the newspapers were reporting in the General Election of 1910 was the state of the battle between the House of Commons and the House of Lords. Once again the Irish had their eyes on Westminster, for Parliament was involved in one of the fiercest struggles, and in this struggle there was an opening for the Irish to strike with their votes. In 1909 the House of Lords threw out Lloyd George's budget. "It amounted to a claim on the part of the Peers to force a General Election whenever they wished; for a Government unable to raise taxes must either resign or dissolve." [24] Because the Lords had been so successful in the past in throwing out Gladstone's Home Rule Bill, they thought that they could fight such domestic issues as a graduated income tax and old-age pensions in the same way they had fought Irish separatism. The result of the General Election was that the Liberals lost one hundred seats, but with the help of the Irish they could hold a majority of over one hundred. The Liberals, therefore, needed a unified bloc of Irish votes if they were to achieve anything as drastic as the reform of the veto power of the House of Lords. Fortunately the Irish Party had been united since 1900 when John Redmond gained control over the Parnellite and anti-Parnellite factions. The General Election of 1910 gave the Irish Party an opportunity it had not had since the days of Parnell. The English were about to pay grievously for the old Act of Union that had brought the Irish into Parliament, for now Liberal reforms such as income tax and insurance were to be bound up with nationalism and religious

[24] G. M. Trevelyan, *British History in the Nineteenth Century and After: 1782-1919* (New York, 1966), p. 448.

bigotry. The situation became impossible: without the Irish the Liberals could not maintain a government, and the price of Irish co-operation was a new Home Rule Bill. In 1911 Prime Minister Asquith, with Redmond's support, succeeded in passing the Parliament Act, which curbed the power of the House of Lords by declaring that a bill, once passed in the Commons, should within two years become law—if the majority in the Commons could maintain itself for the two-year interval.

The passage of this Act made Home Rule seem imminent. The prospect, however, was unacceptable to the north of Ireland, and the threat of a Dublin Parliament made the Protestants of Ulster counter with threats of civil war. Naturally enough the Opposition recognized in Ulster its opportunity to undermine the Liberals. As Trevelyan pointed out, "the natural desire of the Conservatives to revenge their own defeat over the Parliament Act made them all the more willing to support to the utmost limit the action of the Protestant Loyalists in Ireland." [25] As early as 1883 Lord Randolph Churchill had advised countering the threat of Home Rule by "playing the Orange card." This policy of dividing and conquering was most effective, for the north of Ireland, Orange Ulster, was Protestant and industrial, whereas the south, Green Ireland, was Catholic and agricultural. Randolph Churchill, hoping to stir up the natural antagonism, had coined the phrase: "Ulster will fight and Ulster will be right," and the Low-Church North dutifully responded with: "Home Rule is Rome Rule." When Redmond revived the spirit of Parnell, it was inevitable that the Tories would revive the spirit of Lord Randolph Churchill. The barriers of the House of Lords now taken away, the third Home Rule Bill was introduced. It was then that the Tories played their Orange card, and the face on that card was Edward Carson, the man who brought force back into Irish politics.

Edward Carson, though born in the South, had devoted his career as a lawyer to fighting Irish nationalism. During the days of the Land War, he won prominence by prosecuting the men who

[25] Ibid. p. 454.

were active in the battle on the side of the tenants. This activity earned him the title of a "Castle Bloodhound." Carson's aristocratic sympathies were rewarded: he was elected Member of Parliament for the Unionist constituency of Dublin University. Once in Parliament, he became the natural spokesman for Loyalist Ireland, and, therefore, his sphere of influence shifted from Dublin to Belfast. Ulster's reaction to the Parliament Act of 1911 was the formation of the Ulster Volunteers and a Provisional Government under Carson in 1912. The purpose of the Volunteers was to intimidate the Liberals and, if necessary, fight England to remain part of the British Empire, for behind the religious antipathy between Orange North and Green South was the economic dependence of Ulster's industry upon the fortunes of the Empire. If Britannia ruled the waves, Belfast built the ships.

The southern reaction to Carson's Volunteers came at the suggestion of another Ulsterman, Eoin MacNeill, Professor of Ancient Irish at University College, Dublin, and Vice-President of the Gaelic League. In an article in the League's *An Claidheamh Soluis,* entitled "The North Began," MacNeill called for the formation of a Volunteer organization in the South to ensure that the threat of the Ulster Volunteers would not prevent the reintroduction of the Home Rule Bill in March of the coming year. The underground Irish Republican Brotherhood jumped at the chance to form an open Volunteer organization headed by prestigious members of the upper middle class, but secretly staffed by officers from its own ranks.[26] In November 1913 the Irish Volunteers were formed and the original Provisional Committee was expanded to include twenty-eight members. The most socially visible members were such respected constitutionalists as Professor MacNeill; diplomat Sir Roger Casement; T. M. Kettle, M.P.; and a landed gentleman, Colonel Maurice Moore (brother of George Moore). But of the twenty-eight members of the committee, nine were members

---

[26] See F. X. Martin, "Eoin MacNeill on the 1916 Rising," *Irish Historical Studies,* XII, 226-71; see also Diarmuid Lynch, *The I.R.B. and the 1916 Insurrection* (Cork, 1957), p. 23f.

of the Irish Republican Brotherhood, and among them was Padraic Pearse.[27] Now in this game of chess it was the North's move, and it did more than form a committee. In March 1914 forty thousand German rifles were landed in Larne Harbour for the Ulster Volunteers. When orders were given by the Liberal government to disarm this illegal group, the British officers at the Curragh, a military camp in Kildare, threatened to resign their commissions. The matter was not pressed with vigor, for all sorts of embarrassing situations could arise, not the least of which was the fact that an Englishman, General Gough, would have to meet and disarm another Englishman, General Richardson, who commanded the 100,000 Volunteer army of Ulster. Since such open encounter in the field smacked of civil war at a time when Germany was becoming ambitious, the situation was rather delicate. Ulster kept its illegally smuggled arms. Randolph Churchill had said that "Ulster will fight and Ulster will be right," but his son, Winston Churchill, described Carson's Provisional Government of Ulster as "a self-elected body, composed of persons who, to put it plainly, are engaged in a treasonable conspiracy." [28] The son, unlike the father, was at this stage of his career a Liberal, and, as First Lord of the Admiralty, a member of the government. The game continued, and now it was the South's turn. In July 1914 an Englishman, Erskine Childers, ran guns into Howth Harbour on his yacht, the *Asgard,* but this time His Majesty's troops were not insubordinate. The Scottish Borderers did not disarm the Irish Volunteers, but later that day they did fire into a crowd of jeering civilians, killing three. Now in the streets of Dublin a new tune was being sung.

God rest the souls of those who sleep apart from earthly sin,
Including Mrs. Duffy, James Brennan and Patrick Quinn;
But we will yet avenge them and the time will surely come
That we'll make the Scottish Borderers pay for the cowardly deeds
they done.

---

[27] P. S. O'Hegarty, *A History of Ireland Under the Union,* p. 669.
[28] As quoted in J. J. Horgan, *From Parnell to Pearse* (Dublin, 1948), p. 253.

The words of the street ballad tell us that those who were singing it were not the ones who discussed Asquith and Redmond above a silver tea service. If history had thrown the upper-middle classes of Parliamentary Ireland in with the Liberals, it was also throwing Irish Labor in with the nationalists, for the Volunteers under Professor MacNeill were not the only troops in the South.

From August 1913 to February 1914, Dublin had been the scene of one of the greatest strike and lock-out conflicts in the history of organized labor. The leaders in this strike were James Larkin and James Connolly. Larkin was a huge man who had emerged from the ugly world of the Liverpool slums with an Old Testament prophet's wrath against capitalism's "dark satanic mills." Before serving as General Secretary to the Irish Transport and General Workers' Union, Larkin had served his apprenticeship as a labor organizer in Liverpool and Belfast, but a life spent at work in the docks, factories, and slums of these cities was evidently not enough to prepare him for the unique horror of Dublin. Dublin at that time was a city troubled by a great pool of unskilled laborers who had fled the countryside only to encounter the worst slums in Western Europe.

The poor crowded into these foul dwellings in incredible numbers. Nearly 26,000 families lived in 5000 tenements, while over 20,000 families lived in one room, and another 5000 had only two rooms. Of the 5000 tenements, over 1500 were actually condemned as not only unfit for human habitation, but condemned, in fact, as incapable of ever being rendered fit for human habitation. The total of Dublin's "slum jungle" population came to about 87,000 people, or 30 per cent of that city's population of nearly 300,000. . . .

From these festering tenements oozed all the fearful concomitants of Dublin slum life. Death, disease, immorality, insanity, crime, drunkenness, unemployment, low wages, and high rents rolled on in a seemingly interminable vicious cycle. The Dublin death-rate was fantastic.[29]

One of the great difficulties of the economic facts of life in Dublin was that the Irish businessman's chief strategy in competing for

---

[29] Emmet Larkin, *James Larkin: Irish Labour Leader 1876-1947* (Cambridge, 1965), p. 42.

English markets was to take advantage of the cheap labor at hand. To combat this situation Larkin had gathered skilled and un-skilled laborers into the one great Irish Transport and General Workers' Union. Since such an organization reduced the floating supply of casual, day-to-day workers, the Dublin employers at-tempted to crush the union and demanded that all workers have nothing to do with it on pain of losing their jobs. Against the infernal background of the Dublin slums, the strike and lock-out began to stand out as an archetypal conflict. To the poor Larkin seemed an Irish Prometheus bringing an end to the age of Titans. "Through the streets he strode, shouting into every dark and evil-smelling hallway, The great day of a change has come; Circe's swine had a better time than you have; come from your vomit; out into the sun. Larkin is calling you all." [30] To the employers, however, Larkinism was a Godless form of anarchy. The employers were led by William Martin Murphy and his lawyer, Timothy Healy. Since these men had been against Parnell, and more re-cently, against an art gallery for the modern paintings Hugh Lane wished to donate to Dublin, Yeats and other intellectuals looked upon them with the deepest contempt. Whether or not Timothy Healy was an "old foul mouth," and William Martin Murphy an incarnation of ignoble bourgeois avarice, is uncertain. But in any case the Dublin of this period was in one of the ugliest moods of that city's peacetime history, and it is important to keep this sordid-ness in mind as the real background against which Pearse and the others walked into their heroic martyrdom. The Dublin of 1913 was anything but noble and heroic, and Irishmen, rather than fighting the *Sassenach*, were tearing one another to pieces. When Larkin appeared to address a crowd from a window in Murphy's Imperial Hotel on O'Connell Street, the police made a baton charge on the crowd. The police brutality was exceptional, and although hundreds were injured, nothing came of the Parliamen-tary Commission's investigation except a whitewash of the police. When the lock-out began, Murphy spoke to "my friends, the

30 Sean O'Casey, *Autobiographies, I*, p. 572.

workers," and warned them that the shareholders of the company would have three meals a day no matter how long the conflict lasted, but that the workers could not be certain of such security.[31] When this threat of starvation became actual, many sympathetic families in England offered to take in the children of the workers to care for them. The Archbishop of Dublin, William J. Walsh, was disturbed by this offer that would, in effect, take Irish Catholic children into English Protestant homes. Since he felt that this move might endanger their faith, he forbade Catholic mothers to send their children away. Now added to the scenes of police brutality were scenes of police-enforced self-righteousness in which children were taken from the hands of the mothers who attempted to put them on ships bound for England. As A.E. put it, the children were not to be permitted to leave "the Christian atmosphere of the slums." For Yeats, who had hoped with his theater and his friend's art gallery to take one giant step toward making Dublin into a Florence, the police brutality, bourgeois avarice, and religious fanaticism were sickening. The Dublin of the lock-out was not the Dublin of the Celtic Twilight, and in his poem, "September, 1913," Yeats wrote an elegy for the Ireland he had hoped to create.

> What need you, being come to sense,
>   But fumble in a greasy till
> And add the half-pence to the pence
>   And prayer to shivering prayer, until
> You have dried the marrow from the bone;
>   For men were born to pray and save:
> Romantic Ireland's dead and gone,
>   It's with O'Leary in the grave.

The lock-out dragged on for months and ended inconclusively; the employers were able to carry on their businesses, but they were not able to destroy the union. But one thing new did emerge from

31 See *1913: Jim Larkin and the Dublin Lock-Out* (Dublin, 1964). This handsome pamphlet contains important historical and literary material written by Yeats, A.E., and O'Casey. It was published by the Workers' Union of Ireland (29 Parnell Square) for the fiftieth anniversary of the lock-out.

the lock-out and that was the Citizen Army. As the police baton charges went unchecked by Dublin Castle, and people were killed in the streets, a friend of the labor supporter Countess Markiewicz offered fifty pounds toward buying the workers shoes to enable them to drill and form an army. This friend, Captain Jack White, took over the training and command of this defensive group, and A.E. suggested the emblem of the Plough and the Stars for its flag. The workers lost the battle, but the picket-lines became ranks of marching men. In October 1914 Larkin left Dublin to conduct a lecture tour in the United States, and James Connolly became Acting General Secretary of the Union.

In the early days of the Irish Revival, when Connolly was moving in the Celtic Literary Society, Maud Gonne described him as one of the bravest men she knew, but it had taken time for Connolly to find the proper outlet for his courage. He was active in the nationalist societies at the turn of the century, but when, in 1903, he contested a city ward for Labour and lost, he left for the United States. It was not until 1910 that he returned to Ireland and worked with Larkin in Belfast and Dublin. Connolly had begun his campaign against Empire in the jingoist period of the Boer War, for he felt that the plight of the working man could never be improved without severing the connection between the slums of Dublin and the paneled board rooms of London's City. The strike of 24,000 workers had been an attempt to break the power of the Dublin employers, but as the strikers were attacked by the police, it became clearer than ever that Dublin Castle as well as the Dublin employers stood in the way. When the Great War broke out in August 1914, Connolly, now with a small army of his own, agreed with Wolfe Tone and the revolutionary tradition of 1798 that England's difficulty was Ireland's opportunity, and made a promise to himself: "I will not miss this chance." [32] Connolly was a nationalist and a socialist, and in both cases the events of 1914 were sources of extreme despair. In February of

[32] See *Labour and Easter Week: A Selection of the Writings of James Connolly*, ed. Desmond Ryan (Dublin, 1949), p. 1.

1914, Connolly had to endure the virtual defeat of the strike and lock-out; in March of 1914 he had to look on helplessly as John Redmond announced in the Commons that he would accept an amendment to the Home Rule Bill that would, in effect, partition Ireland. "An Ireland without Ulster would be an Ireland without Labour, for without the industrial north, Labour would have no chance in the Home Rule Parliament." And finally with the events of the war before him, he had to sit idly by and observe the break-up of that socialist abstraction, the international working class. As socialism was crushed in the collision of the German and British empires, Connolly's nationalistic hatred of England and his socialistic hatred of the British Empire merged into one passionate rage, a rage that was all the more intense because of its futility. While Britain was making enlistment appeals that spoke of the plight of small nationalities like Belgium, Connolly countered with his own propaganda campaign.

Ireland is rotten with slums, a legacy of Empire. The debt of this war will prevent us from getting money to replace them with sound, clean, healthy homes. Every big gun fired in the Dardanelles fired away at every shot the cost of building a home for a working class family. Ireland has the most inefficient educational system, and the poorest schools in Europe. Empire counsels us to pay pounds for blowing out the brains of others for every farthing it allows us with which to train our own.[33]

Connolly's role in revolution, unlike Pearse's, was not literary or mystical; if Pearse, with his noble profile, looked like a knight on a quest, Connolly, with his round face and walrus moustache, looked like a jovial publican. Completely lacking in the penumbral shades that surround the poet, the labor leader represents the socio-economic realities of the Rising. Connolly was more interested in the Irish means of production than in the Irish language, but both he and Pearse shared the common futility of being nationalists. Pearse had his own mystical reasons for wishing for apoth-

[33] Ibid. p. 109. See also Emmet Larkin, "Socialism and Catholicism in Ireland," *Church History*, XXXIII, p. 480.

eosis; Connolly's revolutionary passions were less exotic, but they were equally irrational. Mystical or Marxist, they both were driven by an intense consciousness of failure. So extreme were Connolly's incitements to open insurrection in the columns of his *Worker's Republic* that the Supreme Council of the Irish Republican Brotherhood was afraid that he would bring on a suppression of nationalist activity and thereby ruin their own plans for a rising. It was not until the I.R.B. revealed these plans and gave a part in them to the two-hundred-man Citizen Army that Connolly calmed down and agreed to wait for the hour chosen by the I.R.B.

The continuity of the Irish revolutionary tradition is clearly seen in the Irish Republican Brotherhood. Founded in America in 1858, its early career was, militarily, not the most brilliant. After the American Civil War, a group of Fenians crossed into Canada and discharged their firearms with little purpose other than the harassment of that part of the British Empire that was closest to hand. The next venture of the I.R.B. was the futile Fenian Rising in Ireland in 1867. After these military failures other tactics were tried, and those that involved sending funds to support Michael Davitt's Land War or Parnell's Home Rule campaign were more intelligent and successful. Many of the belligerent American-Irish were unhappy with these constitutional methods and carried on, in the grand anarchist style, a dynamiting campaign in England. One dynamiter sentenced to life imprisonment was Tom Clarke. Released after fifteen years of his term, Clarke, unrepentant, went to join his friend, John Devoy, in America, and together the two Fenians continued to plot against the Empire. In 1908 Clarke returned to Ireland and made a small tobacconist shop in Parnell Street the headquarters of the I.R.B. Here the Fenians through Clarke and Devoy passed on the ideas and traditions of revolution to a new generation. If John O'Leary was the Fenian hero of nationalist intellectuals because of his moral disapproval of the dynamiting campaign, Clarke was the hero of the militarists. Fifteen years in prison would more than likely make any man dubious of restraint and refinement. Clarke was rather suspicious of Pearse at first, but when he had heard him make a speech he changed his mind: "By God! I never thought there was such stuff in Pearse." [34]

Pearse had joined the I.R.B. in 1913; he had taken his time in associating himself with this secret, oath-bound underground society because he wanted an open and popular rebellion on a large scale. But as events began to move more quickly at the prodding of Carson and the Ulster Volunteers, Pearse could not afford to be particular without running the risk of being left out altogether. When the Irish Volunteers were formed in November 1913, he could have good reason for being happy that he had not held back, for now he was in the thick of things. He was on the Provisional Committee of the Volunteers and was an agent of the I.R.B. Pearse had slowly been winning a reputation in Dublin. As an officer of the Gaelic League and a past editor of its journal, he was well known in the largest nationalist cultural organization. As a Gaelic writer he had published his first book of short stories in 1907, and in 1908 he had founded his school, a school that enrolled the children of some prominent Dubliners. In 1912, while Redmond was addressing a huge crowd gathered in Parnell Square for a demonstration in favor of the new Home Rule Bill, Pearse addressed a smaller group in Irish. His words at this time were parliamentary, and that is one reason why Clarke was dubious about his politics. "I should think myself a traitor to my country if I did not answer the summons to this gathering, for it is clear that the Bill which we support today will be for the good of Ireland and that we shall be stronger with it than without it." Pearse kept open a line of retreat, for he went on to say: "Let the foreigner understand that if we are cheated now there will be red war in Ireland." [35] But if Pearse was known in Irish-speaking circles, he was certainly unknown to that arch-enemy of Irish, Professor John Mahaffy. In 1914 Pearse was invited to speak at the Trinity College centenary of the birth of Thomas Davis, and when

[34] See Desmond Ryan, *The Rising* (Dublin, 1949), p. 7.
[35] Padraic Pearse, *Collected Works: Political Writings and Speeches,* p. 230.

Mahaffy, then Provost, was informed that Pearse had given anti-recruiting speeches, he complained to the student council in charge of the affair that "a man called Pearse" was to speak. When the students persisted in their invitation, Mahaffy forbade them the use of the college. Nevertheless, on November 14, 1914, Pearse shared the platform of the Antient Concert Rooms with W. B. Yeats. Quiet and retiring as he was in private life, Pearse was able to seem the opposite when given a public platform. A year after the Davis centenary, at the gigantic funeral procession for O'Donovan Rossa, the old Fenian leader, Pearse chanted: "They think that they have foreseen everything, provided against everything; but the fools, the fools, the fools!—they have left us our Fenian dead, and while Ireland holds these graves, Ireland unfree shall never be at peace." [36] The romance of the monumental grave, the mysticism of martyrdom, the desire for apotheosis in a tragic death: Pearse lived his life as if he were the hero in a tragedy. And from his speeches, plays, and poems, one gets the impression that he had memorized his lines well in advance of the act. One month before the Rising, Pearse made a farewell speech to his students that expressed the *mythos* of the coming insurrection: "As it took the blood of the Son of God to redeem the world, so it would take the blood of Irishmen to redeem Ireland." [37]

Pearse, of course, was not the only member of the I.R.B., and more practical men like Sean MacDermott helped Clarke turn the organization into something more than a society for Fenian reminiscences. In August 1914 the Supreme Council of the I.R.B. (of which Pearse was not yet a member) decided to "free Ireland by force of arms, to use the Volunteers to that end, and to secure arms from Germany." [38] To use the Volunteers for this purpose, the I.R.B. had to keep the Provisional Committee in the dark. This subterfuge was made doubly difficult when John Redmond, seeing what a political force and problem the Volunteers had be-

36 Ibid. p. 137.
37 Ibid. p. 98.
38 J. J. Horgan, *From Parnell to Pearse* (Dublin, 1948), p. 263. See also Diarmuid Lynch, *The I.R.B. and the 1916 Insurrection* (Cork, 1957), p. 112.

come, insinuated the Irish Party into the government of the Volunteers. Redmond succeeded in packing the committee with twenty-five of his own men, and in this move moderate Ireland followed suit, for the ranks of the Irish Volunteers now swelled to 160,000. But when the war broke out, Redmond attempted to direct the Volunteers toward the battlefields of Europe. Redmond had stood in the House of Commons and offered the services of the Volunteers to defend Ireland so that British troops could be moved to the front. The offer was declined, for the British were not in favor of replacing an army of occupation with Irish troops, but this British lack of interest created problems: nationalist groups misunderstood and thought that Redmond was offering the Volunteers to fight England's war, and pro-British groups were hurt and felt that Britain had no confidence in them. Consequently the Volunteers came to be a troubled group; many British sympathizers enlisted in the army, and these enlistments gave Redmond the appearance of a recruiting agent for the Crown. When, therefore, at his speech at Woodenbridge in September 1914, Redmond defined the field of the Volunteers as existing not only in Ireland, "but wherever the firing line extends," he disturbed the radical wing of the original Volunteers and 10,000 seceded under the leadership of MacNeill and Pearse. In MacNeill's eyes the Volunteers were strictly a defensive organization, and in the original manifesto of the organization it was explicitly stated that "their duties will be defensive and protective and they will not contemplate aggression or domination." [39] MacNeill differed from his I.R.B. colleagues, for he felt that he could secure Home Rule after the war with the flexing of muscle rather than the shedding of blood. He reasoned that England would not turn its existing army on a co-operating Ireland, especially after it had fought a war allegedly dedicated to the protection of small nationalities, but that it would welcome the chance to play the Ulster Volunteers against their Irish counterparts, for in the case of an insurrection it could pretend to save Ireland from civil war, bring in troops,

[39] As quoted in J. J. Horgan, *From Parnell to Pearse*, p. 226.

and postpone self-government for the incorrigible Celts indefi-
nitely. Such a wait-and-see policy of common sense did not appeal
to the radicals of the physical force party; instead they chose the
dangerous strategy of treason and looked to England's enemy for
weapons. And here another impractical, tragic figure enters the
story.

Sir Roger Casement, an Ulsterman, had spent his life-work in
exposing the atrocities committed against the Negroes in the
Congo and the Indians in the South American Putamayo, and for
this work he received his knighthood in 1906. Retired from the
consular service and suffering ill health from his work in South
America, Casement had at first declined to take an active interest
in Irish politics, but as the situation in Ulster became more critical, he became angry at what he considered to be the exploitation
of religious antipathy for the benefit of an English political party.
Perhaps Casement was beginning to see that Ireland was another
land afflicted with the evils of imperial colonialism and felt guilty
that all his work had been done outside his native land. At all
events, Casement's first Irish appearance, though an anonymous
one, was in an ominous article published in 1912 in *The Irish
Review* entitled "Ireland, Germany, and the Next War." There
he argued that Ireland should seize the opportunity of the coming
war to, in effect, play Germany and England against one another,
declare neutrality, and hope to gain international guarantees for
independence because of Ireland's strategic maritime position in
the Atlantic. With this maritime position in mind, Casement saw
an opening for relations with Germany when, in August 1913, the
Cunard Line announced that it would no longer use Cork harbor,
thereby implying that the harbor was unsafe. Casement was a
friend of the Cork Harbour Commissioner, J. J. Horgan, so he
was able both to observe and influence the proceedings. Using his
diplomatic contacts, Casement persuaded the Hamburg-Amerika
Line to announce its intention of using the harbor, thus opening
up the first of what was hoped would be many contacts with Germany. All seemed to be going well from August to December 1913,

and Horgan had the Cork Harbour Board give a vote of thanks to Casement. Then in February 1914, as the threat of war increased, the Hamburg-Amerika Line suddenly abandoned the project. Casement was furious at what he thought was the secret work of the British Foreign Office. In a letter to Horgan he openly expressed his revolutionary sentiments: "Under cover of an offer to Ulster they are going to strip all the flesh off the Home Rule Bill—if we let them ... Don't despair of the arms. I think we can get them. The Irish in America will not desert us in this crisis." [40] The letter is long and highly emotional, and it shows the frame of mind in which Casement went to America to meet the Irish-American leader of the *Clan na Gael,* John Devoy. Casement's poor health and overly emotional idealism did not impress Devoy favorably.[41] Having been unsuccessful in his encounter with Devoy, Casement traveled to Germany to work on a plan to persuade Irish prisoners of war to form an Irish Brigade to fight England. Upon his arrival in Germany, Casement's health failed, and the plans for the Irish Brigade failed as well, for little more than fifty prisoners agreed to join the Brigade. On the whole, Casement's ideas were grandiose and out of keeping with the realities of the war, for he felt that an insurrection could not possibly succeed without 50,000 German troops. To expect that soldiers could slip through the tight British naval blockade was unrealistic, however, and no troops were sent. When Casement learned of the failure of his attempt, he decided to return to Ireland to call off the insurrection, and arranged for his return by German submarine.

Because Devoy could not rely on Casement, he made arrangements to acquire arms without his knowledge, and a shipload of arms was dispatched for Tralee Bay on the German ship *Aud.* Posing as a Norwegian freighter, it made its way to Ireland and succeeded in running the blockade, but because of a confusion of

[40] Ibid. p. 237.
[41] The major sources of my abridged narrative of the insurrection are Desmond Ryan, *The Rising* (Dublin, 1948), and Dorothy Macardle, *The Irish Republic* (American edition, New York, 1965). Ancillary sources are listed in the Bibliography.

dates, the ship was not met by the Irish rebels, and the scheduled rendezvous did not take place. The *Aud* waited in vain; finally it was intercepted by the British. In order to prevent the shipload of arms from falling into enemy hands, the captain of the *Aud* blew up the ship in Cork harbor. Ironically enough, the efforts of the Irish Americans were foiled by the American government, for the German code had been cracked and a warning of the dispatch of the consignment of arms had been sent to the Admiralty on April 17, 1916.

Meanwhile, Casement returned to Ireland and was put ashore on Banna Strand, but he was discovered and placed under arrest on Friday, April 21. The last plan of his life was to call off the futile insurrection, but, once he was placed on trial for treason, he accepted responsibility for the Rising and attempted to gain through his own trial a public hearing for Ireland in the newspapers of the world. Since the British were acutely sensitive to what effect public opinion would have on America's willingness to enter the war, the protests that were seeking to save Casement became a serious problem. To this day there is controversy over the homosexual *Black Diaries* of Casement that were made public during the trial. Their authenticity has not been proved or disproved, and the role of the British government in the affair is still murky. Whatever effect the diaries had on public opinion, they were, of course, totally irrelevant to Casement's heroism and patriotism; they were equally irrelevant in the case of treason. In spite of international protest, Casement was hanged in August 1916.

The failure of the Casement expedition to America and Germany was only the first mishap. When Chief of Staff Eoin Mac-Neill discovered that his Director of Organization, Padraic Pearse, was planning an insurrection behind his back, he was incensed, and he told Pearse that he would do everything in his power, short of informing the British, to call off the irrational slaughter. Mac-Neill had sensed before that his fellow officers of the Irish Volunteers were up to something, and in February of 1916 he wrote an intelligent and articulate memorandum against the policy of insurrection; unfortunately, he was unable to present it himself. It was read in his absence, praised, and ignored. Because MacNeill has been too hastily seen as "the ostrich-minded professor" who countermanded his commands, it is worth considering this memorandum at some length, for it contains the rational perspective of the revolutionary mystique; and thanks to the work of the Irish historian, F. X. Martin, this memorandum has been rescued from obscurity.[42] MacNeill was repelled by the sacrificial cult of the poets and the presuppositions of the militarists that an offensive was always the best strategy. What he felt was disguised in all this mystical and military rhetoric was the simple fact of murder: it was murder to lead one's own men into a hopeless slaughter; it was murder to walk out into the street and begin shooting passing soldiers and policemen. He declared, ". . . the only possible basis for successful revolutionary action is deep and widespread discontent. We have only to look around us in the streets to realize that no such condition exists in Ireland."

I do not care and will not care a rap for maxims or formulae or catchwords or forebodings, or for the reproaches either of our own time or later times. Organization, preparation, calculation are the necessary preliminaries to any decision, except the decision to organize, prepare, and calculate. . . .

There is a feeling in some minds that action is necessary, that lives must be sacrificed, in order to produce an ultimate effect on the national mind. As a principle of action, I have heard that feeling disclaimed, but I did not fully accept the disclaimer. In fact, it is a sounder principle than any of the others that I have dealt with. If the destruction of our nationality was in sight, and if we came to the conclusion that at least the vital principle of nationality was to be saved by laying down our lives, then we should make that sacrifice without hesitation. It would not be a military act in any sense, and it does not come within the scope of our military counsels.

To my mind, those who feel compelled towards military action on any of the grounds that I have stated are really impelled by a sense of

---

[42] F. X. Martin, "Eoin MacNeill on the 1916 Rising," *Irish Historical Studies,* XII (March 1961), 226-71.

feebleness or despondency or fatalism or by an instinct of satisfying their own emotions or escaping from a difficult and complex and trying situation. . . .

We have to remember that what we call our country is not a poetical abstraction, as some of us, perhaps all of us, in the exercise of our highly developed capacity for figurative thought, are sometimes apt to imagine—with the help of our patriotic literature. There is no such person as Caitlín Ní Uallacháin or Roisín Dubh or the Sean-bhean Bhoct, who is calling us to serve her. What we call our country is the Irish nation, which is a concrete and visible reality.[43]

MacNeill had a perfect psychological understanding of the revolutionaries, so perfect, in fact, that their main excuse for concealing their plans from him was that they found him a hard man to approach. MacNeill recognized that behind Pearse's heroism was a fear of complexity. MacNeill recognized in Connolly the rage of frustration: Connolly wished to kick back at all the obstacles he had tripped upon throughout his life. But in each case Mac-Neill thought that "No man has a right to seek relief of his feelings at the expense of his country." It was not surprising that the rebels could not talk to MacNeill, and since they could not talk to him, they used him. As Pearse said to him at their last meeting: "We have used your name and influence for what they were worth, but we have done with you now." [44]

In his memorandum of February, MacNeill had stated that the Volunteers were justified in securing arms and defending these arms by force if they were threatened with confiscation. It was on this principle that the rebels made their final attempt to win MacNeill to their side and prevent him from ruining the insurrection planned for April 23, 1916. On the Monday before Easter, MacNeill was presented with a bogus "Castle Document," probably forged by Joseph Plunkett, that outlined the British preparations to round up all nationalist leaders and suppress the Volunteers. MacNeill was taken in at first, but as the week went on, he began to wonder about certain confusions in the document. On

43 Ibid. pp. 236, 239.
44 Ibid. p. 266.

Thursday he sent out orders giving his trusted associate Bulmer Hobson command over all the Volunteers in the city, and he took other steps to check Pearse's power as Director of Organization. On Friday, Pearse, MacDonagh, and MacDermott saw MacNeill and informed him for the first time of the shipload of arms that was scheduled to land; they were able to convince him that he had little choice but to go along with their plans, or else be a party to the utter wrecking of the Volunteer movement. MacNeill gave in, but on the following day, Saturday, he learned of the failure of the *Aud* and the arrest of Casement. Convinced that the insurrection, which was hopeless in conception, was now stillborn, he issued an order countermanding the parades and movements that were the agreed-upon beginnings of the Rising. On Easter morning *The Sunday Independent* contained a notice from MacNeill canceling the day's maneuvers. Looking at the morning papers, both MacNeill and Dublin Castle could quite rationally think that the threat of insurrection had passed. But on Sunday morning, Clarke, Pearse, MacDermott, and Connolly met in Liberty Hall and decided to go ahead. The British had now enough evidence, forged document or no forged document, to begin the suppression of nationalist leaders. There was nothing left to do but make a protest in arms. It was all that was left to them, that single last desperate act. It had no reason; it was a gesture.

The original plan was that the German arms were to be distributed and that there should be a rising throughout the country, a rising that moving eastward would relieve the besieged Volunteers in Dublin. The arms were not landed, the British had Casement in custody, and now the countermand had ruined everything. With the exception of a few skirmishes in the country, the scene of the Easter Rising was in Dublin. Of the full 16,000 that the Irish Volunteers could muster by April 1916, 1200 went out to hold the capital against the British Empire.[45]

[45] Macardle claims 1200 as the number of the insurgents (p. 165); Desmond Ryan claims 700 at first, 900 by the end of hostilities (p. 129); he quotes Cathal Brugha as saying that at no time were there more than 1000; Diarmuid Lynch's tabulation lists 1575 (p. 143).

Shortly after noon on Easter Monday, April 24, the sacrificial act began. Pearse had invoked the blood of the lamb in his speech at St. Enda's, and now even the unmystical Connolly realized: "We are going out to be slaughtered." [46] The O'Rahilly, a Volunteer leader of MacNeill's faction, had driven all over Ireland on Sunday to cancel the insurrection so that others might not be killed, and then appeared for action in Dublin, for, as he explained: "I have helped to wind the clock, I might as well hear it strike." [47] Of the 1200 men that gathered, many thought they were on the usual practice drill. Few paid attention to the lines of shabbily uniformed men, for the sight had become a familiar one to Dubliners. A few must have laughed, but many took no notice at all. In a ring around the heart of the city, small groups of men were taking up their positions in the public buildings that they were to turn into forts to withstand a siege from the army of the mightiest empire in the world. Pearse and Connolly occupied the General Post Office and made it the General Headquarters of the insurrection. With the poet and the labor leader were Tom Clarke, Sean MacDermott, and another poet, Joseph Plunkett, chief strategist of the insurrection. Weak from a recent operation on his throat, he reclined upon a mattress on the floor. Looking pale and unreal, an unreality that was heightened by the immense rings and bracelets he wore as tokens from his fiancée, Grace Gifford, Plunkett seemed anything but the man who had infuriated the German General Staff with advice on how to run the war. In Jacobs's biscuit factory another poet, Thomas MacDonagh, lecturer at University College, and teacher at St. Enda's, took up his position with the help of Major John MacBride, the estranged husband of Maud Gonne. Sean Heuston, a boy of seventeen, was commanding at the Mendicity Institution. At St. Stephen's Green, Countess Markiewicz and her boy-scout *Fianna* were digging trenches, but the man in charge of the men was Michael Mallin.

[46] *Labour and Easter Week: A Selection of the Writings of James Connolly,* p. 21.
[47] As quoted in Max Caulfield, *The Easter Rebellion* (London, 1963), p. 22. Also in Desmond Ryan, *The Rising,* p. 124.

Eamon De Valera commanded at Boland's Mill, Eamon Ceannt and Cathal Brugha at the South Dublin Union, Edward Daly at the Four Courts, and Michael Malone at Clanwilliam House on the Mount Street Bridge.

The positions secured, Padraic Pearse walked out from the Post Office to the foot of Nelson's Pillar and read to an astonished audience *An Poblacht na hEireann,* the declaration of the Irish Republic.

IRISHMEN AND IRISHWOMEN: In the name of God and of the dead generations from which she receives her old tradition of nationhood, Ireland, through us, summons her children to her flag and strikes for her freedom.

Pearse's friend, Stephen MacKenna, was there in the crowd, raging at his illness and age that prevented him from taking a part, but, as MacKenna records, no such patriotism stirred the other Dubliners who were present. This time Pearse's speeches moved no one, and what should have been the climax of his career became its most painful anticlimax.

I saw him, at about noon, I think, read the Proclamation of the Irish Republic: but for once his magnetism had left him; the response was chilling; a few thin perfunctory cheers, no direct hostility just then, but no enthusiasm whatever.[48]

So very much like a tragic hero, Pearse had confused his own imagination with reality; the vision which had made him kneel and vow to free Ireland was seen by none. And yet even this humiliation before the crowd was part of Pearse's self-created myth, for this moment of encounter had been anticipated: Pearse could never forget the dream he had had of a fool dying in front of a "silent unsympathetic crowd." [49] The encounter completed, he returned to the Post Office. Never the soldier that the realist Connolly was, he had his meditations about Cuchulain in his chariot, but somehow in a war of rifles, grenades, and artillery, he seemed

48 Martin Daly [Stephen MacKenna], "Memories of the Dead," p. 20.
49 Padraic Pearse, *Collected Works: The Story of a Success,* p. 77.

a little incompetent; yet his incompetence was not mixed with fear, and this lack of fear made him an inspiring leader in spite of himself.

Captain Brennan-Whitmore . . . sat back and observed the contrasting behaviour of Pearse and Connolly. Connolly seemed much the more positive character. Forever on the prowl, he was a restless, energetic figure, continually seeking out weaknesses in the defenses, continually demanding more effort from his men. Pearse, on the other hand, appeared to be "lost somewhere in the clouds"; at times "even looked supremely futile." . . . Yet Brennan-Whitmore felt that by his very presence alone, he added an untold value. There was an ambience about him which spread calm confidence. Noticing that, wherever he went, the eyes of the garrison followed, Brennan-Whitmore thought, "If that man had lived in the Middle Ages, he would have been a saint." [50]

The rebels settled down and waited for the fight, the fight that was to become Easter Week, 1916.

In the bright sunshine of that Monday afternoon the insurrection could seem for a moment to be illuminated by the spirit of romance. The boys of the *Fianna Éireann* had attacked the Magazine Fort in Phoenix Park and succeeded in exploding part of their gelignite, although that part was not enough to destroy the Fort or announce the insurrection all over Dublin. An attack was made on Dublin Castle, that symbol of seven centuries of foreign rule, but the attack was itself only symbolic, for the rebels did not realize the Castle was practically deserted and that with a stronger attack they could have taken it, or at least burned it. An hour after Pearse had proclaimed the Republic, a troop of Lancers cantered in precise formation down O'Connell Street. The cavalry officer with his sword had been one of the most effective weapons against crowds of nationalist demonstrators in the past,[51] but with the demonstrators turned into armed rebels safely stationed behind windows and barricades, the beautifully uniformed Lancer became

[50] Max Caulfield, *The Easter Rebellion*, p. 133.
[51] For a description of such an incident, see Sean O'Casey, *Autobiographies, I,* p. 367.

truly a thing of the past; the rebels opened fire. But the British Lancers were not the only ones unprepared for street fighting and modern warfare. The rebels had destroyed the rail lines, but they had left the telephone communications untouched; the British, therefore, merely put in a phone call and the 1200 troops in the city on Monday were increased to 5000 by Tuesday. Connolly had thought that no capitalist army would ever shell capitalist buildings, but one of General Friend's first commands was to dispatch four eighteen-pounders from Athlone.

On Tuesday the artillery was introduced, and some of the minor rebel positions were taken. By extending a line down Dame Street from Dublin Castle to Trinity College, the British were able to break the rebel army in two. But now a third force began to be a problem, for a mob of looters raided shops, interfered with fire-fighting equipment, and tried to steal furniture from the barricades erected by the rebels. Connolly thought that the proletariat would come to the support of the revolutionaries, but the revolutionaries soon had to face a situation that required them to use force against their own countrymen. For Pearse and Connolly, reality was proving to be something other than their own imaginings, but the rebels did not abandon the rhetoric that had inspired them to revolution. On Tuesday, *Irish War News* appeared; it was written in Pearse's celebrative style: "The country is rising in answer to Dublin's call, and the final achievement of Ireland's freedom is now, with God's help, only a matter of days." But other notes had to be sounded along with the trumpet call: "The Provisional Government hopes that its supporters—which means the vast bulk of the people of Dublin—will preserve order and self-restraint. Such looting as has already occurred has been done by hangers-on of the British Army. Ireland must keep her new honour unsmirched." [52]

On Wednesday the artillery bombardment began in earnest. The gun-boat *Helga* demolished Liberty Hall, and guns from Trinity College began to smash the buildings on O'Connell Street.

[52] Dorothy Macardle, *The Irish Republic*, p. 182.

To the south the rebels had already been cleared from St. Stephen's Green and were now barricaded in the Royal College of Surgeons. The digging of trenches in the Green had proved useless, for the British were able to take the Shelbourne Hotel that commanded the Green and train machine guns down on the trenches. Other rebels in the south of Dublin, however, were more successful. On Wednesday the first reinforcements from England, the Sherwood Foresters, had arrived in Kingstown and were beginning their march on Dublin. But when the Foresters attempted to cross the Grand Canal at the Mount Street Bridge, the bloodiest encounter of the Rising took place. Commandant De Valera, who was in charge at Boland's Mill, had decided to use strategy to compensate for the lack of numbers; he ran up the Irish flag on a nearby building and thus concentrated artillery fire on an unoccupied position, and then he scattered his men into smaller groups so that their fire would give the appearance of an extensive entrenchment of men. One of these detachments of men was Michael Malone's party of fourteen, which held Clanwilliam House, 25 Northumberland Road, and the Parochial Hall. The rebels were able to establish a perfect cross fire, and for six hours they were able to keep back 800 of the Sherwood Foresters. At the end of the battle on Wednesday evening, four officers had been killed, fourteen wounded, and, of the enlisted men, 216 were killed or wounded. Three of the fourteen rebels were able to escape to safety. Because of the heavy casualties, and because these British troops had never seen combat before, the march on to Trinity College was postponed until the next day.

On Thursday and Friday the squeeze began and the encirclement of the rebel positions was completed. Now artillery and machine gun fire began to express the power that the Imperial Army could bring to bear upon a ludicrously ill-equipped rebel band. On Friday morning General Sir John Maxwell arrived from England to take command. Since every day the rebels were able to hold out contributed to the reality of revolution in Ireland, it was imperative that the nonsense be stopped at once. In the past the British had enjoyed making fun of the "cabbage patch" revolts of 1848 and 1867, and had boasted in the House of Commons how old soldiers had been able to hold Ireland while England was engaged in the Boer War. Now the soldiers could not be cavalier about the ease with which revolution was snuffed in Ireland. From the perspective of Verdun, Dublin was nothing, but for the Irish it was the greatest revolutionary act of a century. General Maxwell declared that he was ready to level every building in a rebel area, which was defined as "any area occupied by the rebels"; this clumsy and rapid designation did not help the civilians who were trapped there. By Friday evening the Post Office was in flames, and though other rebel positions were still holding, General Headquarters had to order a retreat. Once Pearse was in the street and saw what an indiscriminately murderous weapon a modern machine gun could be, he realized that if he persisted more civilians than Volunteers would be killed. On Saturday, April 29, 1916, at 3:45 P.M., Pearse signed the order for surrender.

In order to prevent the further slaughter of Dublin citizens, and in the hope of saving the lives of our followers now surrounded and hopelessly outnumbered, the members of the Provisional Government present at Headquarters have agreed to an unconditional surrender, and the Commandants of the various districts in the City and Country will order their commands to lay down their arms.

It was over. On the rebel side, fifty-six were killed in action; on the British side, one hundred and thirty. The estimate of civilian dead is over two hundred.[53] Had enough of the Irish been in sympathy with the Rising, (or as De Valera lamented after his surrender: "If only you'd come out with knives and forks"),[54] what was an insurrection might have developed into a full revolution. But the middle classes, with thoughts of their own children who were fighting and dying in the Great War, cheered the British

[53] As quoted in Macardle, *The Irish Republic*, p. 186. A. J. P. Taylor, in *English History 1914-1945* puts total Irish casualties at 450, British casualties at 100.
[54] Max Caulfield, *The Easter Rebellion*, p. 133.

soldiers and served them tea; [55] and the lower classes, rather than rallying around Connolly's Plough and Stars, swarmed out of the slums and fought with one another for the loot that spilled on to the sidewalks from the broken store windows. The imagination of the poet-rebels had been so far beyond the reality of the nation that it took the nation three years to catch up.

The man who helped the Irish nation catch up with the advanced thought of its revolutionaries was General Maxwell. Thoroughly ignorant of the Irish and their centuries' old tradition of reciting the names of the martyrs who had fallen for Ireland, he set out to put down rebellion once and for all in Ireland with the very methods that would most perpetuate it. Had Maxwell made Pearse stand trial and the public condemnation of his fellow countrymen, Pearse would have been destroyed by the one thing serious-minded idealists cannot stand, ridicule. Instead, General Maxwell gave him a soldier's and a martyr's death by executing him at the hands of a firing squad. The man of failure, in failing, became a success, for Pearse received the apotheosis of a tragic death that he had longed for all his life. And with Pearse fourteen other leaders were executed. To make certain that the Irish understood how Great Britain dealt with rebels, the executions were strung out over two weeks. The politicians were giving the military a free hand, hoping blindly that a simple military solution would end a complex political problem. As the executions dragged on, the intellectual Left became outspoken in its protests. Perhaps the most articulate of the protesters was G. B. Shaw. Considering the captured rebels to be entitled to all the rights of prisoners of war, Shaw felt that the militarist solution was both ignorant and immoral.

It is absolutely impossible to slaughter a man in this position without making him a martyr and a hero, even though the day before the rising he may have been only a minor poet. The shot Irishmen will now take

[55] James Stephens, *The Insurrection in Dublin* (Dublin and London, 1919), p. 27.

their places beside Emmet and the Manchester Martyrs in Ireland, and beside the heroes of Poland and Serbia and Belgium in Europe; and nothing in Heaven or earth can prevent it....[56]

It was inevitable that the Irish would soften toward the rebels, and it was inevitable that their own feelings of guilt and shame would make them glorify in death the men that they had ignored in life. After the executions, this change of attitude was inevitable, but the process of idealization was hastened when Plunkett was married to his sweetheart Grace Gifford on the night before his execution, and the wounded Connolly, who could not stand, was executed strapped to a chair.

In his last speech to the military court Pearse claimed that the rebels had "kept faith with the past, and handed a tradition to the future." [57] More than anything, this soldier facing middle age feared that his generation would pass on without a fight, and that his own ideals would sink into the futility of old age. Because there had been no rebellion in Ireland since 1867, it was absolutely necessary that the chance offered by the Great War be seized. Pearse's hopes succeeded, for public sympathy began to swing toward revolution. People now began to be proud that a small Irish army had been no more incompetent than the Imperial Army which had blundered through six days in quelling the insurrection. In the proud ways of tradition the bold men of 1916 fought artillery with rifles as the bold men of 1798 had fought rifles with pikes. Revolution was coming alive again in Ireland. While responsible members of the middle classes were fulminating in their drawing rooms, their children were beginning to wonder. One young boy who was shortly to become an officer in the Irish Republican Army listened to the politics of common sense at his father's dinner table, but sneaked out at night to join the revolution. Commandant Ernie O'Malley has described what Easter 1916 meant to him.

[56] As quoted in Dorothy Macardle, *The Irish Republic*, p. 187, from the *Daily News*, May 10, 1916.
[57] Desmond Ryan, *The Rising*, p. 260.

The executions had caused bitter feeling, and the arrests and the strict enforcement of martial law helped to intensify it. The people as a whole had not changed; but the new spirit was working slowly, half-afraid, yet determined. The leaders had been shot, the fighting men arrested, and the allied organizations disrupted. Without guidance or direction as if to clarify itself, nebulous, forming, reforming, the strange rebirth took shape. It was manifest in flags, badges, songs, speech, all seemingly superficial signs. It was as if the inarticulate attempted to express themselves in any way or by any method; later would come organization and cool-headed reason. Now was the lyrical stage, blood sang and pulsed, a strange love was born that for some was never to die till they lay stiff on the hillside or in the quicklime near a barrack wall.[58]

Another young boy of eighteen years who, like O'Malley, was to become one of the most important Irish officers in the war of independence known as The Troubles, has clearly set forth what Irish patriotism was like before and after 1916. Tom Barry heard of the insurrection while he was fighting with His Majesty's forces in Iraq.

I went to the war for no other reason than I wanted to see what war was like, to get a gun, to see new countries, and to feel a grown man. Above all I went because I knew no Irish history and had no national consciousness. I had never heard of Wolfe Tone or Robert Emmet, though I did know all about the kings of England and when they had come to the British throne. I had never heard of the victory over the Sassanach at Benburb, but I could tell the dates of Waterloo and Trafalgar. I did not know of the spread of Christianity throughout Europe by Irish missionaries and scholars, but did I not know of the blessings of civilization which Clive and the East India Company had brought to dark and heathen India? Thus through the blood sacrifices of the men of 1916, had one Irish youth of eighteen been awakened to Irish Nationality. Let it also be recorded that those sacrifices were equally necessary to awaken the minds of ninety per cent of the Irish people.[59]

The British military did as much as they could for Irish independence, but the politicians were not helpless bystanders. Lloyd

[58] Ernie O'Malley, *On Another Man's Wound* (London, 1961), p. 38.
[59] Tom Barry, *Guerilla Days in Ireland* (Dublin, 1949), p. 2.

George called a convention of leading Irishmen from the Church, business, and education. The situation in Ireland was extremely difficult, for agreement on an Irish policy that would be acceptable to Ulster was virtually impossible in a coalition government which had Carson in the Cabinet. The convention was mainly an attempt to appease the United States and prevent the Irish-Americans from blocking American entry into the war. The Irish Convention on Home Rule met from July of 1917 to April of 1918, but on the day that the Convention issued its report and recommendations to the government, a conscription bill was introduced into Parliament, and this time the bill included Ireland.[60] Public disgust at such political hypocrisy was making converts for *Sinn Fein.*

The English referred to the rebels as *Sinn Feiners* or Shinners, but ironically enough, Griffith and his party were ignorant of and unresponsible for the Rising of 1916. When Griffith and all nationalists of any shade of green were arrested and thrown into a common prison, however, it was only natural that a unified Irish party would emerge upon the release of the prisoners on Christmas of 1916. In 1917 *Sinn Fein* won its first seats in an election, and in December 1918 it won a majority in the south. In January 1919 these non-attending parliamentary ministers met in Dublin and declared themselves to be the *Dail Eireann,* the independent parliament of an independent Ireland. The war was on, for the British government simply could not believe that this group of radicals was representative of the Irish people, and felt that granting Irish independence would represent appeasement and the death of Empire. Lloyd George stood before his fellow countrymen, and in his folksy Welsh way, assured them that the problem in Ireland was the work of a "small body of assassins, a real murder gang, dominating the country and terrorising it." [61] (But, of course, we Americans can no longer afford to be self-righteous on that account, for the style and the strategy have become familiar again.) The Troubles began, and a different war it was.

60 See J. J. Horgan, *From Parnell to Pearse,* p. 325.
61 As quoted in Lord Pakenham, *Peace by Ordeal* (Cork, 1951), p. 33.

Imagination had been satisfied in the blood sacrifice of the Rising. The poets had done their part, now it was time for the realists to take over. If the poet Padraic Pearse is the hero of the Rising, Michael Collins is the hero of The Troubles. Between these two men, one sees the double mind of revolution. Collins's reaction to Easter Week clearly indicates the mentality that took over Ireland. In a letter to Kevin O'Brien, Collins criticizes the incompetent insurrection.

They have died nobly at the hands of the firing squads. So much I grant. But I do not think the Rising week was an appropriate time for the issue of memoranda couched in poetic phrases, nor of actions worked out in a similar fashion. *Looking at it from the inside (I was in the G.P.O.) it had the air of a Greek tragedy about it,* the illusion being more or less completed with the issue of the before mentioned memoranda. Of Pearse and Connolly I admire the latter the most. Connolly was a realist, Pearse the direct opposite. There was an air of earthy directness about Connolly. It impressed me. I would have followed him through hell had such action been necessary. But I honestly doubt very much if I would have followed Pearse—not without some thought anyway.[62] (My italics.)

If imagination had been far beyond reality in the Rising, reality caught up with a vengeance in The Troubles. And Michael Collins, Director of Intelligence and Minister of Finance, conducted the war with brilliant intelligence if with little finance. Collins's program was as simple as it was unpoetic: to bring about a general state of disorder.[63] The English soldiers who were hired to put down rebellion, the notorious "Black and Tans," had gone through the horror of trench warfare only to return to an England where they were useless and fit only for the ranks of the unemployed. Naturally hardened by these experiences, they found attractive the wages offered for subduing Ireland by terror. But through the cleverness of Collins, they themselves were terrified. Trained by trench warfare to expect the enemy to be in front, the British soldiers were frustrated in their attempts to deal with an

[62] See Rex Taylor, *Michael Collins* (London, 1958), p. 77.
[63] See Padraic Colum, *Arthur Griffith*, p. 193.

invisible army in which a civilian walked up, murdered a British
officer, and then disappeared into a crowd of His Majesty's subjects who had not seen a thing. Terrified and expecting death
from all directions, the Tans and Auxies went berserk, and the
more savage they became, the more they played into Collins's
hands. Collins knew the military value of the American and French
newspapers; the world was watching Ireland, and the English, as
he knew only too well, could withstand anything but public opinion. The pacification techniques that would work well in the
colonies simply could not be used in Europe. America, the English
Labour party, the English clergy, and, perhaps most important of
all, King George V, were bringing pressure on Lloyd George's government to stop the murder and counter-murder in Ireland. Meanwhile, Collins, almost as much of a legend alive as Pearse was dead,
was openly cycling the streets of Dublin and eluding his captors
by never hiding. The British secret agents hunted him, but Collins
had his own agents in Dublin Castle, and when the British agents
were closing in on him, fourteen of them were shot in bed of a
Sunday morning.[64] The British responded by machine-gunning the
players and spectators at a football game that afternoon. It was a
different war. Griffith was shocked. Pearse would have been revolted at the sight of a pregnant woman attempting to beat off
the I.R.A. officers who had shot her husband dead at her feet. But
as Collins said, another man could step into a spy's place, but he
could not step into a dead spy's knowledge. The romantic and
incompetent rebels, he thought, could only die for Ireland; they
could never free her. In The Troubles fact replaced myth, and
our own moral judgments tragically have to come to terms with the
success of the *Realpolitik* methods they might condemn. The noble
and stoical Fenian, John O'Leary, had said that "There are things
a man must not do to save a nation," [65] but as Yeats pointed out,
that romantic Ireland was with O'Leary in the grave. Also about
to go into the grave was an Ireland ruled by England.

[64] See James Gleeson, *Bloody Sunday* (London, 1963).
[65] See W. B. Yeats, *Autobiographies*, p. 96.

The English gave in, to a degree, for on December 6, 1921, Collins and Griffith were two of the signers of the Anglo-Irish Treaty that gave limited independence to the south only. Ulster opted out of the new Irish Free State. The situation was acceptable only to a bare majority, and a minority felt that it was better for Ireland to die than for Ireland to lose her honor. The techniques that Collins brought to Ireland were used against him in the Civil War. The murder continued. Collins was killed in August 1922 in his native Cork, and Griffith died of a stroke. If there was ever any doubt that the ideological movement was over, there could be no doubt now. The movement that had sanctified violence in the figures of Cathleen ní Houlihan and Cuchulain was destroyed by violence; the land that had dismissed evil as an un-Irish thing was overwhelmed by it. The romantic movement that had followed upon the death of Parnell was at an end.

PART TWO

THE POETS IN THE EVENT

CHAPTER FOUR

THE MYTH OF THE SELF
IN THE POETRY OF THE REBELS

When that prophetic man, Standish James O'Grady, predicted that the literary movement would be followed by a political and a military movement he was recognizing that art and politics, even when violently opposed to one another, are intimately related in the larger cultural transformations of history. O'Grady could agree with Shelley that "Poets are the unacknowledged legislators of the world," for any specifically acknowledged political act always has its origin in an antecedent consciousness that was the preparation for the political event. Upon that consciousness art, popular or intellectual, exercises a formative influence. To be sure, we all recognize that propagandists are not poets, and that the single-mindedness of the politician eliminates everything that is irrelevant to action, and in that elimination art is forced to escape the pressure of the crowd if it is to survive. But even in escaping to the aloneness of aesthetic contemplation, the artist is not necessarily irrelevant, for in his work the artist can only realize himself politically by being politically insubordinate. Action demands an immediate embodiment of mind, but because no single act can contain the entire consciousness there is always a part of the mind that remains untouched. By refusing to commit himself to political action the artist is insisting on discovering what he senses has been ignored in the politician's demand for an immediate commitment. In bringing this vague and intuitive perception into the distinct and articulate shape of art, the artist is only doing in symbolic form what society at large will do later when it comes to its own awareness (often through the help of the artist himself) and gives this awareness shape in political decision and military action. O'Grady was irrelevant in 1878; he was not in 1916. To an age of social science such as ours it may seem excessively romantic to regard Standish O'Grady as an unacknowledged legislator of the Republic of Ireland; it may seem better to keep literary criticism distinct from historical scholarship (a distinction the New Critics would prefer to keep as well), but in a study of ideology this becomes impossible, for it is difficult to tell where the artistic messianism of O'Grady, A.E., and Yeats leaves off and the political messianism of Pearse begins.

Perhaps the reason that art and politics are often at odds with one another, even when they are embedded in a single ideology, is because great art most often realizes itself in a tragic or comic perception of the nature of human existence. To live out his role the politician must believe or pretend that the next revolution or piece of legislation will make a difference and that the difference is worth living and dying for. The artist, with an older sort of wisdom, knows better. Like the anarchist Bakunin, he sees that the revolution that is to bring about the dictatorship of the proletariat will only bring about the dictatorship of the ex-proletariat. But this avuncular wisdom does not appeal to a younger generation yearning for commitment.

The generation of Pearse, MacDonagh, and Plunkett had no patience with the older artists. They wanted action, engagement, and a total commitment to the revolution. The rebels of 1916 were something like the rebels of the student New Left today. Impatient with the philosophical, the ambiguous, the tragic, and the complex, they demand that issues be approached "at gut level." The career of such a rebel seems to fall into two phases; in the first phase the adolescent rebel attempts to defeat authority at its own game; failing in that, the rebel kicks over the table and attempts to destroy the game itself. The student who at twenty-nine is so violent a member of SNCC was at eighteen trying to write poetry in the manner of T. S. Eliot. Pearse, MacDonagh, and Plunkett were rebels in the same manner. Through them Catholic-nationalist literature hoped to triumph over the Protestant Anglo-Irish literature of Yeats, A.E., Synge, and Lady Gregory. But they failed; despite their feelings of divine election and of moral superiority to the heretical Yeats and A.E., they failed completely. Not only did the rebels fail as poets, but they also made huge critical blunders. They were wrong about Yeats; they were wrong about Synge; and failing to assess the worth of the older generation, they made mistakes with their own. James Joyce once approached Pearse with a mind to learning the language of his country, but because Pearse found it necessary to praise Irish by making contemptuous remarks about the literary insufficiencies of the English language, Joyce left in disgust. No matter how effective Pearse may have been as a teacher of Irish to future soldiers (he once offered a rifle as a prize for the best Irish speaker at St. Enda's), he must also be judged as having played a significant part in convincing the greatest novelist of the century that there was no place for him in the Irish movement. Artistically, the rebels were failures, and their failure could only intensify their yearning for revolutionary satisfaction.

It is easy to criticize Pearse, MacDonagh, and Plunkett as classic examples of the revolutionary as artist *manqué*. It is too easy. Such a judgment, in coming to the defense of art, forgets that the old familiar distinctions between art and reality are blurred in the phenomenon of revolution. When the revolutionary fails as artist, he turns from art to history and attempts to make of the state a work of art. This failure as artist can be seen as a simplification of consciousness in a mind that cannot grasp the essential complexity of human existence, but it can also be seen as a lifting up of history into the realm of aesthetic form in an attempt to make a greater tragic or comic work of art out of the reality of human existence. When a revolutionary attempts to turn reality into a work of art, it is no longer appropriate merely to evaluate his lyrics. Art helps to create a historical consciousness, but once that consciousness exists, it is history itself that becomes the work of art.

Art gives articulate form to the inchoate mass of experience: the lyric teaches us to expect flashes of insight from momentary perceptions; the novel teaches us to think of the ordinary life as a career through time. Once an experience is articulated the mind sees it in form. Since all form has limitation, the mind observes the edges which describe the end of the form and the beginning of something else. *Paradise Lost,* for example, is a sublime articulation of the Christian vision of history; but once that vision is articulated it is easier than ever before to talk *about* the Christian vision of history. Once the form is created we move out of the form to observe it. Art is an agent by which the consciousness is dislocated from what it formerly took to be reality. Now the old reality becomes the work of art. This Hegelian process of *aufheben* is currently much discussed in Marshall McLuhan's terminology: that the sloughed-off environment becomes a work of art in a new environment, which is itself invisible, until it too is articulated into form and thus transcended. Art and reality are, therefore, not static terms, like style and content; they are, like mass and energy, dynamic and interchangeable. *Cathleen ní Houlihan* gave articulate form to Irish nationalism. The new environment, which was invisible to all but the poets and rebels, was the Republic of Ireland. Now if this Hegelian process is real we can expect the present Republic of Ireland to become a work of art in an as yet invisible environment; the Republic will become a cherished relic, like the Mexican Olvera Street that is preserved in the midst of the enormous megalopolis of Los Angeles.

This dislocation of consciousness that springs from making real ity into a work of art comes at a certain price: one must die to be reborn, and the price the revolutionary must pay is his willingness to die and lead others to death so that the state in his imagination can be achieved. It is at this threshold of death that rational, evaluative judgments can be made concerning the rebels. If one values life, the rebels with their Republic of Ireland were insane fanatics who had no understanding of reality; if one values death, then the realistic critics of the fanatics were men of limited vision: standing squarely upon reality they made sensible speeches without realizing that it was precisely reality that the revolutionaries had pulled out from under them.

But before history can be turned into a work of art, the artist must discover his calling. When, in something like a conversion experience, the individual perceives the image of himself as revolutionary, he sees that image against a backdrop of history, and in that projection history is transformed in his imagination into a myth. Myth and imagination are difficult things to discuss, for they take us away from the charts and graphs that keep us afloat in the unknown; but images have their substance, and if we examine the images of the self in the poetry of the rebels we can see the historical imagination of the revolutionary at work in the larger cultural phenomenon of romanticism. In analyzing the manner in which the rebels imaged themselves and their situation in time in their poetry, we can see the way in which they perceived reality. Once we understand the nature of their perceptions we are in a better position to understand their actions.

The role of a rebel is very general, but the way in which the role appears to the imagination of one man is very particular. In the imagination the role is concentrated, intensified, and heightened until it is seen in the moment of its most resonant and symbolic gesture. Out of the general role, the imagination makes an individual work of art, a portrait in which the role's ceremonial robes of office are given its own unique body, face, and expression. The role as individually imagined is the image of the self; the role as individually enacted is the myth of the self.

The self-image of Padraic Pearse was Jesus Christ, for Pearse saw the role of the rebel as the perfect Imitation of Christ. Because these images are not newly created but taken from cultural contexts, they come with burdens of responsibility, for the image demands the one action that can express it. The mythical image of Pearse as savior demanded the reality of crucifixion. Because these burdens of responsibility are unpleasant, most people shirk them or try to muddle the issue, not seeing that one cannot be a good monk by playing the lover, or a good poet by playing the popular rhetorician. The greatness of Padraic Pearse is seen in his refusal to shirk the burden of responsibility that came with the image he had chosen. He wanted to be a savior to his people, and he moved remorselessly and uncomplainingly into myth; perhaps that is why he achieved the apotheosis he desired.

Before Pearse fired a shot, he rehearsed insurrection by writing a play about it. *The Singer* is his most characteristic and most important work, for in it all his literary and nationalistic ideas are fully realized. Here one sees quite clearly that for Pearse the rebel is the perfect imitation of Christ. The pattern of the hero with the thousand faces is sharply evident in the story of the singer Mac-Dara.[1] The patriotic songs of the hero force him into exile, into *separation* from his people of Connacht. Wandering as an alien through the cities of men, MacDara earns his bread as a teacher, until he is again cast out onto the roads. There in the loneliness of the ditch, the despondent hero casts out God and denies the path to crucifixion that has been ordained for him. At the nadir of his despair, MacDara experiences the anguish of Christ in the garden of Gethsemane, but out of this extreme despair comes a new faith, a new birth. After the *separation* comes the *initiation*. The hero in this descent into hell is initiated into a wisdom the common man can never know; he realizes that a gay folly is the highest knowledge, and that to be truly wise one must abandon what the world knows as wisdom to become foolish. Initiated into this gay

1 Joseph Campbell, *The Hero with a Thousand Faces* (New York, 1949).

science (a rather scandalous mixture of Nietzsche and Christianity), the hero *returns* to his people. The son returns to comfort his mother, who is, of course, "Mary mother of us all." MacDara's return to his people, like Christ's return to Jerusalem, is joyous and everywhere is met by crowds. Yet the singer knows he goes to his death. The *Sassenach* are on the march, and the word that is to start the revolution has not been given. The common people would hold back, in prudence and wisdom, but the singer will have no part of this prudence and wisdom which is, in reality, the false security of the terror-stricken. The drama ends with Mac-Dara's exhortation:

One man can free a people as one Man redeemed the world. I will take no pike, I will go into the battle with bare hands. I will stand up before the Gall as Christ hung naked before men on the tree.[2]

One can see why the lawyer and historian J. J. Horgan has called the Easter Rising a mortal sin and Pearse a heretic.[3] Pearse's devotion is extreme, and, like all extreme devotion, it is perilously close to blasphemy. But in his poem, "The Fool," Pearse anticipated these criticisms.

The lawyers have sat in council, the men with the keen,
                                        long faces,
And said, "This man is a fool," and others have said,
                                        "He blasphemeth";
And the wise have pitied the fool that hath striven to give
                                        a life
In the world of time and space among the bulk of actual things,
To a dream that was dreamed in the heart, and that only the
                                        heart could hold.
O wise men, riddle me this: what if the dream come true?
What if the dream come true? and if millions unborn shall dwell
In the house that I shaped in my heart, the noble house of
                                        my thought? . . .

[2] Padraic Pearse, *Collected Works: Plays, Stories, Poems* (Dublin, 1924), p. 44.
[3] J. J. Horgan, *From Parnell to Pearse* (Dublin, 1948), p. 285.

And so I speak.
Yea, ere my hot youth pass, I speak to my people and say:
Ye shall be foolish as I; ye shall scatter, not save.[4]

Whether this is heresy or the imitation of Christ must occupy the minds of the theologians. But even to a layman it would seem that such a direct and mystical relationship between man and God tends to eliminate the intermediary of the Church and its sacraments. It is doubtful that Pearse consulted his confessor before plotting revolution. But Horgan's opposition is a clearer matter than theology; it reflects the familiar social structure of revolution. Horgan was Redmonite and wealthy upper-middle class; Pearse was a member of the intelligentsia in sympathy with peasantry and labor. Pearse was acting in exact imitation of Christ; he was abandoning the rich man who, like the camel, could not pass through the needle's eye, and he was gathering the common and vulgar about him. As another Irishman, G. B. Shaw, pointed out: Christ was what we would now call a Bohemian; the Pharisees did not follow Him, but the proletariat did. In short, no matter how unorthodox Pearse was, he could make a legitimate case for regarding Christ as the greatest revolutionary of all time. Christ's peace came with a sword, and his return is to come with apocalypse. Of course, as one knows only too painfully from history, anything can be proved with Scripture or statistics. Some see in the parables of Christ a call to turn the other cheek and forswear violence; Pearse saw only Christ's terrible swift sword and the overturning of kingdoms in which the meek of Connemara inherited Eire. In the theology of Pearse, Douglas Hyde was the Precursor who had baptized the people with Irish; it was the task of the Messiah to complete their salvation.

I have come to the conclusion that the Gaelic League, as the Gaelic League, is a spent force; and I am glad of it.... it was a prophet, and more than a prophet. But it was not the Messiah. I do not know if the Messiah has yet come, and I am not sure that there will be any visible

---

[4] This poem, and all the poetry of the rebels I shall quote, is taken from *The 1916 Poets*, ed. Desmond Ryan (Dublin, Allen Figgis, 1963).

and personal Messiah in this redemption. The people itself will perhaps be its own Messiah, the people labouring, scourged, crowned with thorns, agonising and dying, to rise again immortal and impassible. . . .
The deed of the generation that has now reached middle life was the Gaelic League: the beginning of the Irish revolution. Let our generation not shirk its deed, which is to accomplish the revolution.[5]

Pearse knew very well that he was a silly figure of black-robed seriousness, but he did not shirk the limitation of personality. Accepting personality as if it were a cross, he tried to make his limitations in society into virtues in his myth. Since the self-image of Christ-like rebel was totally absurd and antisocial, the hostility or resistance the self-image would encounter only intensified the Christ-like nature of Pearse's idea of a rebel. Accused of being foolish, Pearse made a metaphysic out of foolishness. Throughout his plays, poems, and stories, he celebrates children and fools, for in them he is steadfastly resisting maturity. Pearse refused to grow up, because to grow up is to accept the world, to accept the kingdom of this earth instead of the kingdom that is not yet of this world. Pearse did everything in his power to become as a little child; perhaps that is why he abandoned the bar to work with schoolchildren: in them he was trying to perpetuate the boy in himself that had vowed to free Ireland. The boy Christ had confounded the learned doctors, and the boy Cuchulain had confounded the older wariors, and for Pearse, Christ and Cuchulain were not opposed. If it is hard to see Cuchulain, riding in his chariot with the severed heads of his enemies about him, as a Christ-like figure, we must look again, for Pearse most certainly did. He read the Ulster Cycle as allegory, as an image of the story of Calvary. Emain Macha was a kingdom afflicted with a primal sin that was redeemed by the blood sacrifice of Cuchulain.[6] Pearse's writing, political or literary, is filled with the imagery of apocalypse and one must go

[5] Padraic Pearse, "The Coming Revolution" (November 8, 1913), *Collected Works: Political Writings and Speeches* (Dublin, 1924), p. 91ff.
[6] Padraic Pearse, *Collected Works: Songs of the Irish Rebels and Three Lectures on Gaelic Topics*, p. 156.

to Revelation to encounter the Christ-Cuchulain figure that he en-
visioned. (It was this avatar that Yeats called a "rough beast.")
The boy Cuchulain is impetuous and foolish, but his acceptance
of a short life grants him the immortality that he desires. Christ
without the cross is not Christ, and Pearse knew that the rebel-
martyr without death was no hero at all. In his passionate objectivity, Pearse calculated, threw his life into the balance, calculated
again, and decided that his death was not the cost but the reward
of sacrifice. In exactly the same manner as he embraced foolishness
and made a religion out of it, so he embraced death.

A RANN I MADE

A rann I made within my heart
To the rider, to the high king,
A rann I made to my love,
To the king of kings, ancient death.

Brighter to me than light of day
The dark of thy house, tho' black clay;
Sweeter to me than music of trumpets
The quiet of thy house and its eternal silence.

Pearse's patriotism is a *Liebestod,* a mysticism that renounces the
life of body and the life of men in society. For this reason, Pearse's
neo-peasant poetry never worked; his passions were too Alexandrian; he could not rest in the anonymity of the folk of the valleys;
that was repression, not expression; he had to move on to the
transfiguration on the Mount, where all the eyes of the folk were
lifted up to him. Pearse tried to achieve self-fulfillment in the folk,
but he spent far more time in his revolutionary Hermitage in
Rathfarnam than he ever spent in his cottage in Connemara. His
myth required that he give up everything; there was no other way
without abandoning the self-image. In his poem "Renunciation"
this acceptance of the necessity of crucifixion is very dramatically
rendered; for there Pearse renounces the senses one by one, until
nothing is left to distract him from death.

RENUNCIATION

Naked I saw thee,
O beauty of beauty,
And I blinded my eyes
For fear I should fail.

I heard thy music,
O melody of melody,
And I closed my ears
For fear I should falter.

I tasted thy mouth,
O sweetness of sweetness,
And I hardened my heart
And I smothered my desire.

I turned my back
On the vision I had shaped
And to this road before me
I turned my face.

I have turned my face
To this road before me,
To the deed that I see
And the death I shall die.

The perfect service to this beautiful death demands nothing less
than self-immolation. The Irish interpret this poem as an expression of an unflinching devotion to an ideal, a self-sacrifice of the
noblest order, for Pearse, the schoolteacher, had said that the most
important value in education was to inspire "a love and a service
so excessive as to annihilate all thought of self...." [7] The poem
makes immediate sense if we read it from this patriotic point of
view. But for those of us not involved in Irish patriotism, the
poem has more dimensions than one. Beyond its patriotic flatness,
the poem contains a few ironies and one powerful self-accusation,
and it is in its fullness of meaning that the poem becomes a much
more interesting human document. From this perspective, the fear
of failure expressed in the first quatrain is like the religious fa-

[7] Padraic Pearse, *Collected Works: Political Writings and Speeches*, p. 25.

natic's fear of sin: a fear that causes the devout to castrate himself, lest he fall into carnal sin. The imagery of the poem is sexual,
and if Pearse is not exhibiting the classic Freudian symptoms of
self-castration, he is most certainly talking about an immolation
of equal severity. The saint and/or the fanatic is here crying aloud
in anguish and full consciousness of what his sanctity must cost
him. Most people do not gaze upon beauty, and blind themselves;
most people do not hear music, and shut their ears; most people
do not kiss, and smother desire; most people are neither saints nor
fanatics. In Pearse's poem humanity and sanctity are opposed,
violently opposed. Here humanity is seen in the flesh, in the senses,
in the sexuality of the body, and anyone acquainted with Irish
Catholicism knows only too well that the flesh and the senses are
enemies that threaten to cast the soul into eternal damnation for
nothing more than an instant's thought. Pearse's poem was written
in the Irish language and it is rooted in the Irish culture. In that
culture, virginity is considered a higher state than marriage, and
the brother who becomes a priest is a greater and stronger man
than the brother who, out of carnal weakness, marries; the sister
who becomes a nun is closer to God because of the offering up of
her barren womb; and over all the sexual occasions of human life,
a celibate clergy keeps insistent watch. This is the culture of which
Pearse is an almost perfect expression: he dressed in black, he
praised the purity of the peasant, and celebrated the famous chastity of Irish women; if he thought about women, it was always as
mothers, most often as mothers of soldiers, but never as wives.
Pearse is a perfect follower of *Cathleen ní Houlihan:* in "Renunciation" he turns aside from the dull love of the wife to accept the
sharp, transfiguring love of death.

Unlike Pearse, Thomas MacDonagh did not aspire to be a savior
to his people. Uncertain of his self-image, his myth was changeable
and unstable, for he lacked that passionate intensity needed to
lock the will upon a single thing. It was only in the revolution
that he seems to have found at last the self-unity that art could
not provide him. One feels that if fame and success as a poet had

come to Pearse, it would not have distracted him from the martyr-dom that was his truest passion; but MacDonagh seems to have been no such character, and one can see that, in the words of Terence de Vere White, if "the muse had been kinder," Mac-Donagh would have chosen to live longer. Unlike Pearse, Mac-Donagh seems to have been an ordinary human being who desperately wanted to be more than an ordinary human being. Of the three poet-rebels, he alone seems to be the classic example of the revolutionary as artist *manqué*.

MacDonagh seems to have been a companionable person with a lively sense of humor. If there were ever any jokes in St. Enda's, it was MacDonagh and not Pearse who authored them. Pearse seems to have recognized his failings along these lines, for once having written an exceptionally sober number for his school's newspaper, he came to MacDonagh and pleaded for a joke to rescue the issue. Perhaps the best contrast between the two fellow rebels is con-tained in the Dublin legend which has it that MacDonagh took Pearse to a music hall: as MacDonagh would comment upon the admirable qualities of the prettiest legs in the chorus line, Pearse would nod, and admit that, yes, they were the limbs of an angel. Though Pearse tried on many occasions to rejoin the human race, first as a peasant, then as a speaker to crowds, he had in fact elimi-nated his humanity in his remorseless fixation of the will upon martyrdom. Pearse had eliminated everything in himself that did not pertain to his myth; if we subtract the role of the rebel from him, nothing remains. This failing in humanity is strongly pro-nounced in Pearse's prose, for his educational writings are warm, personal, intellectually articulate, and convincing; but his public speeches, especially the graveside orations, are all crowd-rhetoric. Bloodthirsty and insincere, they amount to a kind of intellectual slumming. They are the feeble and pathetic attempts of the shy man who is trying to rejoin the human race, but trying so hard that he loses the relaxed humor and personal spontaneity that would have assured him of success. As a writer of speeches, Pearse was a dismal failure, and it is not surprising that Tom Clarke was moved, while Yeats and Stephen MacKenna were not. The speeches do not express the myth; they are merely necessary means to achieve the myth; they are what Yeats would call pursuits of the false mask. And as the speeches are to Pearse, so the poems are to MacDonagh. We look in vain for traces of that broader humanity, gentleness, and humor that Yeats, James Stephens, and Padraic Colum have described. Speaking of this split in MacDonagh between the man and the work, Colum has said:

A poet with a bent toward abstraction, a scholar with a leaning towards philology—these were the aspects Thomas MacDonagh showed when he expressed himself in letters. But what was fundamental in him rarely went into what he wrote. That fundamental thing was an eager search for something that would have his whole devotion. His dream was always of action—of a man dominating a crowd for a great end.[8]

The split between the man and the work does not by itself indicate that MacDonagh was no poet and could not express himself, for, as Yeats has put it, the art often expresses what the man most lacks. What the poems express is the tortured soul, the suffering romantic, the conventional melancholic. They are freighted with abstraction, and the syntax is twisted all out of shape by the strained inversions needed to fill out a dull meter and a flat rhyme.

THE SONG OF JOY

O mocking voice that dost forbid always
The poems that would win an easy praise,
Favouring with silence but the delicate, strong,
True creatures of inspired natural song,
Only the brood of Art and Life divine,
Thou say'st no fealty to the spurious line
Of phantasies of earth,—to mortal things
That strain to stay the heavens with their wings
And ape the crowned orders at the Throne
Around a graven image of their own,
Setting the casual fact of one poor age
Aloft, enormous in its privilege

8 *Poems of the Irish Republican Brotherhood*, ed. Padraic Colum and E. J. O'Brien (Boston, 1916), p. xxx.

> Of instant being! O voice of the mind
> Wilt thou forbid the songs that come like wind
> Out of the south upon the poet heart,
> Out of the quietude of certain art?
> Now the cross tempests from the boreal frost
> Harry my atmosphere,...

The poetry speaks for itself. The early poetry tries for simple nature lyrics, but as it progresses it seems to harden and become defensive in a declamatory way: the poet keeps insisting that he has visions and sees beyond the veil of mortality.

> O Joy! O secret transport of mystic vision,
> Who hold'st the keys of Ivory and Horn,
> Who join'st the hands of Earth and Faerie!
>
> . . .
>
> The poet guards the philosophic soul
> In contemplation that no importunate thought
> May mar his ecstasy or change his song.

The poems are not self-expression, but self-defense; they are the performances of a man who is trying to convince himself that he feels deeply and intensely, that his soul pulses with a being larger than that of the common lot of man. The poems are what all sensitive men write in their adolescence.

IN CALM

> Not a wind blows and I have cried for storm!
> The night is still and sullen and too bright,
> Still and not cold—the airs around me warm
> Rise, and I hate them, and I hate the night.
>
> Yet I shall hate the day more than the hush
> Henceforth forever, as life more than death;—
> And I have cried to hear the wild winds rush
> To drown my words, to drown my living breath.

All this talk of hate and the pathological inversion of all normal values might mean much, were not the poem such a close imitation of a long established convention of romantic melancholia. Specifically, "In Calm" is very close in spirit and imagery to Coleridge's "Dejection: An Ode." MacDonagh hates the inactivity of the calm and wants violent winds to come because, following Coleridge, he sees the wind as the universal life breath and outward sign of one's own creativity. And yet if the poem is derivative, the question still remains: Why did MacDonagh choose to imitate this kind of poem over another? The imitation, of course, argues for an affinity, and the ideas that come forth in a discussion of the great romantic poems of description and meditation would clarify MacDonagh's work as well, and clarify the cultural situation of the revolutionary as artist *manqué*.

In poems like "Dejection: An Ode" or "Tintern Abbey" the poet is concerned with a crisis in universal order and a crisis in individual creative power. The poet gazes upon nature and calls out across an abyss that separates him from communion with that nature. In his sadness he longs for a mystical ecstasy that will reunite him with the world: Coleridge longs for the creative power of imagination, an imagination that, through the symbolism that is really the language in which God speaks to the world, can put the broken universe back together; Wordsworth longs for the vanished innocence of a childhood in nature. But in each case the poet fails; one man cannot achieve the universe, and no matter what his powers were in youthful innocence or creative adolescence, he must recognize that he no longer has them. The poet, therefore, seeks to return to the humanity he had ignored in the transports of his former ecstasies; he finds, in his own suffering, a sympathy for suffering humanity. Wordsworth, at the end of "Tintern Abbey," turns away from the landscape to the human love that his sister represents; Coleridge, in "Dejection," turns away from the stars to love of his "dear lady," Sara Hutchinson. In each case the poet turns away from the unachieved universe to come down off the mountain to the city of man.

So recurrent is this pattern in romantic art that it practically amounts to a cultural syndrome. The romantic adolescent proclaims his Cosmic Self against a background of burning stars, but once in that empty cosmic space, the self out of culture collapses in upon itself; the individual then realizes that what he really wanted was not the stars but a true human community; running down from the mountain, the romantic embraces the first peasant he comes across and proclaims that he will henceforth build the New Jerusalem in his own backyard. After the contemplative impasse, the man sets to work: Faust takes to the dikes, and *Teufelsdröckh* to the duty nearest at hand. But for the nineteenth century, the most sensational example was set by Byron: after the intellectual impasse came his fight in the Greek revolutionary war against the Turk, and then death. Probably more than any other romantic poet, Byron showed an exalted way out of the dead end of romantic melancholia. To Mazzini and the Russian nihilists, "Byron was the symbol of future destiny; he represented the wonderful blend of thought and action, of heroism and sacrifice." [10] The crisis of order for the romantic in this scheme is not only how to relate ecstasy to endurance in time, but how to relate imagination to reality and the Self to the Other. Passion cries out for a quick relation here and now, but the dreamer finds that he is incompetent with reality, that the ultimate relationships of time and eternity, imagination and reality, Self and the Other, take a prolonged labor that only a saint could master. Failing, the incompetent becomes impatient. Raging at his aloneness, the incompetent dreams up a companionship with the cheering multitudes that he directs toward some overwhelming event. Failing in life, the incompetent discovers that socially successful people are terrified by death and that he can finally become a success if he dies well. Death is, perhaps, the one remaining thing that must be done alone; ironically, then, it is death that proves the life of the self, not solitude, for "man only feels solitary in society for social reasons." [11] It is a public death which gives identity to the private life. This romantic pattern of failed universe and return to humanity informs the career of Thomas MacDonagh, for Mac-

[10] J. L. Talmon, *Political Messianism: Romantic Phase* (New York, 1960), p. 262.
[11] Albert Camus, *The Rebel* (New York, 1956), p. 199.

Donagh's self-image was the tortured soul, his self-myth was a Byronism converted to a Christian cause.

Over and over again the poems rehearse a personal agony, a love that died, a youth that fled, a disappointment with Fate, and over and over again he proclaims against this suffering that he is a mystic caught up in the ineffable joy-sorrow beyond human ken. But the tragedy continues for the revolutionary even after he returns to humanity from his mountain-top vigil; the enthusiastic imagination which had made starlit aloneness seem the answer to all things, now makes the peasant community seem to be the cure for civilization's discontents. In his new dream of companionship with humanity, the romantic revolutionary imagines a simple peasantry that is free of his own divisions and anxieties; he sees a charming peasantry that will tip its soiled cap and give a cheery greeting as the man of books passes by in his atmosphere of sorrow and mystery. This is most certainly "the coming together of classes" that Yeats praised with his talk of Ned the beggar and Sean the fool, and even Pearse shows this attitude in his play *The Singer,* for although the peasants do not understand the hero's talk of spiritual despair, they affirm that the talk must be true and wise, even if it is beyond them. MacDonagh seems to have grown disappointed with the urban Gaelic League and even found the peasantry to be "cold, dark, and reticent, and too polite." [12] In MacDonagh's play *When the Dawn Is Come* there is a painful awareness that the intellectual can be little more than sacrificed in Ireland: the hero, a man of abstractly perfect virtue, is respected by all but his desire to beat the *Sassenach* through intellectually subtle ways leads to disaster. He pretends to be an informer, and almost dies at the hands of his own followers. The intellectual and the ignoramus can, with all good will, rub shoulders in a revolution, in that unnatural time when the excitement of violence and self-sacrifice obscures the harder day-by-day labor of education and endurance. But when the revolutions are over, the peasant, who was essentially only a fellow human when he shared a bar-

12 W. B. Yeats, *Autobiographies,* p. 505.

ricade, becomes the menace with a vote and a seat in the *Dail*. Yeats, who in his early days exalted his fellow countrymen, excoriated them when he discovered as a senator what changes power could bring about in simple men. In the days of the past, when the Irish Revival seemed no bloodier in aspect than the revival of Welsh or Breton, the intellectuals had visions of love and universal humanity, and each one hoped that he might be the chosen one to lead the people out of bondage. Later Yeats grew into a Swiftian contempt for popery and the Irish masses and delighted in saying outrageous things to an incensed Senate of Catholic businessmen. Although Pearse and MacDonagh were saved the agony of passing legislation, one can see the beginnings of the intelligentsia's great disappointment in MacDonagh's unhappiness with the Irish peasantry and the urban Gaelic League. MacDonagh's death may well have been a gesture of despair at his countrymen who were not living up to the expectations he had of them. MacDonagh seems to have been the kind of man who, if given a chance in a different environment, might have lived a full life, but perhaps he wanted more out of life than a professorship, and purchased immortality with the only means at his disposal: his death. Yet even if his death were a gesture of despair, there is a greater courage and self-sacrifice contained in it than in Pearse's deeply cherished apotheosis. Perhaps the attending British officer's words are his best epitaph: "They all died well, but MacDonagh died like a Prince." [13]

Of all the poets and poetic figures who took part in the literary insurrection of 1916, Joseph Mary Plunkett is the most mysterious, and so little is known about him that he is likely to remain the least understood of all the rebel leaders. Caulfield's history makes him out to be a rather adolescent eccentric who covered himself with antique jewelry and imagined himself the kind of counterespionage agent he had read about in popular novels.[14] But perhaps the bracelets were Celtic and intended to serve as talismans of the hero

---

[13] As quoted in James Stephens's Introduction to *Poems by Thomas MacDonagh* (Dublin, 1916), p. xi.
[14] Max Caulfield, *The Easter Rebellion* (London, 1964).

Cuchulain. Still, Caulfield's history may be right. Plunkett's sister admitted that he found the revolution to be quite a bit of fun, and his own journal of his trip to Germany seems to confirm the counterespionage theory of self-dramatization.[15] In this journal, Plunkett records his concern about being trailed by "G Men," and invents elaborate camouflage to cover his contacts in Germany: all of which is very openly noted in the journal.[16] One wonders why agent Plunkett did not chew the paper lest it fall into the hands of his pursuers. In reading the journal it is difficult to imagine Plunkett as a real human being of mature age. Like Maude Gonne, Plunkett seems to have tried to live his life as if it were an adventure novel.

In his charming, easy way he packed, however, enough adventure into his little known life. He had the hero's joy in high escapade, and if there is anything to be said at all of his life it is this, that it was a life of marvellous grist. In spite of ill health, absorbing study, and hard poet-work, he was ever ready to meet the ventures that came his way: in his schooldays at Passy; with his dear friend Asphar at Malta, with the Algerians, amongst whom he was held in such affection; with Stäkler, the tall dark cosmopolitan who taught him Arabic (it was Stäkler's habit to go out of nights amongst the different tribes of the hinterland disguised as one of themselves and be hail-fellow-well-met with the strange guardians of the fringe of the Sahara—a real live Strickland); in the Cercle Republicaine in Algiers, where Plunkett often danced, and where, when a shot went off in the cardroom alongside to punctuate a charge of cheating, no one, girl or gentleman, even turned to look; in the half-French, half-Moorish, skating rink (Plunkett was a finished skater), where there occurred accidents too full bodied, too near the elemental edge of things, to be allowed to redden the pages of a stately review. The reality of all that life became part and parcel of a soul at once impressionable and as hard as nails, for he hated sentimentality, that which he had being of the Spartan type, contemptuous of lambency or paw. And that is the tragedy of his twenty-eight years.[17]

15 Geraldine Plunkett, "Joseph Plunkett: Origins and Background," *University Review*, National University of Ireland, Vol. I, No. 11.
16 "Joseph Plunkett's Diary of His Journey to Germany in 1915," in *University Review*, loc. cit.
17 Peter McBrien, "Poets of the Insurrection III, Joseph Plunkett," *Studies*, V (December 1916), 536-49.

It would seem that for Plunkett revolution was merely one of his many escapades. He seems to have come into contact with the revolution through the chance accident that his mother asked MacDonagh to tutor her son in the basic Irish he needed for matriculation in the National University. We next see Plunkett as a contributor to *The Irish Review,* a review which he came to own and edit through the simple procedure of paying the troubled magazine's debts. Given this scarcity of biographical material, about the only way one can approach the man is through the study of his imagination as it is revealed in his poems, but, of course, such a study tells more about what the man wanted to be than what he actually was. Yet even in a study of the poems, the story is incomplete; the poems show talent, but it is anybody's guess if their baroque and chryselephantine lusciousness could ever be brought under control, and once under control, directed toward greatness. Plunkett was executed at the age of twenty-eight, so it is only fair to him to consider that if Yeats had been executed at that age, a few literary historians might remember the minor poet who had written *The Wanderings of Oisin* and *The Celtic Twilight.*

THE SPLENDOUR OF GOD

The drunken stars stagger across the sky,
The moon wavers and sways like a wind-blown bud,
Beneath my feet the earth like drifting scud
Lapses and slides, wallows and shoots on high;
Immovable things start suddenly flying by,
The city shakes and quavers, a city of mud
And ooze—a brawling cataract is my blood
Of molten metal and fire—like a God am I.

When God crushes his passion-fruit for our thirst
And the universe totters—I have burst the grape
Of the world, and let its powerful blood escape
Untasted—crying whether my vision durst
See God's high glory in a girl's soft shape—
God! Is my worship blessed or accurst.

Desmond Ryan, the chief historian of the Easter Rising and the editor of the 1916 poets, says that Plunkett was deep in a reading of the Christian mystics, Tauler and St. John of the Cross. One almost feels relieved to learn that Plunkett did not dream up these orgies of erotic mysticism by himself, but is trying to express himself within a tradition, albeit a tradition slightly less traveled than the standard romanticism that attracted MacDonagh. Both Mac-Donagh and Plunkett objected to the pagan and occult tone that Yeats and A.E. were giving to modern Irish literature, and both young men strove to write a poetry of the sublime that would be devoutly Catholic. As Yeats went to Swedenborg, so Plunkett went to St. John of the Cross. The stream of Spanish mysticism had existed in the tradition of English poetry since Crashaw and had recently been experiencing a revival in the work of Francis Thompson; it was only reasonable to think that the medievalism of Ireland could do as much for English poetry as the medievalism of Spain had done for English poetry in the seventeenth century. Unfortunately, Plunkett took the tradition to heart in all its entirety. It is perhaps impious to speak of bad taste in such lines as "When God crushes His passion-fruit for our thirst," but the choirs of belching angels that attend Crashaw's poetry seem to blow their trumpets at the four corners of Plunkett's page. Nevertheless, Plunkett manages to write this sort of thing with some energy in image and cadence. *De gustibus non disputandum est,* and one must concede that this young poet has excelled Francis Thompson, for the concreteness and particularity of the chosen image is never blurred by periphrasis. If an image seems elaborate it is often because the image is elaborate in its source, e.g. Revelation. Plunkett's poetry is filled with the thunders and seven seals of Apocalypse, but unlike Yeats's avatar, his is no rough beast, but Christ. Plunkett is obsessed with sacrifice as much as Pearse, but Pearse's vision of sacrifice is dramatic: in his we see a single figure against the plain backdrop of an Irish village, where Plunkett's vision is epic and the sacrificial figure stands against a cosmic background.

ARBOR VITAE

Beside the golden gate there grows a tree
Whose heavy fruit gives entrance to the ways
Of Wonder, and the leaves thereof are days
Of desolation—nights of agony,
The buds and blossom for the fruits to be:
Rooted in terror the dead trunk decays,
The burdened branches drooping to the clays
Clammy with blood of crushed humanity.

But lo the fruit! Sweet-bitter, red and white,
Better than wine—better than timely death
When surfeited with sorrow—Lo the bright
Mansions beyond the gate! And love, thy breath
Fanning our flaming hearts where entereth
Thy Song of Songs with Love's tumultuous light.

The Tree of Life, as used here, is an old epic device taken from
the pages of Blake, Milton, Dr. Dee, Zosimus, Genesis, and Hermes
Trismegistus; and caught up in the implications of such iconography, the poet has difficulty holding on to the syntactical order
that the sonnet requires. The Tree is, of course, the primordial
emblem for the consummation of opposites (as the cross is the
modern emblem for the same consummation); the trunk of the
tree, like the body, is rooted in the terror of darkness, but this
suffering only nourishes the bitter-sweet fruit of mystical love
which flowers aloft in the higher consciousness that is not rooted
in time, so that if one succeeds in the proper polarization of *ida*
and *pingala* that coil about the spine of the trunk, the cosmic force
will ascend from the *kundalini* through the *sushumna* to the thou-
sand-petaled lotus of the coronal *chakra*, though there are some
who take issue with this and prefer to speak of the opposites more
simply in terms of sex. Plunkett seems to prefer the intensification
coupled with familiarity that comes with the simpler lyric of the
love of God for the soul in *The Song of Songs*. In "La Pucelle"
the girl becomes the soul.

> She walks the azure meadows where the stars
> Shed glowing petal on her moon-white feet,

The planets sing to see her, and to greet
Her, nebulae unfold like nenuphars.

No dread eclipse the morn of Heaven mars
But fades before her fearing, lest she meet
With darkness, while the reckless comets beat
A path of gold with flickering scimitars.

The battle-ranks of Heaven are marching past
Squadron by squadron, battalion, and brigade,
Both horse and foot—Soundless their swift parade.

Silent till she appears—then quick they cast
Upon the wind the banner of the Maid,
And Heaven rocks with Gabriel's trumpet-blast.

The love between the Soul and God, like the sexual love between a man and a woman, is a fierce passion, and in this poem
Heaven is about to engage in a cosmic battle for the sake of the
single girl. The title of Plunkett's book was significantly *The Circle
and the Sword*, the crown and the weapon that is to win it, the
phallus and its sheath. The peace of Christ comes with a sword,
and the soul must take up the weapon. But this love requires its
descent into hell, and in his "Heaven and Hell," Plunkett describes
the cosmic conflict, for the Bridegroom has now become a soldier.

> ... There burned
> In heart and eyes a drunken flame
> That sang and clamoured out your name,
> And woke a madness in my head.
> The enemies I had left for dead
> Surrounded me with gibbering eyes
> And mocked me for my blinded eyes.
> I curst them till they rose in rage
> And flung me down a battle gage
> To fight them on the floors of Hell
> Where solely they're assailable ...
>
> To-day, though dimly, I do see,
> My vision has come back to me.
> And I have learnt in deepest Hell
> Of Heavenly mysteries to tell,

> I with terror-twisted eyes
> Have watched you play in Paradise.

In turning the Bridegroom of the *Song of Songs* into a soldier, Plunkett shifts the tradition slightly, for now it is not exactly Christ who is the Bridegroom, and the soul the bride, as much as it is the girl who has become the soul in the state of grace, and the soldier the man struggling to achieve union with that grace. This shift of vision enables Plunkett to turn his love in the real world, Grace Gifford, into an emblem of his desire for salvation in sacramental marriage. Thus before the mortal man is united with grace, he must undergo penitential combat: he must free the maiden in the castle of Ireland from the English dragon of sin. In Plunkett's "The Little Black Rose Shall Be Red at Last," this union of mystical tradition with Irish nationalism becomes quite clear. In addressing himself to the traditional image of conquered Ireland (*Roisin Dubh*), Plunkett is able to achieve a variation upon a traditional theme that is at once strikingly original.

THE LITTLE BLACK ROSE SHALL BE RED AT LAST

> Because we share our sorrows and our joys
> And all your dear and intimate thoughts are mine
> We shall not fear the trumpets and the noise
> Of battle, for we know our dreams divine,
> And when my heart is pillowed on your heart
> And ebb and flowing of their passionate flood
> Shall beat in concord love through every part.
> Of brain and body—when at last the blood
> O'er leaps the final barrier to find
> Only one source wherein to spend its strength.
> And we two lovers, long but one in mind
> And soul, are made one flesh at length;
> Praise God if this my blood fulfils the doom
> When you, dark rose, shall redden into bloom.

What Plunkett is saying here is that his body bleeding into the Irish soil will be a sexual intercourse that will conceive new life, although he will not survive to see the issue of his sacrificial love and death. In Plunkett's imagination Grace Gifford and Cathleen ní Houlihan become one, for the sacramental marriage is achieved in the midnight wedding before his execution, but the marriage is not consummated in life, but death. It becomes the role of the woman to survive him, and in her grief, gather him together again in the resurrection of Ireland. Through the last gesture the couple become mythopoeic, for it is clear from the nature of Plunkett's imagination and its fixation upon a celestial couple that his self-image is the lover as sacrifice and dismembered god. His self-myth is only too clear, for Joseph Plunkett and Grace Gifford become: Venus and Adonis, Ishtar and Tammuz, Osiris and Isis. In spite of all his erotic-mysticism, Plunkett's own epitaph is not greatly different from Pearse's "Renunciation."

> Now I have chosen in the dark
> The desolate way to walk alone
> Yet strive to keep alive one spark
> Of your known grace and grace unknown.
>
> And when I leave you lest my love
> Should seal your spirit's ark with clay
> Spread your bright wings, O shining dove,
> But my way is the darker way.

As different as Pearse, MacDonagh, and Plunkett were from one another, they shared a common desire to live a myth. A certain amount of self-dramatization is natural to man, but few individuals attempt more than a temporary imitation. In one moment they may be imitating one model, and in the next an entirely different model, for the imitation depends more upon the social situation than their own requirements for unity of being. Far from being a myth, the average man's life is a mixed metaphor. When an individual sees his life as an extended narrative or drama into which all incidents must fit naturally or be transformed upon the occasion into an unanticipated relevance, he begins to turn his life into a game. "Into an imperfect world and into the confusion of life" he "brings a temporary, a limited perfection." [18] Culture is

18 Johan Huizinga, *Homo Ludens* (New York, 1955), p. 10.

a game that is no less playful when the stakes are death. In the culture of an Age of Reason when civilization and elegance declare life to be a stylized dance, the hero may be content to let the chance stumbling blocks of life become occasions to display his own wit, intellectual brilliance, and flexibility, for when man figures himself against a perfectly ordered, rational, and mechanical universe, it is his mental flexibility that most defines the uniqueness of his own humanity. Such tasteful self-dramatization does not threaten the social order, but a romantic might find that his enormous passions were not fitted for such dancing. The exaggerated passions of Pearse, MacDonagh, and Plunkett show the self-mythicization that a romantic age finds a more congenial mode of thought. The poet-rebels chose to image themselves as sacrificial heroes taken from the old mythologies of torn gods. If Clarke and MacDermott had been as articulate, we might have found evidence of equally fervid imaginings within the minds of the realists; certainly the legends of Michael Collins show that one realist had a masterful sense of the game. It would be a mistake to regard self-mythicization as the hallucinations of the cranks that historical chance throws into prominence. Chance is always taken account of in the game, but chance is not the game or its explanation. The realist is not necessarily a man without imagination, and it would be stupid to think that political leaders are great to the degree that they lack imagination. Calvin Coolidge in America and Isaac Butt in Ireland were leaders who were most solidly on the ground, but no one would credit them with making, much less understanding, history. Imagination is an ability to concentrate and intensify an enormous amount of knowledge into a few quick lines that others can recognize and act upon. History may not be fiction, but that does not mean it is not a work of imagination.

PART THREE

THREE IMAGES OF THE EVENT

CHAPTER FIVE

THE TRAGIC IMAGE: YEATS

"If it had not been for W. B. Yeats there would be no Irish Free State!" said Dr. Oliver Gogarty when a politician questioned the nomination of a poet to the first Irish Senate.[1] It was an exaggerated claim, for both Yeats and the Irish Free State were the harvest of a previous season, but since Yeats had long since taken his place in the sun, it was conceivable that the new Senate of Ireland's distinguished men should stand a little in his shade. Dr. Gogarty, in his literary awareness, could appreciate the historical importance of *Cathleen ni Houlihan*, but the other statesmen and politicians, no doubt, did not think in those terms. A year later, in 1923, when Yeats became the first Irishman to win the Nobel Prize, Lord Glenavy, the chairman of the Senate, revealed the particular kind of respect the haughty, arrogant, mob-baiting director of the Abbey Theatre could command. Speaking of the Senate's tribute to the new prize winner, the chairman said:

[1] *The Senate Speeches of W. B. Yeats*, ed. Donald R. Pearce (London, 1961), p. 15.

... [it is] a fitting recognition of his great literary gifts, but we take the greater pride in it on account of the courage and patriotism which induced him twelve months ago to cast in his lot with his own people here at home, under conditions which were then very critical and called for the exercise of great moral courage.[2]

Yeats had given up his home in Oxford to return to Ireland and had accepted a seat in the new Senate in a time of civil war when to be a Senator required a bodyguard. The poet who had issued the dangerous call to arms in 1902 was on hand in 1922 to help Ireland in "the slow, exciting work of creating institutions," but he had not been on hand in 1916.

The riots over *The Playboy of the Western World* led to Yeats's expulsion by Arthur Griffith from the cause of Irish nationalism. In Synge's death two years later in 1909, Yeats, in his symbolic mode of living, saw another example of genius brought down by the mob. For Yeats the period around the time of the death of Synge was a time of "Estrangement," and the passing of time only intensified his sense of alienation. The controversy over *The Playboy* was followed by the controversy over the Lane Pictures. And the grim spectacle of industrial warfare in the strike and Lock-Out finally convinced Yeats that Dublin could never be Florence. There was no longer any question of being an artist in Ireland, for Yeats felt that all his priceless things were "but a post the passing dogs defile."

Yeats gave up the attempt to create a great community with a great and popular theater. In March 1916 he was rehearsing his dance play *At the Hawk's Well* for a private showing in Lady Cunard's drawing room.[3] He had come a long way from the simple nationalism of his youth, and if once he dreamed of becoming the poet of a new insurrection, nothing was further from his mind in the early spring of 1916. Three weeks before the Rising, Yeats's state of mind was a fatigued one:

2 Ibid. p. 155.
3 Joseph Hone, *W. B. Yeats: 1865-1939* (London, 1962), p. 297.

I hope I am not incoherent but I am tired out with the excitement of rehearsing my new play—*At the Hawk's Well* in which masks are being used for the first time in serious drama in the modern world.[4]

And even after the performance, there was no time to learn of the plans of an organization to which Yeats once belonged. While the Irish Republican Brotherhood was busy with plans to land arms in Tralee Bay, Yeats was busy with another kind of work.

Now that it is over I find myself overwhelmed with work—introduction to books of Japanese [plays] for my sisters—two books of verse by Tagore to revise for Macmillan who has no notion of the job it is, and a revision of a book of my own verse for Macmillan, so I hope I may delay another week with your proofs.[5]

.

In London Yeats was moving in the society of peers and Prime Ministers, and doing his best to prevent them from giving him a knighthood, lest his fellow countrymen say: "only for a ribbon he left us." [6] If his fellow Dubliners stopped to think of the fifty-one-year-old man, it might be to comment upon the decline of a great poet whose inspiration seemed to have been as delicate as the dew of a Celtic twilight.

... I was sorry for Yeats and for his inspiration which did not seem to have survived his youth ... I remembered my prediction when Symons had showed me "Rosa Alchemica," "His inspiration," I had said, "is at an end, for he talks about how he is going to write."[7]

In *Rosa Alchemica,* that first intuition of *A Vision,* Yeats was searching for a ritual, for a dance that the mythical Michael Robartes could teach, a dance that would be the intersection of the timeless with time. But history, as well as eternity, has its way of startling, and the sudden force that flung open the door of Yeats's study was neither eternity nor poltergeist; it was the event. After the executions, Yeats wrote to Lady Gregory.

---

[4] *The Letters of W. B. Yeats,* ed. Allan Wade (London, 1954), p. 610.
[5] Ibid. p. 612.
[6] Joseph Hone, *W. B. Yeats: 1865-1939,* p. 291.
[7] See George Moore's hasty postmortem in *Vale* (New York, 1914), p. 178.

I am trying to write a poem on the men executed—"terrible beauty has been born again." If the English Conservative Party had made a declaration that they did not intend to rescind Home Rule, there would have been no Rebellion. I had no idea that any public event could so deeply move me—and I am very despondent about the future. At the moment I feel that all the work of years has been overturned, all the bringing together of classes, all the freeing of Irish literature and criticism from politics.[8]

To John Quinn he wrote:

A world seems to have been swept away. I keep going over the past in my mind and wondering if I could have done anything to turn these young men in some other direction.[9]

The note of guilt and personal responsibility had appeared; it would stay with him for a long time. Maud Gonne reminded Yeats of her vision of O'Connell Street in ruins, and perhaps they remembered that day at Drumcondra in 1900 during Queen Victoria's visit, when Maud Gonne had sworn the children to the undying hatred of England. Yeats could wonder "how many of these children will carry bomb and rifle when a little under or a little over thirty." [10] The Ireland that Yeats had pushed out of his mind suddenly and violently burst in upon his reverie. With his feelings of personal responsibility, the Dublin crisis became Yeats's crisis, for Yeats found himself in a position where he was being entertained by the leaders of British society at the time when the followers of his movement back home were being executed. Pearse was known personally to him, and he had shared a public platform with him for the Thomas Davis Centenary in 1914. Before that Yeats had offered Pearse the use of the Abbey Theatre for a charity performance for his school. Yeats was impressed by Mac-Donagh, and the Abbey had performed his *When the Dawn Is Come*. Joseph Plunkett, as editor of *The Irish Review,* was also an acquaintance, and Connolly was known to him and Maud Gonne

8 *The Letters of W. B. Yeats,* p. 613.
9 Ibid. p. 614.
10 Edward Malins, "Yeats and the Easter Rising," Dolmen Press Yeats Centenary Papers No. 1 (Dublin, 1965), p. 6.

from the old days of their work in the Celtic Literary Society. Major MacBride was only too familiar, for he was the estranged husband of Maud Gonne, the man who had taken her away from Yeats. Memories of Drumcondra and the 1898 celebrations would only tend to strengthen Yeats's feelings of uneasiness; they would remind him of the painful dream of his early love and his desire to light a city with the torch of his poems; no doubt, he hoped this would finally light the fire in his love. To recall the futility of those wasted years was always a painful experience, but now added to it, was the remorse for all the accusations he had heaped upon the needs of his "fool-driven land" when he had turned away from the attempt to burn up personal anxiety in a public event. Yeats had sided against Maud Gonne and her fanatic republicanism, and in his poem, "No Second Troy," the criticism of her and her movement is clear. Now, with O'Connell Street in flames and young men marching to imprisonment and execution in a captured city, it could seem that there was another Troy and a beautiful older woman to preside over its high funeral gleam. In 1902 Maud Gonne had played the beautiful woman disguised as the Shan Van Vocht in Yeats's *Cathleen ni Houlihan;* she had played the woman who seduced the young man away from his marriage bed. Now her estranged husband and the children from Drumcondra were dead. An ancient heroism had returned with all of its frightening passion; something was left in Ireland beyond the paudeens who fumbled in their greasy tills. If Dublin could not achieve the grace and confident beauty of Urbino, it showed that it could achieve the more Northern, terrible beauty of death. Clearly Yeats had to make some sort of amends for his condemnation of his country.

Yeats was reported to have fretted somewhat that he was not consulted before the insurrection was undertaken; this must have been an expression of the self-dramatizing Yeats attempting to impress his English host with his underground, revolutionary connections. Certainly he knew he was out of touch with recent developments, and, certainly, he was no great admirer of the new

leaders of the younger generation. "To Rothenstein he spoke of
innocent and patriotic theorists carried away by the belief that
they must sacrifice themselves to an abstraction." [11] On the one
hand Yeats was pulled in the direction of London and intellectual
civilization and could see from the perspective of that world how
comic the patriots were; but guilt and personal responsibility
pulled him by the other hand back to Dublin, for it was his native
Dublin that had now involved him in an actual event, in the stuff
of history as opposed to the speeches of literary banquets. It is
this antithetical pull between intellect and imagination, between
comedy and tragedy, between London and Dublin that gives Yeats's
poem on the Easter Rising its supreme double consciousness, and
not, as some critics have suggested, its unresolved ambiguity or
uncertainty.[12] Seen from a distance, the Rising is a second Troy
and Maud Gonne is its Helen; seen close up, the event is a tragicomedy: the Dublin streets a far cry from the topless towers of
Ilium, and Maud Gonne's face far too old and wrinkled to launch
a thousand ships. But sophisticated dismissal could not be very
satisfying; the crime of Maud Gonne's beauty had been committed
in 1902. As symbol she could indeed seem to be a "fierce virgin"
who required men for no amorous passion. In his diary, "Estrangement," Yeats pondered on this relationship between repressed
sexuality and expressed violence.

The root of it all is that the political class in Ireland—the lower middle
class from which the patriotic associations have drawn their journalists
and their leaders for the last ten years—have suffered through the cultivation of hatred as the one energy of their movement, a deprivation which
is the intellectual equivalent to a certain surgical operation. Hence the
shrillness of their voices. They contemplate all creative power as the
eunuchs contemplate Don Juan as he passed through Hell on the white
horse. . . .
  . . . Hatred as a basis of imagination, in ways which one could explain

11 Joseph Hone, *W. B. Yeats: 1865-1939*, p. 299.
12 Herbert Howarth, *The Irish Writers: Literature Under Parnell's Star*
(London, 1958), p. 140. Though I quarrel with Howarth's reading of Yeats's
poem, I have found much that is exciting in the book, and, clearly, my study
of the Rising mythos has been influenced by his treatment of the Parnell myth.

even without magic, helps to dry up the nature and make the sexual abstinence, so common among young men and women in Ireland, possible. This abstinence reacts in its turn on the imagination, so that we get at last that strange eunuch-like tone and temper. For the last ten or twenty years there has been a perpetual drying of the Irish mind with the resultant dust-cloud.[13]

Looking back on his own youth, Yeats could see how much of youth's passion had been sublimated into the creation of that national collective representation, Cathleen ní Houlihan. In the play one sees the pull of two loves, the dull, domestic *agapé* of the wife, and the sharp, transfiguring *eros* of the primitive tempt-ress and destroyer of men. Symbolically, Cathleen is the negative of the Blessed Virgin; she is a black madonna, a fierce virgin of a religion much older than Christianity. For the husband, relation with the wife of the play means an acceptance of life and things as they are, politically and ontologically; relation with the beau-tiful woman under the thin disguise of an old woman means ecstasy and transfiguration out of life. If Yeats's theory of sex and violence seems to be a psychoanalytic conjecture, it is one that is based upon a long-established traditional belief: the belief that lovers grow fat, relaxed, and at peace with the world in an easy bridegroom sleep, but that a man with his manhood remaining to be proved is anxious, alert, on edge; in the extreme, willing to smash the face of the first man who hints at his inexperience or lusts after his sister as he does after another's. For the most part, so much is common knowledge. Yeats was willing to take the tradi-tional belief as an explanation of national behavior. He saw in Ireland's furious chastity the wasted nights of his youth that led to the violent days with crowds; [14] he saw in the cultivation of hatred an increasing petrification of the heart. In 1909, Yeats wrote in his diary: "The soul of Ireland has become a vapour and her

---

[13] W. B. Yeats, *Autobiographies* (London, 1961), p. 486f.
[14] See Yeats's letter to Olivia Shakespear, *The Letters of W. B. Yeats*, p. 790, as well as the other late letters to Mrs. Shakespear and Dorothy Wellesley in which Yeats discusses his psychology of sexual desire.

body a stone." [15] The use of the stone as metaphor for the heart
seized hold of Yeats's imagination, for the stone found its way
into other contexts before it settled into place as the stone that
troubled the living stream.

After a while, in a land that has given itself to agitation overmuch,
abstract thoughts are raised up between man's minds and Nature, who
never does the same thing twice, or makes one man like another, till
minds, whose patriotism is perhaps great enough to carry them to the
scaffold, cry down natural impulse with the morbid persistence of minds
unsettled by some fixed idea. They are preoccupied with the nation's
future, with heroes, poets, soldiers, painters, armies, fleets, but only as
these things are understood by a child in a National School, while a
secret feeling that what is so unreal needs continual defence makes them
bitter and restless. They are like some State which has only paper money,
and seeks by punishments to make it buy whatever gold can buy. They
no longer love, for only life is loved, and at last a generation is like
an hysterical woman who will make unmeasured accusations and believe
impossible things, because of some logical deduction from a solitary
thought which has turned a portion of her mind to stone.[16]

When Yeats watched the hysterical mobs at the Abbey, when
he saw the fury with which Hugh Lane was accused of decadence
because he wanted to give Dublin a collection of paintings, when
he saw the transformation hatred worked upon the once lovely
women, Maud Gonne and Countess Markiewicz, he wondered
about the reality of the Ireland upon which he had based his art.

When I think, too, of Synge dying at this moment of their bitterness
and ignorance, as I believe, I wonder if I have been right to shape
my style to sweetness and serenity.[17]

The teas and literary banquets which failed to bring out the total
man brought forth only the socially accepted image of the dreamy
poet with flowing tie and limpid verse, but the mob soon hammered
Yeats's thought into unity. The resistance of the mob completed

15 W. B. Yeats, *Autobiographies*, p. 488.
16 W. B. Yeats, "J. M. Synge and the Ireland of His Time," *Essays and Introductions* (New York, 1961), p. 313f.
17 W. B. Yeats, *Autobiographies*, p. 482.

the man in a way that the indulgence of the well-bred could never do. Yeats defined himself by the object of his hatred, and in the intensity of his combat he discovered the totality of the myth of his self. He was not a dreamy Pre-Raphaelite, or a Buddhist or Christian saint; he was an artist concerned with the intellectual and imaginative transformation of material; he was a man of action, and the values of the warrior were most appropriate to his situation: nobility, strength, courage, and gentleness. He saw himself as Oisin, the man who journeyed out of time with the temptress, but returned to sing to a mob-ruled, priest-ridden world of the greatness of the people of Finn, the people of Burke, the people of Grattan, the people of Swift, of Berkeley, of Emmet, and of Parnell.[18] At sixty-seven, Yeats could look back over all his poetry and say: "The swordsman throughout repudiates the saint, but not without vacillation. Is that perhaps the sole theme— Usheen and Patrick—...?"[19] It was in conflict that Yeats outgrew the simplifications of the aesthete and his flight from necessity. One side of Yeats praised flight, another thrust him into the midst of action, but until middle age, there was no thought as to how this could be. After the conflicts of 1907, 1909, and 1913, Yeats had time to absorb the battle into himself, and there come to terms with it. And perhaps this process describes the development of Yeats's almost unbelievable greatness.

Few contemporary poets have been so deeply rooted in historical events, and those that have, have participated in actions that took them away from art. Yeats's amazing self-mastery (and, indeed, mastery of society) seems to have been the result of his dialectical method of experiencing the world. First he would immerse himself in action, and let it overwhelm him completely, then slowly he would reverse the process to have the Self completely envelop the Other and lift history up into the region of myth. Because he lived a myth, history became the myth in which he found himself. At first this dialectic was instinctive and unconscious, but in the

18 See Yeats's Senate speech on divorce in *Senate Speeches*, p. 99.
19 *The Letters of W. B. Yeats*, p. 798.

introspection after the battles of 1913, Yeats attempted to articulate his own theory of personality. And when George Moore's
mocking comedy of the literary revival appeared in 1914, Yeats
was pushed further into the corner of autobiographical defense,
and this, too, helped to articulate the unique quality of life as
he lived it. Four months before the Rising, his coming to terms
was becoming poetry. In the verse prologue to *Per Amica Silentae
Lunae,* he wrote:

Hic

Yet surely there are men who have made their art
Out of no tragic war, lovers of life,
Impulsive men that look for happiness
And sing when they have found it.

Ille

No, not sing
For those that love the world serve it in action,
Grow rich, popular and full of influence,
And should they paint or write, still it is action:
The struggle of the fly in marmalade.
The rhetorician would deceive his neighbours,
The sentimentalist himself; while art
Is but a vision of reality.
What portion in the world can the artist have
Who has awakened from the common dream
But dissipation and despair.[20]

In the fatigue of battle, Yeats would always imagine a place that
was free of conflict; here in reviewing the battle with propaganda
and the cant of the patriotic societies, Yeats imagined that any art
put to service in the world must be debased. Pegasus cannot pull
Maud Gonne's bandwagon. In reviewing, for his own autobiog-
raphy, the Tragic Generation of Dowson, Wilde, and Johnson,
Yeats saw the artist as one who perished because he no longer
could believe in the common dream; his greater intensity consumed him in the gross atmosphere of society. This romantic

[20] See *Per Amica Silentae Lunae,* in *Mythologies* (New York, 1959).

view of the artist as suffering soul was the approved and orthodox position of artists of the time, but even as Yeats expounds it, he expresses dissatisfaction with it. The deadly sweetness of the fly in marmalade is that "extravagant style He had learnt from Pater." The artists of the Aesthetic period perished in their gem-like flames because their denial of external reality caused the self to collapse in upon itself. In their view there was only sensation and its object, and in this aesthetic solipsism, each man was locked in his private world of discontinuous sensations. It was this alienated, cerebral, decadent role that had set Yeats longing for the cultural role of the bard or the poet of an insurrection; it was this longing that made him welcome Irish culture and the building of a great community as the way of salvation. The alternative was the life of such decadents as Huysmans's Des Esseintes. Self-mastery was not the destruction of the other by the self, or the annihilation of the self in the other; it was imaginative creation in the face of "loss."

The distinction between man and art breaks down when we speak of this dialectic of the self for the Self becomes a creation like the poem. Yeats lost Maud Gonne, and failing to be a success at rallies, he created a public theater; losing his public, he created his Eleusinian drama of apparition; failing to create an Anglo-Irish civilization in a Catholic state, he took to his Tower to prepare for the ascent out of time, and in those Tantric, sexual "Supernatural Songs" of his old age, he sought to excite sexual passion so that he could cast it up in the face of death, and escape rebirth, for he knew that it was not by the shadow of the hair that time held man. The pull between creation in time and escape out of time is the great tension and excitement in Yeats's poetry. In the period before the Rising, Yeats was celebrating the escape from conflict; he advised Lady Gregory, after the defeat of her nephew's plans to establish a Dublin gallery, to turn away.

> And like a laughing string
> Whereon mad fingers play
> Amid a place of stone,

> Be secret and exult,
> Because of all things known
> That is most difficult.

Each time that Yeats turned his back on the world, the celebration of escape became more profound than the time before. The "Song of the Stolen Child" is followed by "The Lake Isle of Innisfree." "Innisfree" is followed by "To a Friend Whose Work Has Come to Nothing," but between this 1913 poem and the later great celebrations of escape like "Sailing to Byzantium" comes the violent encounter of the Rising. Yeats had turned away from Ireland and condemned it, but he found that his nerves were still connected to time, history, and country, for in the aftermath of the executions, the pain of guilt and responsibility brought him back from his escape.

Significantly, "Easter 1916" does not begin with a lament, with the "ochone, ochone" of the Young Ireland school of poetry; having criticized propaganda, the responsibility fell upon Yeats, not only to retract his condemnations, but to write a true poem on a contemporary event. When Yeats read the early versions of the poem to Maud Gonne, she thought them not strong enough; no doubt she expected a cry of grief and rage, but Yeats's whispered beginning, his low tone of self-accusation is at once the original and imaginative departure from the elegiac formulas of Irish and English poetry and the deeply emotional and personal connection of the poet to the event. "Easter 1916" is not an occasional poem in any casual sense. Whatever jokes on the rebels Yeats indulged in had now come back to him, for he fought only with words, and these men, with another kind of passion, had turned their own mortality into a weapon. They had seized their opposites in action; they had won that beauty which Yeats sought in toil.

... The Daimon comes not as like but seeking its own opposite, for man and Daimon feed the hunger in one another's hearts. Because the ghost is simple, the man is heterogeneous and confused; they are but knit together when the man has found a mask whose lineaments permit the expression of all the man most lacks, and it may be dreads.[21]

21 See W. B. Yeats, *Mythologies*, p. 335.

Yeats was elaborating a theory of personality based upon opposites to explain his own contradictions to himself, but when the
Rising occurred, he had only to project his personal meditation
onto the screen of history to understand how the ridiculous
patriots he had known had suddenly become noble and tragic.
They had achieved unity in the mask of the revolutionary martyr,
and whatever fears, stupidities, or other personal limitations they
possessed disappeared the moment the impersonal, tragic mask
was on. But the tragic mask was not mere escape from the ordinary face, for it was held in place by blood. When the patriots
kept "vivid faces" amid gray, eighteenth-century houses, they were
ridiculous; they nurtured in themselves a passion that was totally
out of keeping with the tawdry Dublin of petty commerce. But
in persisting in immaturity, the patriots transformed and set fire
to those gray, eighteenth-century houses. In being able to call in
the army of the British Empire, and not merely the police, in
achieving a death by firing squad, they had been "changed
utterly."

The central metaphor of the poem is the oxymoron, a "terrible
beauty," for in the oxymoron rests the double consciousness of the
poem. Yeats establishes, in keeping with his antithetical theory of
personality, an antithetical structure in the poem, a conflict between man and poet, intellect and imagination, England and Ireland. The man knew the patriots as actors in a "casual comedy";
now the Irish poet is forced to see them as heroes in the long
line of Irishmen who have died fighting England. The beauty of
their action is terrible because it is senseless, unnecessary, and
stupid; but the beauty of the terror continually ruins the argument; death puts down the voice of reason, and passionate imaginings describe the reality the patriots saw as they marched into
sacrifice. As Yeats put it in the ballad he wrote in association with
"Easter 1916,"

> And is their logic to outweigh
> MacDonagh's bony thumb?

It is death that transforms them utterly from *living* comedians to *dead* heroes. This double consciousness that Yeats has of the event becomes part of the subject matter of the poem in the third stanza. If the poet's consciousness is double, these patriots are men of a different order, for they have "hearts of one purpose alone." Their hearts have become stones, and throughout the changes of season, and amidst all the distractions of a nature teeming in its variety and motion, they persist in their petrified immobility. And yet the common stone, in its stillness, is complete in itself; it is not involved in the flux and contradictions of motion. But man and all living things move; they are caught up in the movements of a world of paradox, of contradiction, of conflicting opposites where heart and mind tear man apart in the minute by minute changes of multiple desire. In the midst of all the wild movement of life: the clouds, the hens, the horse and rider, is the stone—death. Man's tragedy is that he cannot win this reconciliation of opposites without death, or without a living death: a loss of humanity, a loss of the warmth, flexibility, and compassion for man's limitations and things as they are. The fanatic is a reformer who must eliminate his subjective humanity in a remorseless fixation of the will on a single act. The protraction of this brooding changes the heart to stone. "Too long a sacrifice / Can make a stone of the heart." As a poet and a man of wisdom, Yeats cannot share the simple myth that supports the action of the patriots; he sees too well the tragic nature of human existence, the tragic way in which man is crucified on irreconcilable opposites.

In the fourth stanza the tension between man and poet is severely tightened. The conventional movement of the elegy requires that grief should be brought under control, that sorrow should be lessened by religious knowledge. Yeats makes a gesture toward bringing the tragedy under control by asking "O when may it suffice?" The antecedent of "it" is sufficiently general that the question can apply not only to a time when sacrifice will be sufficient for redemption, but when human life is no longer torn apart by irreconcilable opposites. But Yeats sees no way out, for it is not

simply that man is good but has a few bad traits, or is bad but has
a few good traits. Man is damned by his good traits: only a man
like Pearse with strong passion and firm will could persist in his
war against things as they are; weaker men would be content to
fumble in their greasy tills. Pearse is noble and heroic, but he has
maimed himself drastically to become so. Yeats's question is therefore addressed to the very root of human existence; he is asking
for a different order. An ordinary poet would be quick to invoke
the stale formulas that the dead now know a better rest and are
happier in the world above. Yeats will not, however, offer such
assuagement of grief. The question is hardly out, when the line
of thinking it suggests is stopped. "That is Heaven's part." There
must be no quick apotheosis, no glib rationalization of human
grief by superhuman wisdom. Sacrifice for A.E. is a freeing of the
bonds of mortality, but Yeats is an artist and has the tragic vision
of a Homer or a Sophocles. His vision of the remorseless nature of
human suffering will not permit him to accept supernatural con-
solations. Yeats refuses to recite the formulas of theosophy or
Christianity, but at the end of the poem Yeats stands up to his
ancient task of reciting the names of those who have fallen for
Ireland, and in this act, man and poet come together: together
they become William Butler Yeats. An ordinary Irishman would
say that the patriots are with God in heaven and that Ireland has
been redeemed by their sacrifice; Yeats does not.

> What is it but nightfall?
> No, no, not night but death;

Yeats stands and speaks with his own voice, and the voice is
genuine and human; its tragic dignity is all the greater as one
realizes what is kept down, what is not said. The mind would
question with ordinary prudence whether England might not have
kept faith in its pledge to grant Home Rule, but Yeats knows
beyond the perspective of London that there are things beyond
the truths of prudence and reason.

> We know their dreams; enough
> To know they dreamed and are dead;
> And what if excess of love
> Bewildered them till they died?

Yeats, knowing their dream, recants. Before, he had said that "only life is loved"; now he accepts the genuineness of the patriots' intentions. Whatever their personal faces were like, they are now covered by the mask of death. The patriot's fixation may have blinded him; his desire for his opposite led him to seek a heroic death even when it was unnecessary, but the prudent man does not want beauty; he does not wish to have that dismembering transfiguration. The prudent man would settle for life, however tawdry, but these men did not, and the bare fact that they dreamed is "enough" to elevate them beyond their ordinary countrymen. The fact that they were willing to purchase their dreams with their own mortality elevates them into History. They march into tragedy with all the slain Irish patriots of the past. Yeats rises to his task in reciting their names; he keeps down doubt with dignity and respect; he bows his head and accepts his own tradition, even to the point of the invocation "wherever green is worn," but the speaking voice is unmistakably his own.

> I write it out in a verse—
> MacDonagh and MacBride,
> Connolly and Pearse
> Now and in time to be
> Wherever green is worn,
> Are changed, changed utterly,
> A terrible beauty is born.

In Yeats's poem there are real men and not idealized figures sentimentalized by nationalism, and the greatest tribute that Yeats paid these men was to speak about them in a genuine and human voice. These real men rest in the paradoxes and agonies of man's tragic condition, and the double consciousness of their acts does not lessen the reality of their deaths; it only relates it to us. If one wishes to see the poem as an ambiguous one, then he must recognize that this poem is merely one step closer to the later poems in which language is intentionally made ambiguous so that it can render the double consciousness of reality, "doubled in history, world history, personal history." [22] But there are too many pejorative associations in the word "ambiguous" to use it lightly in reference to "Easter 1916." The double consciousness that Yeats has is certainly closer to the historical actuality of the insurrection than almost anything that has been written about it. As a work of art Yeats's poem is amazing, for it lifts an actual historical event into a tragic consciousness without any falsification. It is difficult enough to write a good occasional poem, but to write a great poem in which the event is not mangled to fit into a poetic shape is astonishing. The glib, condescending remarks that have been made about Yeats's view of history seem to overlook the fact that Yeats's view of things is clear, hard, and sharp. In his double consciousness that lifted the event into a tragedy, Yeats at once related the poem to his own antithetical anxieties, and thus empowered it, and made the poem deeply significant to readers who have never heard of Connolly and Pearse, MacDonagh and Mac-Bride.

In considering the death of the patriots, Yeats tried to repress all supernatural thoughts, all deeply personal points of view that were for "my students only." "Easter 1916" was a gift, a public poem that was a retraction and atonement. But in the ballads that he wrote in association with the poem, and in the play he wrote in 1917, *The Dreaming of the Bones,* Yeats's spiritualism began to assert itself. Yet even this most idiosyncratic side of Yeats was in keeping with the historical situation of Ireland after the Rising. The air was filled with formless excitements and anticipations; something was about to happen.[23] Important things were beginning to take shape; perhaps it was only natural that a man who thought in terms of shape-changers would embody the ethos of Post-Rising Ireland in a ghost-play. The Event had given Yeats

22 *The Letters of W. B. Yeats,* p. 887.
23 See Ernie O'Malley's remarks as quoted above on p. 105.

"the touch," for now in his excited anticipations, his imagination raced. If violence was coming, then all the prophecies of his youth were right. The mythical qualities of the Rising took on a new attraction. If, to his host Sir William Rothenstein, Yeats had mocked Pearse's idea of sacrifice, the poetic attraction of such sacrifice overcame him, and became "The Rose Tree." If death is the ultimate reality beyond which the mind of man cannot go in "Easter 1916," in "Sixteen Dead Men" it is again open to the living. Yeats is again viewing the dreams of the dead, the brooding visions of ghosts, as forces in the soul of the world that drive the living into the completion of their dreams. Dead, the patriots of 1916 now converse with the FitzGeralds and Wolfe Tone.

> How could you dream they'd listen
> That have an ear alone
> For those new comrades they have found,
> Lord Edward and Wolfe Tone,
> Or meddle with our give and take
> That converse bone to bone.

In *The Dreaming of the Bones,* Yeats continues to use the metaphor of the dead bones that prod the living into their tragedy.[24] In the play the three musicians raise no curtain, for there is no such separation between life and death, reality and imagination; they merely unfold the cloth that is history's weaving. The musicians are bloodless nightwatchers who observe the spilling of blood. A soldier has escaped from the Post Office to Galway rock, and there he encounters the shades of the adulterers of seven centuries past, Diarmuid and Dervorgilla. Still they hope, these dead lovers who first brought the Normans in, to consummate their love in a kiss, but their own self-inflicted remorse casts up their sin between them; they are prevented from achieving peace until some Irishman forgive them their disastrous sin. They ask the young soldier to forgive, but he cannot; passion nails him into his dream; he is no more free alive than they are dead. The ghostly dreamers of

24 For a Neo-Platonic explication of the play, see F. A. C. Wilson's chapter in *Yeats's Iconography* (New York, 1960).

the past must dream on, creating new deaths in a dream of seven centuries of hate. The revolution has suddenly vanished from the world of the newspapers, and men now appear as mere agents of unearthly will.

> What finger first began
> Music of a lost kingdom?
> They dreamed that laughed in the sun.
> Dry bones that dream are bitter.
> They dream and darken our sun.

The nightwanderers hear new discordant music, music of a lost kingdom, of a kingdom that is about to fall apart. Birds crow; the March birds of equinoctial sacrifice cry a new era. The executions blooden the moon; something is about to begin. In a stark, prophetic image, Yeats sees in the revolution in Ireland, the beginning of the end of two thousand years of Christian civilization.

> I have heard from far below
> The strong March birds a-crow.
> Stretch neck and clap the wing,
> Red cocks, and crow!

Easter 1916 marks a turning point in the history of Ireland; romanticism ends, the dreamers are replaced by men who master the modern techniques of guerilla warfare. Equally, "Easter 1916" marks a turning point in the poetry of Yeats, and, equally in touch with history, the turning is a movement away from nineteenth-century romanticism to the stark perceptions of a very different age. Excess of love bewildered the men of 1916; General Maxwell notwithstanding, they willed their own deaths, and the General gave them a soldier's end before a firing squad. They were not tied to trucks and dragged to bits. That was to come when General Maxwell was replaced by the Black and Tans. The executions of the patriots of 1916 do not put an irrational and savage face upon the universe. We feel sorrow, grief, but the emotions are ennobled and eased by the magnificence of the manner in which the men died: terrible, but beautiful. As time passes, however, the double

view of history, the view from London and Dublin, becomes the
more cosmic view of history seen from Yeats's Tower. Beauty fades,
and the terrible becomes Terror. As Yeats wrote to a friend from
the Tower: "I wonder will literature be much changed by that
most momentous of events, the return of evil." [25]

Volumes have been written about the work of the later Yeats, so
I shall not attempt to set down on a few pages that immense vision
of Terror. Suffice it to say that the insurrection of 1916 is the drop
of the knife that halves the early work and the late, for in the
blood sacrifice Yeats was startled into a vision as the nation was
stunned into a revolution. As he compared "the half-read wisdom
of daemonic images" with "That dead young soldier in his blood"
... "they trundled down the road," [26] he could see that, in some
occult form of imagining, he and the nation were preoccupied
with an even larger terror. With an imagination like a philoso-
phers' stone, Yeats took history as his *prima materia* and worked
until he achieved a myth that was, not false, but "a fiery short-
hand" of actuality. Long ago his imagination had turned Maud
Gonne into *Cathleen ni Houlihan,* and now that the nation had
caught up with his imaginings Yeats was working in the alembic
of his mind upon the shape of things to come. Cathleen underwent a reincarnation and came up as "that fierce virgin."

> Another Troy must rise and set,
> Another lineage feed the crow,
> Another Argo's painted prow
> Drive to a flashier bauble yet.
> The Roman Empire stood appalled:
> It dropped the reins of peace and war
> When that fierce virgin and her star
> Out of the fabulous darkness called.

In the play from which the song is taken, *The Resurrection,* a
Greek, who is a proud, aristocratic, "antithetical" man of civiliza-

25 *The Letters of W. B. Yeats,* p. 680.
26 See W. B. Yeats, "Meditations in Time of Civil War," *Collected Poems* (New
York, 1957), p. 202.

tion like Yeats himself, cannot believe that God is anything but a Platonic Idea. He does not believe that a real Christ has risen; the idea of God as a suffering, mangled thing to him is an unspeakable, barbaric vulgarity. When the silent Christ appears and his own hand discovers His beating heart, he screams in terror and repulsion. As a man of intellect, no *thought* could have brought him to think that the relation between man and God was rape. But the uncontrollable mystery that writhes, copulates, or gyres upon the floor is something that the Syrian, with his Asiatic mind, can understand. He sees what lies outside civilization.

> THE SYRIAN. What if there is always something that lies outside knowledge, outside order? What if at the moment when knowledge and order seem complete that something appears.
>
> [*He has begun to laugh.*]
>
> THE HEBREW. Stop laughing.
>
> THE SYRIAN. What if the irrational return? [27]

What knowledge could seem more complete than Victorian science, Victorian progress, with its Empire that defied the setting sun? Yeats, thinking of the dreams of his youth, the vision of A.E., and the prophecies of MacGregor Mathers, saw the drama of Empire and Tribe repeat itself once more. If barbarian energy and innumerable Asiatic tribes had broken up an empire with a faith that seemed brute and vulgar to a Roman or an Alexandrian Greek, what would the new faith be like?

> And what rough beast, its hour come round at last
> Slouches towards Bethlehem to be born?

The beast is shapeless and undefined, which only increases the terror of the vision.

The Rising of 1916 was a resurrection of Cuchulain; it was a touch of the beating heart for Yeats, the encounter of the irrational. The longer Yeats thought of the men of 1916, the more their deaths took on the tragic joy that Yeats esteemed as the

[27] See W. B. Yeats, *Collected Plays* (New York, 1962), p. 371.

highest wisdom man could embody in action. And what could not be so embodied was mere topical opinion, for the things that men adore and loathe are their sole reality.[28] In "The Statues," written ten months before he died, Yeats gave the Easter Rising a place in that four-stanza history of Western Civilization. The Irish, proud and "antithetical" as the Greeks, watch the British Empire go under, exactly as the Alexandrian Greeks watched the Roman Empire. The gong rings out the end of a Platonic Year of two thousand years. Grimalkin, the witch's cat and crude god for the man of the first quadrant of the moon who has barely learned to walk upright, crawls toward the imageless God of Buddha's contemplation; the first quadrant of the moon becomes the fourth, and humanity is about to shatter in pieces back into God. The Irish share with the ancient Greeks number and intellect; the statue of Cuchulain, the statue of Apollo, the Greek-influenced statues of Buddha, like all dreams of the soul "End in a beautiful man's or woman's body." They end in a body when the moon is at the full, not in the early phases of Grimalkin's ugliness, or in the late phases of Buddha's nothingness. European Civilization was fathered by Greece upon female Asia, but now the situation may be reversed and upon the rape of Europe and America, Asia and Africa may beget another lineage to feed the crow.

> When Pearse summoned Cuchulain to his side,
> What stalked through the Post Office? What intellect,
> What calculation, number, measurement, replied?
> We Irish, born into that ancient sect
> But thrown upon this filthy modern tide
> And by its formless spawning fury wrecked,
> Climb to our proper dark, that we may trace
> The lineaments of a plummet-measured face.

For Yeats the relationship of the irrational with history is always violent and terrifying, whether it is "the uncontrollable mystery on the bestial floor," the "shudder in the loins," or "What sacred

28 See the closing lines to *The Death of Cuchulain,* in *Collected Plays,* p. 445.

drama through her body heaved," or, here, "What stalked through
the Post Office." All are formless images of terror, for the tide that
the Greeks held back in order to create European Civilization has
returned to wreck Ireland and all the West. What remains to be
done in the face of such terror, but "Climb to our proper dark"?
Yeats climbed his winding stair in the Tower. True to his tragic
vision of history, Yeats celebrated his own defeat in a tragic joy.
He was not frightened into abandoning Western Civilization that
Africa and Asia might be satisfied; he did not offer to burn the
libraries that the illiterate might be content.[29] Yeats's gesture was
a flourish of the sword overhead as all that it stood for was about
to go under. Knowing that everything vanishes, he chose to sing
of that most vanished thing of all: Anglo-Irish civilization. Yeats's
last testament to Irish poets was to:

> Sing the peasantry, and then
> Hard riding country gentlemen.

A silly thing to say in 1938—if we read it with a Victorian seriousness that Yeats never had.

The affirmative mockery of Yeats has given much trouble to his
readers: to the pious, Yeats's Ribh is a little unsettling; to the
political Left, Yeats's wheels, gyres, and aristocratic pose are exas-
perating. Out of the dilemma of Yeats, two clearly marked *exits*
have been shown by critics. There is the way out of the New
Criticism, which has lifted the typical Yeats poem into a sort of
middle air where, with all its configurations of meaning and high
tensions of paradox and irony, it vibrates harmlessly. The other is
the way out of the exponents of irony and ambiguity, as if Yeats's
Vision were but a joke. If *A Vision* is a joke, then all of Yeats's life
was, which, of course, it was; but the laughter of Krishna is not
the drollery of George Moore. The wheels and gyres of Yeats's
A Vision are, like the elementary particles of the quantum me-
chanics, "no longer real in the same sense as the objects of daily
life, trees or stones, but appear as abstractions derived from the

[29] See W. B. Yeats, *"On the Boiler," Explorations* (New York, 1962), p. 437.

real material of observation in the true sense." [30] *A Vision*, with its dramatic theory of history and man, is the full expression of Yeats's thought and life. It is more than an eclectic collection of metaphors to be sprinkled into verse. It is the ultimate mocking affirmation of all that is most antithetical to our age; as such we ignore it at our peril.

[30] Werner Heisenberg, "Planck's Discovery and the Philosophical Problems of Atomic Physics," *On Modern Physics* (New York, 1962), p. 20.

CHAPTER SIX

THE MYSTIC IMAGE: A.E.

Because George William Russell was Dublin's most famous visionary, one would think that his first reaction to the Easter Rebellion would have been exultation at the return of an ancient heroism to contemporary Ireland. His response, however, was far more workaday than would be expected.

Most of us in Ireland feel as if the soul had been out on some wild nightmare adventure during the past month, and the intensity of that nightmare emotion had lasted over the wakening and left us shaken and made it almost impossible to settle down to the business of life, which, however, will not be denied and makes its implacable claims upon us all. We have, however moved by emotion, to go back to our work.[1]

Despite the casual reference to the occult phenomenon of astral projection, the passage shows a realist's concern for the present and the immediate future. But categories like realist or romantic fail to apply to A.E.; they are useful conveniences in contrasting a Pearse and a Collins, but they fail to describe a man who spent a

[1] A.E., *The Irish Homestead*, XXIII (May 20, 1916), 305.

lifetime in trying to resolve the conflict between the lift of the
spirit and the weight of the body. A.E.'s call to return to work is
addressed to himself as well as to his fellow Irishmen, for the
insurrection had astonished him. Away from Dublin during Easter
Week, he returned to find the city transformed by the physical
forces he had not thought about. "I confess I did not at first take
the militant nationalism very seriously. I was temperamentally
a pacifist, more interested in the national culture than the state." [2]
A.E. had forgotten the violent prophecies of his youth, or, at least,
had the good manners not to crow. Twenty years had elapsed since
he had had the vision of the avatar in which the incarnation came
with signs and portents of great wars and the destruction of empires. Now, of the older generation, A.E. looked on in amazement
at the dedicated and deadly idealism of the young rebels. "Their
ideals were not mine but I take off my hat to people who die for
their ideals." [3] This amazement and simple praise was the initial
reaction that stirred A.E. to write the elegy for the executed rebels
entitled "Salutation." The poem, unfortunately, is noteworthy
neither in sentiment nor expression, and he eventually chose to
exclude it from his *Selected Poems.* The elegy merely accords the
patriots an almost businesslike accolade: "You paid the price.
You paid the price." The response was simple and immediate, but
ultimately unsatisfying.

A.E. continued to brood upon the Rising, brooding in such a
way that all the major issues and conflicts of his life seemed to be
involved in answering any questions about the event. Perhaps in
this brooding he remembered his vision of the avatar, and, wondering, perhaps asked himself how much the work of his generation had enkindled the imaginations of the young men whose
bodies now lay in quicklime. A.E. had not written the call to arms
of Yeats's *Cathleen ni Houlihan,* but his own *Deirdre* had shared
the boards on that night of April 1902, and in that play the sacred

[2] See A.E., "Twenty-five Years of Irish Nationality," *Foreign Affairs,* January
1929.
[3] Letter to Ernest Boyd, June 7, 1916, as quoted in *Colby Library Quarterly,*
IV (May 1955), 42.

name of Cuchulain was pronounced upon a public stage for the first time. A.E. never felt Yeats's sense of guilt, for he had never thought of the Irish Revival as his movement and he knew that he was better known as an editor and agricultural organizer than as a poet and painter, but, for all that, the older man must have recalled the young enthusiast who stood at the foaming tide-line of the sea at Bray and preached to the people about the return of the pagan gods to Ireland.

In those long-past days of the 'eighties, Yeats had discovered his rival in A.E. Always on the look-out for disciples, Yeats had discovered at his own Metropolitan Art School a true visionary who did not paint the model before him but the sprites of the astral plane that figured in his visions. In these gauze-like creatures who were neither men nor women but apparitions of auras and resplendent light, Yeats saw the *sidhe,* the fairies of Ireland, and rejoiced that this young man possessed the combination of mysticism and things Irish that Yeats longed for. He was delighted with the open and unashamed manner in which Russell spoke of his visions, but when, after a short time at the art school, Russell announced that he was giving up art because it weakened the will and distracted one from the perfection of the total man, Yeats, the aesthete, must have been dismayed, for his amazement and consequent mixed emotions continued long after.[4] But in those days Russell only seemed to be someone too good to be overlooked for the movement. Russell made his first appearance in the world of letters in Yeats's *Celtic Twilight,* and there he is presented as the character whose pleasure it was "to wander about upon the hills, talking to half-mad and visionary peasants."[5] The temptation to borrow the visionary for the movement was naturally irresistible, and Russell was not unco-operative. The two young men shared the Celtic enthusiasms that the older generation had made public. Yeats was powerfully influenced by the work of O'Grady, although

[4] See Yeats's poem, "A Choice," and his letter on the death of A.E. in the *Collected Letters,* p. 838; see also his "My Friend's Book," in *Essays and Introductions,* and his *Autobiographies,* p. 239.
[5] W. B. Yeats, *Mythologies* (New York, 1959), p. 13.

he saw more immediate possibilities for his own work in the not
fully realized Celtic poetry of Sir Samuel Ferguson. Russell's debt
to O'Grady was clearer, for he said of that historian that "Whatever is Irish in me, he kindled to life. . . . It was the memory of
race which rose up within me, and I felt exalted as one who learns
he is among the children of kings." [6] Russell's metaphor is revealing, for it refers to the Indian folklore motif in which the story
of the soul's coming to consciousness of the *atman* (spirit) is told
through the allegory of a king's child who, abducted, spends his
life in a jungle only to discover much later his true kinship. In
reading Standish O'Grady's history, Russell saw in the mist-hidden
figures of the pagan gods the forms and features of the beings that
visited his own dreams and visions; he came to see that his own
personal and heretic religion of the Earth Mother was, in reality,
the religion of his ancestors. It was the recollection of this ancestral
memory that he re-created in his own poems and paintings. Confused, crude, uneducated, and scarcely articulate, Russell as a
young man thrashed about in an attempt to find the external
corroboration and articulation of his own internal life. In the
messianic history of O'Grady, he found the culture in which he
could thrive as an individual and the medium through which
he could discover a relationship with his fellow countrymen. But
Russell saw more in O'Grady's histories than the author himself
did, for Russell had discovered other books in his undirected reading; he had found the sacred books of the East. For the young
romantic these two literatures from opposite ends of the world,
the ancient Indian and the ancient Irish, receded into the common Aryan ancestral darkness of the race. And undirected reading
in Dublin libraries of the time would only reinforce such happy
thoughts, for the reader would eventually come upon the bizarre
histories of Ireland like General Vallancey's. Vallancey had confused O'Grady's early research, but as a Trinity scholar and a
gentleman, O'Grady had access to the library of the Royal Irish

[6] See Hugh Art O'Grady, *Standish James O'Grady, The Man and Writer*
(Dublin, 1929), p. 64.

Academy, and there the librarian put him upon the right path to
O'Curry, the great translator and cataloguer. Russell, not being a
university man and, therefore, not a gentleman, had to fend for
himself in the public library. And so, to Russell, free of the restraint of scholarship, the Druid designs on the mounds along the
Boyne could naturally suggest the civilization along the Ganges.
Such syncretism was in keeping with the general drift of thought
at the time, and it was inevitable that such thought would bring
A.E. as well as Yeats into the arms of that most syncretic religion,
theosophy. So it was that a year after Russell made his anonymous
debut in *The Celtic Twilight,* he followed his friend's example
of uniting Celticism and mysticism and secured a place in the
Irish Literary Renaissance by publishing the theosophical poetry
of *Homeward: Songs by the Way.* Russell chose to continue in
the anonymity that Yeats had given him, for he signed the poems
"Aeon," but the printer could not make out his hand, and so
Russell became and has remained A.E.

The poems were well received and for a while it seemed that
there were two pre-eminent poets in Ireland. By 1897 with the
appearance of A.E.'s second book, *The Earth Breath,* Yeats was
beginning to fidget, generously, but fidget nonetheless.

I think you will yet out sing us all and sing in the ears of generations
to come. Absorb Ireland and her tragedy and you will be the poet of
the people, perhaps the poet of a new insurrection.[7]

Yeats said this in the excitement of the centenary celebration of
the Rising of 1798, and, in a magnanimous attempt to cheer up a
despondent A.E., he bestowed upon his rival his own most cherished ambition. The fires in A.E.'s imagination, however, were not
the fires of a burning city, but the ethereal vibrations that glowed
upon the summits of the holy mountains of Ireland. In wishing
to instill a new pagan idealism in the Irish, A.E. cared little that
the English ruled their bodies, although he did care that the priests
ruled their minds. Arthur Griffith wanted the Irish to be free so

[7] *The Letters of W. B. Yeats,* ed. Allan Wade (London, 1954), p. 295.

that they could make their own pots and pans, but A.E. was afraid that in accepting prosperity, the Irish would shut themselves out from their "primitive sources of power." "Modernism leads away from Nature and Great Mother."[8] His atavism was as clear a rejection of civilization as Hyde's resuscitation of a language in which abstract thought was impossible.

What use would it be to you or to me if our ships sailed on every sea and our wealth rivalled the antique Ind, if we ourselves were unchanged, had no more kingly consciousness of life, nor that overtopping grandeur of soul indifferent whether it dwells in a palace or a cottage.[9]

The young theosophist was an evangelist of idealism, and he called to others to help him in this high work. The call was not rhetorical, for at the end of the essay, A.E. printed his address. In his youth, A.E.'s eyes took in only a land of dreams, a rural landscape in which pagan gods appeared in auras of colors never seen in the gray streets of Dublin. The vision sustained the young clerk as he toiled away in his unheavenly job with Pim's Drapers, but one job was about to give way to another that was to change his life and his visions.

In 1897 Sir Horace Plunkett was looking for someone to help him promote agricultural co-operation among the Irish farmers. Impressed by the model of Danish co-operatives, Sir Horace wanted to reform the primitive structure of Irish agriculture, but being both well-bred and somewhat inarticulate, he needed a public relations officer who could convince the common man of the advantages of co-operative purchasing and distribution. Plunkett first approached Yeats, thinking that a man who could write and make public speeches was just the thing, but Yeats preferred to support himself by occasional critical and editorial work and seemed to agree with his father that a steady job was the death of many a good artist. Refusing Plunkett's offer, Yeats suggested A.E. for the position. Yeats thought that the job would give him "a great

8 A.E., "The Future of Ireland and the Awakening of the Fires," *Irish Theosophist* V (1897), 66.
9 Ibid.

knowledge of Ireland and take him out of the narrow groove of theosophical opinion." [10] The work involved bicycling all over Ireland to give speeches, sit in on dinners, and help in the establishment of rural banks for the Irish Agriculture Organizational Society, and it was a work that A.E. did not take to immediately. He complained to Yeats, and Yeats attempted to cheer him on in the position he himself had declined.

But remember always that now you are face to face with Ireland, its tragedy and its poverty, and if we would express Ireland we must know her to the heart in all her moods. You will be a far more powerful mystic and poet and teacher because of this knowledge.[11]

And Yeats, speaking *ex cathedra* as usual, was right again. The work did change A.E. entirely, and if it did not affect him in the religious retreats of his painting and poetry, it showed in his prose. For over eight years he traveled all over Ireland and came face to face with the shining radiance of her holy mountains and the squalor and meanness of her depressing plains. It was a knowledge that could not be bound in green leather and decorated with gold shamrocks, and it helped rid him of the polite, Matthew Arnold view of the Celt.

A.E.'s difficult apprenticeship came to an end in 1906 when he took over the editorship of *The Irish Homestead,* the journal of the I.A.O.S. (Irish Agriculture Organizational Society). With this editorship, A.E. managed to pass on the latest news about modern egg packaging along with some poetic asides, and the combination contributed to his fame, for slowly he was becoming an international figure known to farmers in Kansas as well as Kerry. The apparent contradiction between egg packaging and theosophical poetry appealed to A.E.'s sense of irony and his desire for a Whitmanesque inclusiveness, but it did not prevent him from expending great imaginative effort in resolving the conflict between beauty and necessity. Never a disciple of Pater, A.E.'s sense of beauty was based upon an intense consciousness of moral responsibility, and when-

10 *The Letters of W. B. Yeats,* p. 291.
11 Ibid. p. 294.

ever his mystical vision of the beautiful was interrupted by the socially ugly, he could respond with the biblical wrath that, for example, he poured upon the Masters of Dublin in the lock-out of 1913. A.E.'s work became, therefore, not merely the forming of agricultural co-operatives, but the building up of a great rural civilization. Throwing all the force of his romanticism, celticism, and mysticism into his work, A.E. labored to bring about a body politic that would not be pock-marked with factories and slums. For A.E. as well as Yeats, development was a dialectical process in which the fantasies of youth were destroyed by reality, but out of the destruction came the imaginative synthesis of one who was man enough to survive the destruction of his dreams; personal fantasy was replaced by historical vision. This growth of thought is nowhere more apparent than in the contrast between two of his books that appeared within a year of one another. In 1915, A.E., at the publisher's instigation, gathered up the numerous essays that had circulated about Dublin in various magazines and pamphlets. *Imaginations and Reveries* is full of the opalescent qualities of his early *Irish Theosophist* prose, and for all its spirituality, it lacks the clarity of his meditational style in his *Candle of Vision*. A year later, however, in early 1916, A.E. published *The National Being*. The dedication to Sir Horace Plunkett clearly reveals the author's attempt to achieve a higher unity of opposites.

A good many years ago you grafted a slip of poetry on your economic tree. I do not know if you expected a hybrid. This essay may not be economics in your sense of the word. It certainly is not poetry in my sense.[12]

The book is a definite growth in thought, *on A.E.'s terms,* not on society's. Not economics and not poetry, the book is a mixture of geography, history, and prophecy. This 1916 work still displays the Standish O'Grady messianic vision of history, but A.E.'s perception of current events has forced him to articulate the anatomy of history in a Viconian system.

12 A.E., *The National Being* (Dublin and London, 1916).

In Ireland our history begins with the most ancient of any in a mythical era when earth mingled with heaven. The gods departed, the half-gods also, hero and saint after that, and we have dwindled down to a petty peasant nationality, rural and urban life alike mean in their externals.[13]

Whether from a direct reading of Vico, or from indirect knowledge gained in conversation during one of those famous Sunday nights, A.E.'s imaginative vision has now taken on the clear four-part cycle of the Viconian theory; it is possible, however, that the cyclical elaboration comes from the traditional division of civilizations into golden, silver, bronze, and iron ages, a traditional distinction which was preserved in theosophical historiography. Whatever the source, A.E. now sees Ireland, not as a land of gods and heroes, but a land of chaos and little men.

The national soul in a theocratic state is a god; in an aristocratic age it assumes the character of a hero; and in a democracy it becomes a multitudinous being, definite in character if the democracy is a real social organism. But where the democracy is only loosely held together by the social order, the national being is vague in character, is a mood too feeble to inspire large masses of men to high policies in times of peace, and in times of war it communicates frenzy, panic and delirium.[14]

A.E. was a democrat and a lover of Whitman's poetry (a poetry which had been reviewed in Ireland with high praise as early as .875 by O'Grady),[15] but his recent experiences made him fear the unruly forces of inegalitarian democracies. He feared the revolution that was brooding in the frustrated and embittered minds of the Dublin workers. Looking at the body politic as he looked at his own mind in meditation, A.E. tried to bring about a lifting of the forces at the base of society so that there could be a flowering at the top. Fearing the chaos of a slum insurrection, A.E. worked for a moral revolution.

13 Ibid. p. 14.
14 Ibid. p. 15.
15 "He is the noblest literary product of modern times, and his influence is invigorating and refining beyond expression." In *Standish O'Grady: Selected Essays and Passages* (Dublin, 1918), p. 290.

There is danger in revolution if the revolutionary spirit is much more advanced than the intellectual and moral qualities which alone can secure the success of a revolt. These intellectual and moral qualities— the skill to organize, the wisdom to control large undertakings, are not natural gifts but the results of experience.[16]

Hard work, as opposed to sudden apotheosis, became the virtue of old age; A.E. left the hastiness of his younger enthusiasms to the younger generation. Traveling around Ireland had convinced him that neither theosophy nor an indifference to Ireland's physical situation would solve all its problems; now he felt that before Ireland decided it was fit to rule itself, it might be wise to improve the conditions it tolerated with the indifference he had once thought of as a mark of the overtopping grandeur of soul. Age had brought its wisdom to A.E., and for many he became *the* wise old man of Dublin. But while he was giving his weekly monologues to the followers that came to his Sunday nights, Pearse and Connolly were addressing a younger and more immediate appeal to large audiences. A.E. had his answer ready for the enthusiasts of the new generation.

It will appear to the idealist who has contemplated the heavens more closely than the earth that the policy I advocate is one which only tardily could be put into operation, and could be paltry and inadequate as a basis for society. The idealist with the Golden Age already in his heart believes he has only to erect the Golden Banner and display it for the multitudes to array themselves beneath its folds; therefore he advocates not, as I do, a way to the life, but the life itself.[17]

A.E. was an excellent critic of the young, for, tongue in his bearded cheek, he was criticizing in them his own youth. Now he was skeptical about the sudden illumination of a whole people; he still believed that one man could be struck from his horse by the light of God, but not entire nations. The road to heaven was long and certainly uphill.

16 A.E., *The National Being,* p. 81.
17 Ibid., p. 99.

Not by revolutions can humanity be perfected. I might quote from an old oracle, "The gods are never so turned away from man as when he ascends to them by disorderly methods." [18]

A.E. was quoting himself, and the quotation shows the way in which his prose was moving from melodiously seraphic utterance to a tighter style that holds real objects in a sharp focus. Whatever limitations he had as a poet or a painter, or whatever limitations he had as an ostentatiously humble person,[19] A.E. must be taken quite seriously as a social critic, visions and all, for it is as a social critic that he was able to achieve the fullest engagement of his faculties. Nothing of his youth was denied or cast away in this new role; his mysticism only developed muscles from the exercise of bicycling all over Ireland. If as a poet, A.E. refused to abandon the lilt of his early *Homeward,* he admitted the world into his prose, and strove for a tougher style.

We can no more deduce the political character of the Irish from the history of the past seven hundred years than we can estimate the quality of genius in an artist whom we have only seen when grappling with a burglar.[20]

Dubliners still like to recall the shabby, bearded figure that would go down the street muttering poetry (usually his own), but if A.E. was a sputterer, he sometimes sputtered out sparks. One of his programs of reform in *The National Being* was not laughed at in America, for in 1935 Henry Wallace and Franklin D. Roosevelt took A.E. seriously enough to bring him to Washington, D.C. His tossed-off idea was:

Why should not every young man in Ireland give up two years of his life in comradeship of labour with other young men, and be employed under skilled direction in great works of public utility, in the erection of public buildings, the beautifying of our cities, reclamation of waste lands, afforestation, and other desirable objects.[21]

18 Ibid. p. 99.
19 The fiercest attack on A.E. as a man is Sean O'Casey's, in his *Autobiographies, II* (London, 1963), p. 167.
20 A.E., *The National Being,* p. 122.
21 Ibid. p. 143.

For an allegedly irresponsible mystic such programs were fairly precise and down to earth. A.E.'s program was rational because, contrary to the popular view of mystics, A.E. and Yeats were the most rational of men. Once having mastered the diffuse and irrational energy of their youth, they learned something that was relevant in the battle of bringing the diffuse and irrational energy of society into the form that was necessary for civilization. The complexity of civilization no longer frightened A.E. and Yeats in their maturity, for they had already come to terms with the complexity within themselves. A.E. had come to terms with the irrational within himself, but his optimistic faith in human goodness led him to believe that the nation would follow his example with little difficulty. He was far-sighted in politics; he could see history prophetically in its larger patterns, but he was apt to miss the close-up details of crudeness and rough texture. Yet his prophecies have their excitement, for they enable one to enjoy an unacademic mode of historical speculation. A.E. had a messianic vision of Ireland and the overturning of empires, and, indeed, what Ireland started, India, Burma, Palestine, and Africa finished. Now, seventy years after A.E.'s vision, we can see that the sceptre has indeed fallen from the hand of the British Monarch. A.E.'s ostentatiously humble manner caused him to be dismissed as a crank by some and accepted as a saint by others. He was neither. As an imaginative man, he thought in myth and symbol, and it was only natural that a man with this sort of mind should be able to perceive the ideologies (more precisely the mythologies) that were beginning to surface in Europe and America. Henry Wallace remembered one prediction of A.E.'s that came toward the end of *The National Being,* and brooding on it, recalled it in his eulogy after A.E.'s death. The ideas expressed in the prediction have since become more familiar to us, perhaps in the terms of Jung's idea of *recollectivization;* essentially the idea grows out of romanticism and phenomenology, and like the ideas of romanticism, no man can claim to be the sole author.

It seems inevitable that the domination of the individual by the State must become even greater. It is in the evolutionary process. The amalgamation of individuals into nationalities and empires is as much in the cosmic plan as the development of highly organized beings out of unicellular organisms. I believe this process will continue until humanity itself is so psychically knit together that, as a being, it will manifest some form of cosmic consciousness in which the individual will share.[22]

Cosmic consciousness is an idea that has been bandied about by hundreds of occult groups and dramatized in such popular science-fiction novels as Arthur C. Clarke's *Childhood's End;* it is, therefore, all the more startling to find a man as irreligious as Sigmund Freud coming to the following conclusions, which should be set alongside A.E.'s thoughts.

I may now add that civilization is a process in the service of Eros, whose purpose is to combine single human individuals, and after that families, then races, peoples and nations, into one great unity, the unity of mankind. Why this has to happen, we do not know; the work of Eros is precisely this. These collections of men are to be libidinally bound to one another. Necessity alone, the advantages of work in common, will not hold them together.[23]

A defense of A.E. based upon an invocation of Freud will, of course, not gain support from anyone who regards Freud's theories to be as nonsensical as the visions of A.E. or the *mysterium tremendum* of Jung, but the very fact that such an idea could occur to men of such radically different and strongly opposed positions argues, at the very least, for a hearing. To return to A.E.:

[22] A. E., *The National Being*, p. 159. "Henry Wallace, in a speech he delivered after A.E.'s death, tells how much impressed he was in his youth by a prophetic statement of A.E.—'in which A.E. declared the inevitability of the greater role of the State in the life of the individual. A.E. was not a statistician, nor a classical economist, but in his preoccupation with the intangibles which give beauty and direction to life, he nevertheless had a sense of social trends.'" Oliver St. John Gogarty, "An Angelic Anarchist," *Colby Library Quarterly* IV (May 1955), 27. This issue also contains a brief memoir of A.E. by Wallace himself.

[23] Sigmund Freud, *Civilization and Its Discontents*, trans. James Strachey (New York, 1961), p. 69.

Our spiritual intuitions and the great religions of the world alike indicate some such goal as that to which this turbulent cavalcade of humanity
is wending. A knowledge of this must be in our subconscious being, or
we would find the sacrifices men make for the State otherwise inex-
plicable. The State, though now ostensibly secular, makes more imperious
claims on man than the ancient gods did. It lays hold of life. It asserts
the right to take father, brother and son, and to send them to meet
death in its own defense. It denies them a choice or judgment as to
whether its action is right or wrong. Right or wrong the individual
must be prepared to give his body for the commonwealth, and when
one gives the body unresistingly, one gives the soul also. The marvelous
thing about the authority of the State is that it is recognized by the vast
majority of citizens. During eras of peace the citizen may be always in
conflict with the policy of the State. He may call it a tyranny, but yet
when it is in peril he will die to preserve for it an immortal life. The
hold the State establishes over the spirit of man is the more wonderful
when we look rearward on history, and see with what labour and sacrifice the State was established. But we see also how readily, once the
union has been brought about, men will die to preserve it, even though
it is a tyranny, a bad State. For what do they die unless the spirit in man
has some inner certitude that the divine event to which humanity tends
is a unity of its multitudinous life, and that a State—even a bad State—
must be preserved by its citizens, because it is at least an attempt at
organic unity? It is a simulacrum of the ideal; it contains the germ
or possibility of that to which the spirit of man is traveling. It dis-
ciplines the individual in its service to that greater being in which it
will find its fulfillment, and a bad State is better than no State at all.
To be without a State is to prowl backwards from the divinity before us
to the beast behind us....
... Something, a real life above the individual, acts through the national being, and would almost suggest to us that Heaven cannot fully
manifest its will to humanity through the individual, but must utter itself through multitudes. There must be an orchestration of humanity
ere it can echo divine melodies.[24]

Whether A.E. took this vision of the State from a reading of
Hegel, or from a mental reading of the tablets on the astral plane,
would be difficult to determine. Perhaps a few remarks from philo-
sophically more learned friends corroborated his own intuitions,

[24] A.E., *The National Being*, p. 159ff.

as O'Grady's history had done in the past. But the most interesting thing about this philosophy of the State is not its source. The philosophy tells us something about A.E. that is always overlooked: that rather than being a dogmatist, he was a thinker who was fascinated by the way in which *conflicting* philosophies and points of view can be *simultaneously* true. Personally, A.E. was not a materialist or an apologist for the Total State; his life's work was in privately initiated, self-help programs for agricultural reform. And he showed himself to be an outspoken champion of individual civil liberties in the lock-out of 1913. But the older he grew, the more fascinated he became with the implications of a materialistic World State, the more he began to wonder if God was on the side of his enemy. As a young romantic, A.E. had a horror of industrial empire and hoped to lead men back to pagan, rural Ireland; as a middle-aged man with some experience of rural Ireland, he hoped to manage, at least, the compromise of a more socially organized rural civilization; but as an old man he began to see that the remorseless march of history was against him, and he began to have a glimmering that, beyond the industrial empire, was the millennium. Finding mysticism in the popularized physics of Jeans and Eddington, and seeing something new on the horizon in the technological offspring of the Industrial Revolution, he exchanged the romanticism of the past for the romanticism of the future. And once A.E. could see even the slightest glimmering of the millennium, he no longer bothered with the tribulation all about him, but leapt ecstatically over the present into the future. Forgetting the apocalypse of his youthful vision, he spoke only of "the divine event" that the State was to pull screaming from the womb of time.

Fifty years have passed since A.E. uttered his prophecy, and we, regarding his words in the light of the recollectivized unities of the Third Reich, the Soviet Union, and China, have some reason for not jumping with excitement at the talk of divine events. A.E.'s vision of the organic unity of the State does not seem to be the collectivization by terror of the modern totalitarian state; or, if it was, A.E. merely dismissed the terror as temporary, like the Dark Ages. It would seem that A.E. was constitutionally incapable of anything resembling a tragic vision of history, so strong were his mystic affirmations in the face of suffering. As a political critic he held views totally opposite to those of George Orwell, and the author of *1984* * might have said of A.E., as he said of Gandhi, that "Saints should always be judged guilty until they are proved innocent."

But we cannot leave it grandly at that. Accepting A.E.'s premise, we must grant him his point if only on the basis of a coherence theory of truth. Admittedly, no one would want to speak up in a seminar on political science to propose A.E.'s definition that "The state is a physical body prepared for the incarnation of the soul of a race." [25] But we can admit A.E.'s visions in court as legitimate sociological evidence, exactly in the same manner that George Orwell admitted penny post cards into a profound sociological analysis of England.[26] Both A.E. and Orwell were trying to get at the central ideological crisis of the twentieth century: the dislocation of the individual from an integral culture and the resultant fragmentation of the self. It was this fragmentation that was soon to encourage the formation of the hysterical unities of the mythologized states, and A.E.'s intuitive variant of Hegelianism shows that he was thinking, not in the clouds, but in the heart of the darkness to come, for when Germany later invaded Russia, some historians saw but the violent encounter of the right and left wing of Hegel's philosophy.[27]

Although *The National Being* was A.E.'s most widely read book, and the book used by the members of the Roosevelt Administration, *The Interpreters* is the most important politico-mystical work. This book appeared in 1922 and is, therefore, a document not only of the Rising, but the Troubles and the Civil War as well,

---

* Banned in the Soviet Union and the Republic of Ireland.
25 A.E., *The National Being*, p. 2.
26 See George Orwell, "The Art of Donald McGill," *A Collection of Essays by George Orwell* (New York, 1954).
27 See Ernst Cassirer, *The Myth of the State* (New Haven, 1961), p. 249.

when even the beatific Mr. Russell had to admit that the devil
was loose in the land of the saints and scholars. The Rising had
taken A.E. completely by surprise, and, stunned by the violence
and the executions of the younger men he had known, he began
to brood upon the meaning of it all. Dissatisfied with his first verse
tribute in "Salutation," he began to summon his deepest thoughts
to answer for the event. As he contemplated the fires and ruins of
Dublin, A.E. remembered that very old man who had set him on
fire in his own youth. Aged and infirm, Standish O'Grady had
retired from the scene of Irish events, but A.E. knew that, just as
O'Grady did not sympathize with the mysticism that his history
had enkindled in A.E., O'Grady did not sympathize with or even
"know what his own work meant to Padraic Pearse."

O'Grady said of the ancient legends of Ireland that they were less
history than prophecy, and I who knew how deep was Pearse's love for
the Cuchulain whom O'Grady discovered or invented, remembered after
Easter Week that he had been solitary against a great host in imagination with Cuchulain, long before circumstance permitted him to stand
for his nation with so few companions against so great a power.[28]

The myth of Pearse as incarnation of Cuchulain began to absorb
A.E.'s meditation until it came to the surface in "Michael," [29] a
dream-inspired poem on the Rising. But the poem did not put an
end to Russell's concern with the Rising, for from 1919 to 1922
A.E. continued to work on a book that would express the complete mind of a revolution. Perhaps he felt that he needed a setting
for the poem, or perhaps his thoughts on politics and history
demanded a more definite expression than his own verse could
permit him. The earlier *National Being* had not adequately come
to terms with violence and the romantic politics of violence; now
that the democratic age of chaos was bringing forth new gods and
heroes to spin the Viconian cycle over again, a new chapter in the
biography of the national being had to be written. On more personal terms, A.E.'s own attempts to achieve unity of being de-

[28] A.E., *The Living Torch*, ed. Monk Gibbon (London, 1938), p. 145.
[29] See A.E., *Song and Its Fountains* (New York, 1932), pp. 58, 99.

manded that he resolve the apparent contradiction of recent Irish
history, for death seemed to be the bitter crop of the idealism
that he had helped to sow in Ireland. Carrying on a dialogue
within himself, it was natural that a dialogue should become the
medium of this mystic's attempt to understand history on his own
terms.

The scene of *The Interpreters* is set in the unspecified future,
a few centuries after the Easter Rising. Once again an insurrection
against the British Empire is in progress, and once again the huge
power of the Empire is brought to bear against Ireland. As figures
move about in the darkness of the streets, the immense aircraft of
The Empire hover above the insurgent city. Several of the rebels
are captured, and, by mistake, one imperialist who is a captain of
the air industry. In the darkness of the prison, a darkness made
slightly visible by the fires and explosions in the city, the captured
rebels gather and begin to discuss the great event. The knowledge
that each is about to be executed shortly acts as a psychological
release and soon each man is discussing his innermost thoughts and
motivations. The symposium of these men thus becomes the necessary document for understanding revolution.

As the characters begin to speak it becomes clear that humanity
is represented in all its variety, for the characters are not individuals as much as types. There is Lavelle, a poet and fervent nationalist in love with the culture of the tiny nation; he is obviously the
mask of Padraic Pearse. There is Culain the socialist; he is James
Larkin. There is Brehon, an aged man whose histories of long ago
had discovered the buried culture of the nation; he is Standish
James O'Grady. There is Leroy, the great dissenter to all popular
movements, religious or political; he is the heretic, A.E. himself.
A man of action is present; he is so impatient with the philosophic
talk of his fellow prisoners that he recalls Michael Collins, who
once interrupted one of A.E.'s monologues on mystical politics
with the abrupt: "Your point, Mr. Russell?" And there is Rian,
the aesthete, a man who would tear down the empire because it
builds such hideous public buildings. His Irish counterpart eludes

me; perhaps he is merely a man of the ranks, for his characterization does not suggest any obvious commanding figure. He sounds
like William Morris, so perhaps A.E. is characterizing the young
Yeats he had known as disciple of Pater and Morris, for it was as
a young man that Yeats referred to the British Empire as "that
master-work and dream of the middle class"; [30] but since Yeats
had a personality that could not possibly be confused with another
man's (indeed, that was his chief reason for creating it) Rian
should be looked upon as the mask of a role that Yeats had out-
grown. At all events, the correspondence between literary character
and historical personage is only part of the total characterization,
for all the major characters are also separate aspects of A.E.'s own
personality. The dialogue in the prison is, most probably, the
dialogue that had taken place in A.E.'s mind as he watched History
come to possess besieged Dublin. Leroy is clearly A.E.'s heretical
self, for A.E. puts into his speeches his own mystical dreams, but
the central conversion experience of A.E.'s life, the visitation of
the Earth Breath as he lay under a tree, is given to the poet Lavelle.
The historian, Brehon, is O'Grady, but he becomes the mouth-
piece of A.E.'s philosophy of history. And Culain, the socialist
James Larkin, is a mystic motivated by an absolutely Christian
compassion for the slum dwellers of the city. A.E. knew Larkin
well and his portrait of Larkin's religious nature is true to life,
but it does seem doubtful that all the participants of the Rising
were really mystics. Even the mistakenly captured industrialist and
man of Empire, Heyt (William Martin Murphy), is presented as
a scientific mystic entranced with the elegance of the abstract. One
can regard this as a failure of characterization, a lack of imaginative sympathy on the part of an author who cannot imagine a man
different from himself; however, in this particular work, which is
not a novel but a Platonic dialogue, the fact that personality in
facing death reveals itself to be a mystical impersonality is part
of the theme of the book. Each of the men is driven by God or by
a god-surrogate; none silhouettes his actions against the void; none
30 W. B. Yeats, *Ideals in Ireland*, ed. Lady Gregory (London, 1901), p. 90.

believes he moves through a random and undirected universe. Each in the motivation of his life assumes a universe of high purpose, a purpose that is continuous with his own.

Having little to do until the morning and doubting the likelihood of sleep on such a night, the heretic Leroy opens the symposium by asking: "What are we guilty of before Heaven? What relation have the politics of time to the politics of eternity?" And this is the central question, for A.E., the pacifist, is disturbed by the efficiency of violence in bringing about historical change and progress and is trying to find the politics that are compatible with ethics.[31] The poet Lavelle attempts to answer Leroy's question with the faith we have seen expressed in the works of Padraic Pearse. Rian seems to think that the ugliness of Empire is reason sufficient to destroy it, but Leroy sees in the objections of Lavelle and Rian only the attempt to replace one tyranny with another.

Rian is fighting for beauty. He is a creature of aesthetic passions. Put power into his hands and he would arrest people for wearing inharmonious colours in the streets. Our great Culain is a socialist. He has an economic ideal while you have a cultural ideal. I think every one who is with us turned different faces to Heaven in their prayers. Does Heaven accept them in the cosmic plan? If it approves of everything, it designs nothing.[32]

Leroy is skeptical of those fighters for freedom who merely want to establish one cultural mood in a nation, a mood in keeping with their own sensibilities. The absurdity of the position does not escape his comment, and he mocks the exalted virtue of the nationalist movement. He tells them of a dream he once had in which the Almighty asked him to explain the local goings-on.

And I explained that the people of the earth were at war to decide whether they would receive their culture from such organs of public opinion as "The Horn of Empire" or "The Clarion of the People" and

---

[31] See A.E., "Twenty-five Years of Irish Nationality," *Foreign Affairs* (January 1929).
[32] A.E., *The Interpreters* (London, 1922), p. 22.

old God looked at me and looked through me, and He burst out laughing....[33]

The old historian, Brehon, enters the discussion and he does not view the revolution as a mere projection of personal desire, but as the embodiment of a spiritual concept. At this point the examination of conscience begins and each man begins to confess the motivation of his life. Rian, the artist *manqué*, wanted to see the palaces of his imagination realized on earth; Lavelle's soul revolted against the Empire and wanted to revive the humble culture of the nation that was suffocating from the enemy's materialism; Culain saw a woman weep because, in her own starving fatigue, she could not help a dying woman, and moved by the pity of that scene, the socialist decided to destroy the system that let such things happen. Each has his personal vision and turns an individual face to God. Each one justifies his action by bringing in divinity. Brehon is moved to ask:

An idea may be heaven inspired, but is the will to enforce it by violence part of that inspiration?

Lavelle answers the question as Pearse would.

Every idea which arises in the heaven world consciousness must ally itself with an appropriate force if it is to be born in this world. When we devise anything for ourselves our thought allies itself with force to move the body, and in carrying out what we devise we must often suppress energies and passions which would impell the body to contrary action. So the national genius, if it is to move the body politic, must ally itself with force to overbear what is hostile to it. How else can right find its appropriate might? [34]

The argument is advanced, but the word "appropriate" begs the question, for what we really want to know is that if Pearse's violence was right, was Collins's? And if his was right, what about the violence of those vestigial patriots of the I.R.A. whose acts against Northern Ireland invoke the same ethics used by Pearse

33 Ibid. p. 22.
34 Ibid. p. 57.

in his campaign against England? The question is the great question that Ivan Karamazov put forth: Can the golden age be justly brought about if it must come at the cost of the murder of a single babe? It is at this interesting point of the debate that the imperialist, Heyt, enters the symposium. Heyt has no patience with the atavism of Lavelle and his sweet love of the culture of the tiny nation, for he says: "The tribal communities are gone behind time irrevocably and are like fossils in human memory."

Heyt is an example of A.E.'s prophetic imagination at its best, for Heyt represents an age in which the Viconian cycle has spun back to the beginnings of theocratic civilization; he is of the ruling class in an empire in which the priests who advise the secular arm of the government are scientists. Heyt's religious vision is essentially one of power, a cosmic vision of the triumph of knowledge over the once inscrutable energies of the universe. Fascinated by the mathematician's sense of elegance and the physicist's grasp of the abstract nature of atomic energies, Heyt has little patience with Lavelle's desire to speak Gaelic, a language in which abstract thought is impossible. For the imperialist, the ethics of politics are clear-cut; his position is the old "Whatever is, is Right." With a lofty contempt for the others, Heyt addresses them.

You intellectuals are in your political thinking like those mathematicians who pursue the elements beyond aether into mathematical space, and when their calculations are worked out are unable to find the material analogue of the result. The intention of nature is seen in the forms it creates and not in the dreams of its creatures.... If Nature was with your thought it would have bestowed power on it, but the world soul has decreed the world state.[35]

Heyt, like all the others, is a mystic. One does not find a simple, down-to-earth power-mindedness in him, for he is a Promethean figure who would eventually like to storm the Gates of Paradise, coming forth to do battle with divinity with the weapons of a superhuman science. In A.E.'s hands even a captain of industry

[35] Ibid. p. 64.

becomes an exalted hero, so incapable is he of expressing a materialistic view of life.

Leroy comes to the attack of the totalitarian state, and one begins to see in the argument between Leroy and Heyt the opposite poles of A.E.'s theory of history, which held that the conflict between the freedom of the individual and the solidarity of humanity would be resolved in the cosmic consciousness at the end of history. Leroy will have no part of solidarity; he is all for the individual.

> Though there be one thousand millions in your world state does it equal in its totality one Shakespeare? I am with Lavelle in the struggle for national freedom, and if the nation wins I shall fight in it for the freedom of the local community and for the greatest richness and variety in life.[36]

Heyt counters with sociology: he claims that culture moulds and forms the individual and that the myth of the sovereignty of the individual is a pleasant fiction. Heyt, like A.E. himself, argues for a psychic sociology in which the State is seen as an organism in which the individual mind is but one cell. Heyt finds evidence of this collective consciousness in the patterns of scientific research.

> In the great laboratories of the state men seem at first to be absorbed in special studies, but when they confer later, they find their special labours were only contributing to great discoveries made in common and all had unconsciously worked to one end.[37]

Leroy counters with the thrust that the unity of nature alleged by Heyt and the surrender of the cell to the organism are merely ideological camouflage for brute economic domination. Heyt does not deny this, but claims that such domination is temporary and necessary: the quantitative change will result in a qualitative transformation. Heyt's political views, symbolized by his name, are based on hate—on an aristocratic contempt for the body that hinders his pursuit of the mystery of the abstract, and on a con-

36 Ibid. p. 75.
37 Ibid. p. 77.

tempt for the scum at the bottom of society who care little for his science. In a towering rapture, Heyt points out the window to the aircraft of the Empire and haughtily asks the rebels: "What power can you invoke mighty enough to overcome that power?" Speaking out of the darkness of his corner, Culain, the socialist, now enters the discussion, and says: "It will be overcome by pity."

The power of empire does not descend from any sky god, but is earth born and sucked up from human depths where millions pay tribute in labour and pain. You breathe the magnificence, but do not feel the agony out of which it is born. Pity for that human agony has grown until it has become mightier than empire.[38]

Culain's is the politics of love, of pity and compassion; but the opposition between Culain and Heyt in the symposium begins to look like collusion, for Heyt is busy in the reification of a system that Culain intends to transform into a spiritual unity based, not upon contempt and aristocracy, but compassion and a classless society. History is repeating itself, for the Roman Empire built the roads upon which the Christian missionaries traveled to conquer a world by pity. Culain's words begin to sound like the words of another, more or less mystical, Irish poet.

> In pity for man's darkening thought
> He walked that room and issued thence
> In Galilean turbulence.

And the opposition between Heyt and Culain as well suggests Yeats's conflict between *antithetical* and *primary* men and eras as expressed in *A Vision.* A.E. and Yeats were two theosophists living through the terror in Ireland and brooding deeply upon the shape of things to come. At the time Yeats and his wife were at work on *A Vision,* A.E. was brooding with his own book. Interestingly enough, the Troubles in Ireland had brought the two friend-enemies into a tentative correspondence, and in one letter, Yeats tried to lord it over A.E. by dropping little bits of knowledge from

[38] Ibid. p. 85.

his secret system.[39] The two dreamers who had survived the destruction of their early fantasies, now, as old men, saw their early visions of the fall of empires gain a sudden relevance. As men were being murdered in the streets the two mystics were working out a theory of history that could never affect history, were attaining a secret knowledge that could never make public sense.

Now in *The Interpreters*, as passionate Heyt and compassionate Culain reach the impasse created by their intense attachment to life, the aged Brehon comes forth to expound the occult theory of revolution. Leroy had vigorously protested Heyt's spiritual transformation brought about by material means, but Leroy, as the great dissenter, has ultimately no politics at all. Against this inadequacy, Lavelle had proposed the politics of romantic violence and sacrifice.

I believe the ideals for which men are not ready to die soon perish, for they have not drawn nourishment from what is immortal in them. If we do not throw life into the scale we are outweighed by those who are ready for this sacrifice. If we become philosophical onlookers, our nation, its culture and ideals, perish being undefended, and an unresisted materialism takes its place.[40]

This point of view is perfect Pearse: it expresses the politics of youth and heroism. But the historian Brehon counters with a wisdom that is taken from a reading of history as much as from the experience of age.

You will find that every great conflict has been followed by an era of materialism in which the ideals for which the conflict ostensibly was waged were submerged.[41]

This was certainly true of the Civil War in Ireland, as it was true for the Reign of Terror in France, Bolshevik Russia, and modern Cuba. A.E. and Yeats watched the executions that occupied postrevolutionary Russia when the socialists began killing the men who stood in the way of a love of Man. Brehon sees this negative

39 See *The Letters of W. B. Yeats*, p. 666.
40 A.E., *The Interpreters*, p. 134.
41 Ibid. p. 136.

afterimage as something not merely restricted to revolutions but common to all wars.

> By intensity of hatred nations create in themselves the characters they imagine in their enemies. Hence it is that all passionate conflicts result in the interchange of characteristics.[42]

"We become what we hate" is a *Yoga* maxim, but the notion is really common sense dressed up in a loin cloth, for hate is as severe a form of bondage as love. If one hates something, he is not free of it; if one hates something with the full force of his being, then the hated object blocks out everything else in sight, until the individual has been distracted from the values he cherished in opposition to the hated object. The lover of freedom destroys the Constitution in fighting communists; the judicially unchecked chief of police becomes a criminal in fighting crime; the celibate becomes pathologically lascivious in fighting lust. The exchange of opposites in passionate conflicts is a common part of personal experience, but Brehon is willing to extend it to revolutions and wars. Brehon's position has its base in common experience, but the summit is definitely beyond the common level of experience, for it points upward to an almost Buddhistic state of non-attachment to human life. Since violence destroys its agent, Brehon concludes that nations must wage psychic and moral wars to conquer as Christ and Buddha conquered.

> ... if we shut any out of our heart by making emotional or intellectual boundaries to human brotherhood, if any race or class is excluded, we pervert the spiritual energies whose natural flow is from each to all; and these energies, diverted from their natural goal, turn backwards and downwards, and poison the very deeps of life, and there generate spiritual pestilences, hates, frenzies, madnesses, and the sinister ecstacy making for destruction which is the divine power turned to infernal uses. Through ignorance of spiritual law idealists who take to warfare are perpetually defeated, for they do not realize the dark shadow which follows all conflict and which must follow this present conflict. ... Therefore we ought to regard none who differ from us as enemies, but

[42] Ibid. p. 137.

to contemplate them rather with yearning as those who possess some power or vision from which we are shut out but which we ought to share. If we seek for the fulness there can be no decay of what is beautiful in the world, for what is right always exercises its appropriate might.[43]

For A.E., this was the relation of the politics of time to the politics of eternity, and if it seems like something that would not exactly stop a mob or quell a riot, we may console ourselves with the knowledge that it was not humanly possible for George William Russell either, for he had his own passions and his own enemies. This philosophy of history is a strange one, for it sees in the passionate conflicts of time a drama moving toward a climax in a cosmic consciousness, yet it exhorts us to abandon the passionate conflicts that are supposed to be impelling us toward the divine event. The politics of eternity thus become an apology for, and an argument against, history. No doubt A.E. realized that "spiritual law" was not likely to affect human laws, for one of the common rebels, Rudd (the Michael Collins figure), punctuates such seraphic utterance with animal impatience and shouted curses.

The revolution, as A.E. presents it, is clearly a drama with men of different types filling the stage, but it is also something more. As a drama receives its unity from the mind of the dramatist, revolution, from A.E.'s point of view, finds its unity in the mind of the national being. As the protagonists of *The Interpreters* relate their life stories, one cannot help remembering Yeats's theory of the dream.[44] The revolution takes on the quality of Yeats's dream of the centaur; the total myth is too large for a single imagination, but pieces of it, the pieces of it that are in sympathy with an individual's particular temperament, can animate an individual's imagination. And as these individuals gather, each driven by a different dream, the pieces fit together, and the total dream of the nation or culture emerges. The dream is pieced together in the gathering of the many, and the gathering of the many in Sackville

43 Ibid. p. 148.
44 See W. B. Yeats, *Autobiographies* (London, 1961), p. 372.

Street is the beginning of the revolution. But even that one national dream, that revolution, may itself be but a piece of a larger dream, may be but one event in universal history. The difficulty, however, is that one cannot decide whether it is the revolution that determines the dreams of individuals, or the "needs and drives" of individuals that determine the revolution. Most probably, as in all self and culture relationships, both processes go on at once: the individual breathes in the cultural atmosphere, but it is his own breath that he gives back, and this becomes part of the air all others breathe. A.E.'s psychic theory of revolution has its fascination in providing a metaphoric explanation for the peculiar animus that appears in revolutions, nativistic movements, or, most simply, riots. Naturally, the piece of the total idea of Revolution that comes most easily to A.E.'s imagination is the mystical. A.E. can understand and keenly perceive the romanticism of O'Grady or the messianic nationalism of Pearse, but he distorts William Martin Murphy into his personal focus, and he scarcely sees Michael Collins at all. As a religious thinker there were always two subjects that A.E. never pursued intellectually: sex and evil. As a student of Eastern thought, he knew that excited violence was a sexual passion, for that is what he means when he refers to the poisoned "deeps of life" and the "sinister ecstasy," but he preferred to blot out these subjects by a meditation upon their opposites of love and goodness. Perhaps he was right; this may have been the only possible personal solution for him, but for us, who come upon history after Buchenwald and Hiroshima, it is not enough. Terror has become so much a part of our reality that we cannot accept a view of history that lacks the vision of terror. Perhaps this is why A.E. ultimately fails to hold us, fascinating though he is, and why we turn away to the tougher perceptions of other writers. There are, of course, simpler reasons, for A.E. never mastered English prose; there is always a sense of strain and stiffness, as if he were trying to round off a neat period in the manner of Dr. Johnson. A.E. could rise to a few eloquent moments, but his writing is nowhere as graceful as Yeats's in *A Vision*. The speeches, though weighted against one another with a sense of drama, do not reach the level of the drama of ideas in Shaw's *Don Juan in Hell,* and as a work of political fiction, *The Interpreters* cannot be compared in quality to either *1984* or *The Magic Mountain*. And yet, for all the work's limitations, A.E. succeeds admirably in showing how five men of conflicting philosophies can all be simultaneously right, and that is the work's singular merit. If A.E. had the blind spots of the religious thinker, he at least did not have the blindness of the moralist who can see the truth of no position other than his own.

Perhaps because each man does have his say in the symposium, A.E. felt a personal need to attempt a leap beyond prose, for having given a historical setting and an intellectual framework to his subject, A.E. concludes the work with his earlier composed poem, "Michael." As the men break up their talk, each to go to sleep or meditation in his own corner, the poet Lavelle attempts to finish his work upon the Easter Rising of centuries past. Whether A.E. was a mystic, a painter, or an agricultural organizer, it is as a poet that he chose to have the last word on revolution, and it is as a poet that we must now consider him.

A.E.'s theory of history, which traces political movements back to their origin in the anima mundi, is appropriate to the origin of "Michael," for A.E. woke up one morning with half the poem already written in dream. The opening of the poem is one of his best; for once the color imagery is effective, the meter is sufficiently varied, and the rhymes are uncommon.

> A wind blew by from icy hills,
> Shook with cold breath the daffodils,
> And shivered as with silver mist
> The lake's pale leaden amethyst.
> It pinched the barely budded trees,
> And rent the twilight tapestries,
> Left for one hallowed instant bare
> A single star in lonely air.

The structure of the poem contains an alternation between a narrative and an interrogative voice; one presents the action, the other inquires into its meaning. The poem begins with a pastoral setting, like Wordsworth's "Michael," but the direction of the poem is away from the mystical presences of nature to the broken life of the city. The fisher folk of A.E.'s pastoral setting tell the old tales, like *The Voyage of Bran,* and preserve the mystery of earth and ancient Ireland. In line 25, after the presentation of the pastoral setting, the interrogative voice appears to ask what the relation is between the deeps of the skies and the deeps of the waters, for these deeps command more attention in the country than they would in the city. In A.E.'s theosophical lore, the deeps of the waters are symbolical of the astral plane, the anima mundi, whereas the deeps of the skies, The Land of Many Colors, are symbolical of the solar plane, the land of light and harmony beyond the elemental vibrations of the lower subconscious. Both these realms meet in the soul of man, for the spirit is continuous with nature. In this mystical setting of nature, Michael hears "older mother cry," which is A.E.'s "Mighty Mother," the pagan spirit of earth. But the poem is a poem of journey, and Michael must leave this land.

Michael takes his farewell from the presences of nature on a sea cliff that overlooks the immensity of sea and sky, and in this farewell, Michael is permitted an ecstatic vision of the Land of Many Colors. The interrogative voice returns in line 87 to question the nature of visions: are they merely psychological projections, or are they bestowed from without? The question is not answered. In the aloneness of his ecstatic vision, Michael is initiated into the mysteries; his mind makes a voyage of Bran to the Islands of Happiness, but the vision is fleeting and Michael is not permitted to see the divinities who people the towers of his vision. Michael cannot enter fully into this heaven, for imagination finds that "height too infinite too scan." When Michael again opens his eyes, he sees that the bird he saw one moment before his vision has hardly moved in flight. Here A.E. indulges in the "lapse of time in fairy land" motif, a motif that he encountered in the Indian tales as well as the Irish legends. The hero goes through a lifetime of experience only to find that he has been dreaming and that merely an instant of time has truly passed. "Can a second suffice / To hurry us to paradise?" After his mystical initiation, Michael leaves the country to move to "the city's dingy air." With an autobiographical similarity to A.E.'s own work at Pim's Drapers, Michael works in a dark warehouse where he maintains his contact with nature by conjuring up his past visions before his eyes. But "memory is a fading fire" and he might have forgotten the Land of Many Colors had not he encountered the legendary cycles of his race. Myth and art become symbolic surrogates for lost mystical experience. The peasant in a community enjoys a whole life in a whole society, but the fragmentary life of man in the collective of the city breaks culture and breaks the self; therefore, art helps to put man back together again. Alone in the city, Michael finds other unhappy men who have banded together in the culture of the older, Gaelic mind.

> The army of the Gaelic mind
> Still holding throughout the Iron Age
> The spiritual heritage,
> The story from the gods that ran
> Through many a cycle down to man.
> And soon with them had Michael read
> The legend of the famous dead,
> For him who with his single sword
> Stayed a great army at the ford,
> Down to the vagrant poets, those
> Who gave their hearts to the Dark Rose.

The Irish legends, especially the epic *Cattle Raid of Cooley*, and the poetry of the bards sustain Michael in his exalted heritage. The interrogative voice returns to ask: "How may the past if it be dead, / Its light within the living shed?" For A.E. all the past and all past memories still exist in the anima mundi with which the soul is in contact in sleep and vision. But now in the city Michael leaves the innocence of his childhood behind, and with it the sweeter stories of Bran and the Happy Islands; he enters the world of experience, and his new hero is not the lonely traveler, but the man of action, of violence, the warrior Cuchulain. The imaginative vision of Cuchulain enables Michael to keep his sight in the world of the blind. He lives for three years in the city, presumably as a member of the army of the Gaelic mind. Then Easter comes. On a pagan and Christian holy day, the Lord of Man rises in the spirit of Michael; from the sepulcher of life in the Iron Age of the British Empire, Cuchulain returns. Michael becomes the lamb of sacrifice. In the midst of the gunfire of the Rising, Michael has another vision of the Land of Many Colors, and this vision protects him from the fear of death: Myth enters the world. Eternity explodes into time. On A.E.'s terms, the politics of eternity take over the politics of time.

The Rising had lain asleep in the dreams of the Irish for seven centuries; it had grown in anima mundi until it burst into consciousness and reality.

Great wars are the results of conflicting imaginations, which are anterior to wars as causes precede effects.... What is a nation but an imagination common to millions of people.[45]

From this perspective war becomes a ritual, a warrior's play that seeks to bring about the truths of imagination and myth in the actual world. The skies open, and Michael, in death, is reunited with eternity. Michael, as half man and half god, becomes himself the intersection of time and eternity. It is important that Michael's first hero was Bran, the hero of innocence, for the *Voyage of Bran* is fantasy: it is a voyage away from time to the Happy Islands; there is no return, for when the sailors step on land again, they turn to ashes as if they were hundreds of years old. Bran learns that he has truly left time, for the story of his voyage is now in the ancient legends of his people; he cannot return, but must move on toward unknown wanderings. Bran's movements lead out of time,

45 A.E., *The Living Torch*, p. 134.

but Cuchulain is a hero who unites time and eternity. In taking
Cuchulain as hero, Michael has passed from fantasy to the reconciliation of experience which realizes that all actions are but part
of a cosmic dance.

A.E. does not end his poem with the patriotic apotheosis of
Michael, but continues it even farther. The interrogative voice
returns to say that the cause for which Michael died was not important; it was merely an excuse for the everlasting to work its
will. "The slayer and the slain may be / Knit in secret harmony."
This is a paraphrase of an aphorism of Patanjale; and with it,
A.E. adds a new dimension to the poem. Patanjale said: "Let the
seer slay reality, then slay the slayer." The meaning is that the
mind in meditation must slay the physical world, and then slay
the self that is conscious of such action. When the barriers of the
limited self are thus removed, the universal mind floods in. When
A.E.'s poem is seen in relation to the paraphrased aphorism, it
takes on an esoteric meaning; the battle in this light becomes
symbolic of the battle of meditation. A.E. is fashioning his war
poem after the great war poem, the *Bhagavad Gita*. As the *Gita* is,
on the surface, about the Indian wars, so "Michael" is, on the surface, about the Rising; but as all actions in time relate to eternity,
this war is not merely a war. For the initiated reader, Krishna
(Cuchulain) is the *Brahman* speaking to the worldly self, Arjuna
(Michael) or *atman*. Krishna asks Arjuna to slay his relatives,
which is not so much a call to fratricide, as it is a call to slay the
self's material relatedness, its *karma*. Against the old tradition of
renunciation of the world, the *Gita* proposed action in the world,
but an action without passionate attachment or a desired goal.
The actor was to rejoice in the act for the act. Michael acts, but
not for the fictional loves and hatreds that patriotic men require.
He can fight the English dispassionately, knowing that the slayer
and the slain "may be knit in secret harmony." This is what the
Easter Rising meant for a mystic.

Ironically, a few months before the Rising, A.E. had declared
that no public man in Ireland could possibly be the hero of an

epic and that none could be even the subject of a "genuine lyric." [46]
The voluntary sacrifice took him so much by surprise, as it did
everyone else, that he labored to withdraw his own detracting
words by writing the lyric himself. It was the most appropriate
tribute he could make. The sacrificial act, coming as it did in an
otherwise sordid period, seemed to reawaken the prophetic fires
of A.E.'s youth, for he now began to see signs of a great intellectual
awakening in the land he had hitherto described as mean. But,
as usual, mystic vision appeared where physical reality had been
blackened out. In an article in which he tried to explain Ireland's
Troubles to America, A.E. looked at the young revolutionaries in
their slouch hats, trench coats, and, if they were lucky, stolen
Webleys, and predicted a great flowering of culture for the period
that was to become the Civil War.[47] As usual, A.E. suffered from
vatic myopia. It was not that he tried to gloss over the ugliness,
for he admitted that "Ireland is by no means an Island of Saints,
and things have been done by Irishmen which I at least will not
attempt to defend"; it was merely that human suffering never
disturbed his transcendentalism. Certainly the time would have
turned any half-mystic into an incarnation of rage, bitterness, and
violent hatred, for A.E. and Sir Horace Plunkett had to look on
in utter helplessness as their most unmilitary installations, the
creameries they had established, were burned by the Black and
Tans. A.E. kept his faith, but he began to realize that the events
of his visions were not in the immediate future, and that his prophecies were denied by the present. A.E. predicted that his native
Ulster would not opt out of the Free State, and was wrong. He
predicted a new and great period of idealism, and when he saw
that the new generation of Irish writers, men like O'Casey, O'Connor, O'Flaherty, and James Joyce, were the most intense realists,
he looked beyond them to a period fifty years in the future when
Ulysses would be forgotten and the Irish writers of the time would

---

[46] A.E., *The National Being*, p. 13.
[47] A.E., "The Inner and the Outer Ireland," Pamphlet (Dublin, 1921), taken
from *Pearson's Magazine*.

be returning to the truer idealism of their grandparents. But the idealistic movement was finished, and A.E.'s own last work, *The Avatars,* showed only too well that the *Weltgeist* was laboring to become conscious of itself through the tougher perceptions of the younger realists. The bleakness of Post-Revolutionary Ireland finally came home to the seer. The young no longer came to his Sunday nights, for he was growing old, and the monologues began to repeat themselves. And with independence going to its head, Catholic Ireland made up for the poverty of the old Penal Law days in a *nouveau riche* spree of Catholic legislation. Whatever flowering of Irish culture was to take place would not be in Ireland, but in London, Paris, and New York. The jingoism of the new Ireland was not a congenial place for a theosophical mystic of Low Church background, and so A.E. left. Never the slightest bit interested in material goods, A.E. nonetheless loved a following, no matter how small. The invitation from the American Department of Agriculture came at a welcome time, and the mystic, before leaving for eternity, was able to enjoy being the lion of Washington dinner parties. A.E. traveled from coast to coast, speaking at universities, and he broadcast talks for the national networks. Dubliners had heard it all before, but for Americans, it was something new. His two trips to America were brief moments of glory, but poor health shortened his second trip. He did not return to Ireland, but went to England, where, in July 1935, he died.

CHAPTER SEVEN

THE NATURALISTIC IMAGE: O'CASEY

In the deadly symbiosis of Ireland and the artist, the two organisms, like the black and white gyres of Yeats's system, live one another's death. It is not simply that one wishes to live without the other; the relationship is far more passionate than that, for Ireland in Saturnine fashion must devour its young, and the young, with a child's guilt, long to be devoured.

> Come fix upon me that accusing eye.
> I thirst for accusation. All that was sung,
> All that was said in Ireland is a lie.[1]

The artist requires the peculiar soil that is Ireland; it is the ground of his art's moral being, and Ireland requires art if it is to grow out of darkness into a freer consciousness of itself. The growth is, of course, a form of death, a dying in order to be reborn, and for this reason, the images of art are often as morbid as the iconography of religion. Whatever beauty this Irish art has, it would seem that there is always some ugliness sustaining it: the

1 W. B. Yeats, *Collected Poems* (New York, 1957), p. 275.

terror of a Catholic upbringing beneath Joyce, the ignorance of the mob beneath Yeats, the ugliness of the slums beneath O'Casey. The hate of each artist was strong, and precisely for that reason none could get along without the hated enemy, for his passion had made that enemy an inseparable part of his art's being. Joyce without the liturgical worship of the word is not Joyce. Yeats without savage indignation, without rider and horse, elevated man and elemental mob, is not Yeats. O'Casey without the Dublin slums is not O'Casey.

The tragedy of O'Casey is that, with the reflexive rage of Lear, he but slenderly knew himself, for the great mass of his work is outside the province of the Dublin slums, and, therefore, outside the province of his genius. In his old age what should have been rage became merely the rant of a testy old man. But in the last testament of his rant, O'Casey records one incident that dramatizes the maiming hatred that mastered those who could not lift hatred into a rage at man's entire condition.

The police were summoned, and the play began again—two plays, in fact: one on the stage, the other in the auditorium. Yeats tore down the stairs and rushed on to the stage to hold the fort till the constables came. The whole place became a mass of moving, roaring people, and Yeats roared louder than any of them. Rowdy, clenching, but well-groomed hands reached up to drag down the fading black-and-gold front curtain; others, snarling curiously, tried to tug up the very chairs from the roots in the auditorium; while some, in frenzy, pushed at the stout walls to force them down. Steamy fumes ascended here and there in the theatre, and a sickly stench crept all over the place, turning healthy-looking faces pale. The high, hysterical, distorted voices of women kept squealing that Irish girls were noted over the world for their modesty, and that Ireland's name was holy; that the Republican flag had never seen the inside of a public house; that this slander of the Irish race would mean the end of the Abbey Theatre; and that Ireland was Ireland through joy and through tears. Up in the balcony, a section was busily bawling out *The Soldier's Song,* while a tall fellow frantically beat time on the balcony-rail with a walking-stick. Barry Fitzgerald became a genuine Fluther Good, and fought as Fluther himself would fight, sending an enemy, who had climbed on the stage,

flying into the stalls with a flutherian punch on the jaw. And in the
midst of the fume, the fighting, the stench, the shouting, Yeats, as mad
as the maddest there, pranced on the stage, shouting out his scorn, his
contempt; his anger making him like unto an aged Cuchullain in his
hero-rage; his long hair waving, he stormed in utter disregard of all
around him, confronting all those who cursed and cried out shame
and vengeance on the theatre, as he conjured up a vision for them of
O'Casey on a cloud, with Fluther on his right hand and Rosie Redmond
on his left, rising upwards to Olympus to get from the waiting gods and
goddesses a triumphant apotheosis for a work well done in the name of
Ireland and of art. . . .

For the first time in his life, Sean felt a surge of hatred for Cathleen
ní Houlihan sweeping over him. He saw how that the one who had
the walk of a queen could be a bitch at times. She galled the hearts of
her children who dared to be above the ordinary, and she often slew
her best ones. She had hounded Parnell to death; she had yelled and
torn at Yeats, at Synge, and now she was doing the same to him. What
an old snarly gob she could be at times; an ignorant one too.[2]

The uproar was over the image O'Casey presented of the Easter
Rising in his play, *The Plough and the Stars*. Lacking the deadly
symbiosis of artist and society in America (perhaps because we
don't take art that seriously), we run the risk of oversimplifying
the issue, either by laughing at the Yahoos who could riot at a
play, or by giving the artist a hero's welcome in the society that
did not produce him. What we must keep in mind about the Irish
is not that they are unartistic, but that for them art is redundant;
their gaze is already locked in an imaginative vision of Ireland.
The artist who cannot stand to see his landscape reduced to the
size of a holy card must turn aside from this oppressive social
reality to create an imaginative vision of art. Precisely because the
Irishman's mode of apprehension is romantic and not materialistic
(though this is changing), he takes art seriously and objects to an
art that does not copy the little holy card in his head. The artist
has freedom of choice: he can copy and be praised or create and
be damned. For centuries a few harmless white lies had been all
that was left to the Irish in their extreme misery; now that they

[2] Sean O'Casey, *Autobiographies, II* (London, 1963), p. 149ff.

had come to power there was a danger that the art that had once assuaged the pain of reality would obscure the promise of it. There was a danger that the old white lies would become political myths used by an Irish upper class to keep the lower classes in line. O'Casey's was a voice out of the slums that spoke of the rebellion, not as a holy rising enkindled by Saint Pearse with a leaf from Irish legend, but as a class struggle lit by a page torn from the book of Marx. The rioters in the Abbey (that non-Catholic theater of Protestants Yeats, Lady Gregory, Synge, and now O'Casey) had a real quarrel with the new playwright, for O'Casey was no youngster beginning his career with a piece of sensationalism. O'Casey became known as a playwright in 1923, but before that he had written articles for *The Irish Worker* and a history of the Citizen Army in which he sided against that army's involvement in the cause of Irish nationalism. By 1926, the time of *The Plough and the Stars,* O'Casey was a middle-aged man with a long trail of scraps and quarrels behind him, and the play that quarreled with the popular heroic view of the Rising can perhaps best be seen in the light of the quarrels O'Casey had had with the ideological movement of Irish nationalism.

O'Casey's first major publication was his *Story of the Irish Citizen Army.*[3] O'Casey was in a good position to write the book, for he had served as Secretary to the council of the army; but the book was not intended to advance his position so much as it was intended to justify his side of the rift that had forced him to resign from the office. The Citizen Army had been founded to protect the workers from the assaults of the police during the lock-out of 1913; thus, at first, its position was defensive, but when the leader of the strike, James Larkin, left for America in 1914, the Secretaryship of the Irish Transport and General Workers' Union devolved on Connolly, and with each passing week Connolly's ambitions became more and more nationalistic. The Great War had destroyed his and other socialists' hopes for the international unity of the working classes. Watching the international proletariat break up

[3] P. O'Cathasaigh (Dublin and London, 1919).

into nationalities, Connolly became more and more hostile to the capitalistic colossus of the British Empire and decided to seize the opportunity of the war to strike England while she was distracted by Germany. When Connolly added his Citizen Army to the force of the radical Volunteers, O'Casey felt that the cause of socialism had been sold out, that the proletariat had thrown in its lot with the bourgeoisie.[4] O'Casey was no mere Marxist dogmatist incensed by an abstract violation of communist doctrine. The opposition between the Citizen Army and the Volunteers was a real one, for many who belonged to the prestigious Volunteers had been the bourgeois capitalists who had tried to starve the workers into sub-mission in the lock-out. Because the Volunteers were headed by an executive committee of respectable gentlemen like Sir Roger Case-ment, Professor Eoin MacNeill, and Colonel Maurice Moore, many of the aspiring members of the shabby genteel quit the vulgar union's army to ingratiate themselves with men of influence, thus hoping to gain better jobs for themselves through the social club of Irish patriotism. O'Casey was understandably livid. But when, in September 1914, the Volunteers split over Redmond's enlist-ment speech at Woodenbridge, the union of the radical wing of the Volunteers under MacNeill and Pearse and the Citizen Army under Connolly was made easier, for Pearse was more compassion-ately concerned with the problems of the Dublin workers than the Parliamentarians had ever been. O'Casey's quarrel, however, had arisen before this *rapprochement;* his argument was with that "sput-tering Catherine-wheel of irresponsibility," the Countess Markie-wicz. The Countess belonged to the Volunteers and the Citizen Army because both groups were Irish and revolutionary, and she was an Irish revolutionary. O'Casey felt that this serving of two masters was as absurd as being a capitalist and a communist at the same time. As secretary he moved that the Countess be asked to resign from one organization. This was an extremely embar-rassing motion to the union, for the Countess had manned the soup-kitchens during the lock-out, and it was her friend, Captain

4 Ibid. p. 55.

Jack White, who had started the Citizen Army with fifty pounds
of his own money. Larkin asked O'Casey to apologize, and since
apologies were never O'Casey's strong point, he resigned.

His resignation put him completely out in the cold. O'Casey had
always hated the bourgeois jingoism of Arthur Griffith, so he had
nothing to do with *Sinn Fein*. He couldn't stand A.E., so he
couldn't ingratiate himself with the literary lights that revolved
about the esteemed editor. He had disagreed with and criticized
the Irish Republican Brotherhood until he was asked to leave and
be quiet. He had scoffed at Connolly's idea that an English capitalist army would never use artillery on Irish private property,
and he had opposed Captain Jack White's introduction of uni-
forms for an army that O'Casey thought should be an invisible
guerrilla band. Unable to get along with any party, O'Casey played
no part in the Easter Rising. He was held a short time by the
British soldiers, then finally released. O'Casey could console himself by saying "I told you so" as his old comrades emerged from
the rubble of an artillery bombardment, but as they marched to
execution and imprisonment, it is doubtful that he exulted; more
than likely he felt some guilt in having survived.

The Easter Rising had pulled down a dark curtain of eternal separation
between him and his best friends; and the few that had remained alive
and delightful, now lay deep, with their convivial virtues, under the
smoking rubblement of the Civil War.[5]

Snubbed by members of the upper class, rejected by members of
his own working class, O'Casey had no choice but to give up his
attempt to gain power and influence in the world of politics and
action. Exactly the opposite of the poets Pearse, MacDonagh, and
Plunkett, O'Casey failed in the world of action and turned aside
to justify himself in the world of art.

He had shifted away from the active Ireland, and was growing con-
tentedly active in himself. Instead of trying to form Ireland's life, he
would shape his own.[6]

[5] Sean O'Casey, *Autobiographies, II*, p. 244.
[6] Ibid. p. 95.

Unfortunately for his life in Ireland, O'Casey used Ireland for material, and in his ungentle hands, Ireland became a most resisting medium. All those who had not participated in Easter Week (and, probably, those who had never taken Irish nationalism seriously) loudly praised those who had, and gave the returning warriors a hero's welcome upon their release at Christmas of 1916. When O'Casey, certainly no conspicuous patriot, took the Rising as material for a naturalistic play, he was only asking for trouble, and no doubt he knew it. It could only seem to the Catholic middle classes that the Abbey, already notorious for its apparent Protestant slander on peasant Catholic Ireland, was intentionally trying to bait them. Swearing allegiance to no one party, O'Casey stood outside the crowd and watched. The picture he saw infuriated saloon and salon alike, for the mob rioted, and "the new school" of Irish writers, F. R. Higgins, Liam O'Flaherty, and Austin Clarke, attacked the play in the columns of A.E.'s journal.[7]

The first scene of *The Plough and the Stars* is set neither in the General Post Office of history nor the humble thatched cottage of Irish dramatic tradition. It is set in a tenement, and from the beginning we sense a confinement, a closing-in in which life does not have quite enough room to behave in a proper manner. Mrs. Gogan is receiving someone else's package and opening it up for inspection and comment; Peter is wandering around in various stages of dress. Fluther is fixing a door, and when the Covey enters, an argument breaks out between them, while Peter curses in trying to fix his collar. O'Casey thus keeps up three independent lines of action within the single room, and this independence of simultaneous action contributes to a comic stylization of the characters' behavior. In the first act, O'Casey dwells upon the comic possibilities of slum life, upon the manner in which the socially expected thing is not quite possible in so cramped a space. For the moment, suffering is kept off stage.

But as soon as the audience has accepted the tenement for what

---

[7] See *The Irish Statesman*, V (February 20, 1926), 739-40; also March 6, 1926, 798.

it is, then the affectations of the characters appear, and the appearance increases the ridiculousness of their behavior. The Covey, who is modeled upon Shakespeare's Fluellen, has pretensions of intellectualism and quotes continually from his favorite book on the evolutionary idea of the proletariat. Peter, in his Forester's uniform, is the comedy natural to this Irish version of a Shriner; his aspirations are toward the middle class. Jack wants to cut a hussar-like figure in the uniform of the Citizen Army. When Jack's wife Nora enters, with her broken grammar and proud attention to refinements, the genteel scene is complete. Each of the characters is lost in a private dream of self-importance, but each lacks a definite, effective, relationship with his world. Since they are lower class, they lack power; since they lack power, they have atrophied wills; since they have atrophied wills, they dream themselves into the places where they matter. The vice is natural to the situation; the satirical bite of the comedy is, however, that the vice applies to the nation, and not merely its lower class.

The tenement now begins to take on an existence of its own, a prismatic one, for things that we know about, the history that is happening outside the window, take on a different color and quality as they pass through the windows and doors of the room in front of us. The characters talk about the great torchlight procession and parade around places sacred to Irish patriots' memory. It was this parade on Sunday, October 25, 1915 that effected the reconciliation between the working-class Citizen Army under Connolly and the middle-class radical Volunteers under Pearse. We are viewing a historical event through the windows of a tenement. We are also viewing the tenement's participant in that event, Jack Clitheroe, through the eyes of the less exalted members of the proletariat, Fluther and Mrs. Gogan. The technique is, of course, as old as Greek drama, but here the incommensurate relation between the on-stage world and the beyond-stage world is not because of a physical inadequacy of the stage to accommodate a large action; it is a suggestive use of dramatic space that is one of the central symbols in the play.

A quarrelsome scene has been set by the interlopers in the room of the Clitheroes, but when Jack and Nora finally come on stage, the quarrel is intensified and defined: Jack and Nora are suffering from a post-honeymoon disappointment. As Mrs. Gogan says: "after a month or two, th' wonder of a woman wears off." Fluther's opinion, on the man's side of things, is: "when a man finds th' wonder of one woman beginnin' to die, it's usually beginnin' to live in another." The other woman for Jack, however, is Cathleen ní Houlihan. Disappointed that marriage isn't everything, Jack longs for the glory of an officer's role in the Citizen Army. Nora, of course, wants no part of trouble. A real woman, and not a mythic one, she wants her man alive, not bleeding into a dirt made sacred because of its nationality. Unfortunately, Nora, the real woman, does not really confront the mythic Cathleen to fight for Life; she cries and whines, and is a tender frail thing who cannot understand a man's desire for glory. In short, Nora is a cliché taken untransformed from the melodramas upon which O'Casey's apprentice years were fed. Nevertheless, though the conflict between Nora and the daughter of Houlihan is not as fully realized as it could be, the opposition is no mere subterranean movement in the play. Jack is presented as a man losing interest in his young wife after only a few months of marriage; were he an ordinary Irishman of the working class, he would be slipping out to spend his nights in the pub while his wife was occupied with pregnancy. But Jack is no ordinary man; his gaze is directed beyond the pub to Liberty Hall. Jack does leave his home and his wife's side, but only because she deliberately failed to pass on the news that he had been made a commandant in the Citizen Army. Nora, in attempting to hold Jack, loses him. Disturbed by the problem of a woman of flesh and emotion, Jack leaves in anger and offers his services to the abstract woman of black. As the warrior leaves, the female characters take over the stage: little Mollser, the consumptive child who seeks company to protect her from a lonely death; Bessie Burgess, the Protestant whose son has enlisted in the English army and is fighting in the trenches; and Nora. The women are left, not yet to keen, but to keep a kind of deathwatch. The curtain for Act One comes down on this grim chorus of women.

At the end of the first act we have both a comedy based upon the traditional device of social affectation and a melodrama that threatens to become a tragedy. The comedy itself is one that creates instantaneous laughter, but the afterimage of the laugh is a formless and dark uneasiness. The comedy darkens as one abandons the necessary comic distance and approaches the characters for a closer look. Each of the characters suffers from some delusion or futile dream, and even the two men who are trying to assert their wills in a definite action do not really seem capable of changing their situation. O'Casey tells us that Jack has "a face in which is the desire for authority, without the power to attain it." And The Covey, the intellectual Marxist, is such a caricature that he cannot be taken seriously at all; his pretensions and his one book, Jenersky's *Thesis on th' Origin, Development, an' Consolidation, of th' Evolutionary Idea of th' Proletariat,* are mere farce. Interestingly enough (and most uncharacteristically for O'Casey, who in the *Autobiographies* sentimentalized himself and his opinions) all of O'Casey's personal opinions about Irish nationalism, communism, and the Citizen Army are placed in the mouth of The Covey. The Plough and the Stars, the flag of the Citizen Army, is a labor flag, and The Covey regards Connolly's nationalism as a sell-out of the proletariat. Though communist, The Covey's dream of power and glory differs little from the dreams of the others. Nora has dreams of respectability, but her actual efforts to achieve respectability and gentility only incur the scorn and resentment of Mrs. Gogan and Bessie Burgess, and her own husband is too busy with his dream to bother about respectability. Mrs. Gogan is a Catholic busybody, and Mrs. Burgess is a Protestant drunk. Though all the tenement-dwellers share a common Georgian home, they cannot agree upon a common dream. In fact, even beyond disagreement, all the characters fail in their relationships with one another. The failure of the marital relationship between Jack and Nora highlights the human failure of all the characters. In the first act we see nothing but bickerings and quarrels; the characters do not have enough room to move about in freedom and peace. However comic the first act may be, the image of Irish life that O'Casey presents, with all its futile dreams, broken wills, and alienation of the sexes, is not a pleasant one. Though not giving the audience cause to riot, he places them in the proper mood.

The curtain in Act One falls upon three sorrowful women, but the curtain for Act Two rises upon an entirely different kind of woman: Rosie Redmond, the prostitute. The scene has shifted from the tenement-hearth where the women live, to the pub where the men live. The night is not a profitable one for a prostitute, for the men are "all thinkin' of higher things than a girl's garters." The openness of Rosie's talk and the actual presentation of a prostitute upon a public stage was a piece of naturalism that was bound to offend an Irish audience, but the casual manner in which her existence is taken for granted would seem intentionally insulting. Rosie describes how hard it is for her to make a living, not because men are sinless, but because her landlord raises the rent when she brings a man home. This involvement of the middle classes in the vices of the working classes would not please a theater-going audience. The most maddening feature of this riot-inciting second act is that the whore's speech is followed by the words of Pearse, whose speech to the crowd outside can be heard within the pub. The juxtaposition of prostitute and patriot is unkind, and O'Casey does not weaken the force of his irony, for he chooses to use the most absurd, the most banally saber-rattling, the most ignorantly heroic speech in all of Pearse's four volumes. "... bloodshed is a cleansing and sanctifying thing," says the Catholic patriot, but what the rioters didn't realize was that O'Casey's three dots did a service to Pearse. What O'Casey neglects to quote are the preceding words: "We may make mistakes in the beginning and shoot the wrong people; but bloodshed is a cleansing and sanctifying thing, and the nation which regards it as the final horror has lost its manhood. There are many things more horrible than bloodshed; and slavery is one of them." [8] Lieutenant-Colonel Ferguson-Smith once gave similar counsel to the Royal Irish Constabulary in June 1920: "Sinn Fein has had all the sport up to the present, and we are going to have the sport now.... You may make mistakes occasionally and innocent persons may be shot, but that cannot be helped, and you are bound to get the right parties sometime." [9] A few days later the Colonel was shot dead while sipping his whiskey in his club in Cork, but his remarks made marvelous propaganda. The Collins-Childers organization made the most of it, thus winning Ireland's freedom by converting America, the English Church, the Labour Party, and King George V to the side of Ireland against Lloyd George's government. O'Casey could have attacked Pearse more fiercely, had he wished to do so, for it is obvious that the Irish patriots were trying to claim that the murder of innocents by Irishmen was an act of heroism, but the murder of innocents by the English was a world-shocking atrocity. But for once in his life, O'Casey had the prudence to restrain himself. The 'twenties in Ireland was a time of mutual assassination, not critical retrospection.

Pearse's speech is heartily endorsed by the prostitute; perhaps as a white slave to an economic system, Rosie agrees that slavery is worse than bloodshed, but Pearse would have been embarrassed to receive her endorsement. Again the juxtaposition of prostitution and patriotism is provoking, but simple juxtaposition is not O'Casey's only technique. Peter and Fluther come rushing into the pub, flushed with the excitement that Pearse's speech has inspired in them, and as the speech is repeated and handled by these comic characters, the sacred becomes profane and the speech contagiously becomes infected with the comedy of the absurd buffoons who have been lifted to such heights of enthusiasm. Here again the relation between the on-stage and off-stage actions allows a symbolic use of space. In the first act we felt confinement; society was seen from the inside of a tenement; now we observe the revolu-

[8] See Padraic Pearse, *Collected Works: Political Writings and Speeches,* p. 99.
[9] See Brigadier-General Crozier, *Ireland For Ever* (London, 1932), p. 286.

tion from the inside of a pub, and whatever ideological purity and sincerity are present in Pearse's thought cannot pass through the dark window of the pub. In the play we cannot see the noble face of Pearse; we can only perceive a disembodied voice, and we watch that voice take on, tragically but believably, the bodies of the characters before our eyes. The speech presented is not Pearse at his noblest, but Pearse in his very worst attempt at stirring oratory. Whatever ideals the man had cannot be exchanged with the listening mob; his language fails him. The mob hears what it wants to hear and goes about its business with new slogans to rationalize private desires. Necessarily, the revolution breaks away from the revolutionary. Fluther and Peter gulp their drinks and hurry out for the headier wine of patriotism.

Dropping the green thread of action, O'Casey now picks up the red. In rushes The Covey, who is sickened at the sight of the proletariat cheering on the bourgeoisie. The Covey's denouncements, however, do not add up to a serious alternative, for The Covey is as simple-minded a zealot as his nationalistic comrades. Rosie Redmond slides over to him and begins her solicitation, and here, perhaps, O'Casey is having a little fun. The whore's name suggests the rose of England and the leader of Ireland's pro-England Parliamentary party. At this moment of history, Redmond was busy trying to win recruits for England. Keating once described Ireland as the harlot of England, so perhaps one can infer a joke into the text: the English seduction of the Irish working classes. O'Casey makes fun of both sides, but he does not allow such abstractions to blur the comedy, for in the particular case of The Covey, the attempted seduction is futile. The Covey is so taken up by the doctrines of his system of thought that he can no longer perceive the reality of his situation: namely, that he is getting a come-all-ye from a whore. The Covey's response is to offer to lend Rosie his copy of Jenersky's thesis. Rosie has little left to do but throw off her shawl to expose the top of her bosom in open proclamation of her calling. Ironically, this Marxist is more a prude than an advocate of free love; the concrete is more than he can handle, so The Covey retreats back quickly into the abstract. The Covey waves a different banner and chants different slogans, but he does not add up to a free thinker or a free lover. Having achieved a minor resolution of one line of action, O'Casey sends The Covey hurrying off stage and returns to the green thread.

Peter and Fluther return to the pub, but this time they are accompanied by Mrs. Gogan. Mrs. Gogan has been visibly awed by the parade and the speeches, especially by the beautiful green uniform of the Irish Foresters, and her womanly comments return to the theme of sacrificial death for Ireland and Cathleen ní Houlihan.

> ... The lovliest part of the dress, I think, is th' osthriches plume. ... When yous are goin' along, an' I see them wavin' an' noddin' an' waggin', I seem to be lookin' at each of yous hangin' at th' and of a rope, your eyes bulgin' an' your legs twistin' an' jerkin', gaspin' an' gaspin' for breath while yous are thryin' to die for Ireland!

Here sacrifice for Ireland is seen to be comic because of a shift in point of view. From the human point of view, life is what counts, and living for Ireland is the supreme value. From the supra-human point of view, dying for Ireland is salvation, but the pretentious-ness of the appeal, this affectation of being beyond humanity, is as much a source of comedy as Fielding's peasant playing the lord. Fluther, as well as Mrs. Gogan, is willing to puncture the Forester's bladder of hot air, for he comments that he doubts patriotism would be the actual crime for which a Forester would be hanged. The bickering begins again. O'Casey's skill in this act is singularly fine, for he handles his dramatic action with considerable energy and variation by quickly introducing a vigorous action, arresting it, then introducing another line of action. No sooner are Fluther and Peter at it again, than in walk Mrs. Burgess and The Covey, and Peter and Fluther's quarrel subsides while Mrs. Burgess and Mrs. Gogan have a go at it. The women, however, are a little more fierce. Bessie Burgess accuses the Catholics of bad faith since the Irish Catholics have not enlisted in the war that is to help poor

little Belgium. A row is on, but before the fight can progress, the
figure of Pearse reappears in the window, and, appropriately, he
is speaking of the current war in Europe with all its magnificent
spilling of blood: "When the war comes to Ireland she must welcome it as she would welcome the Angel of God." As Pearse dis-
appears, the women resume their fight. The sight of two old hags
brawling with one another about their virtue—and this after the
lofty words of Pearse—is a fierce image, an image, perhaps, of
Civil-War Ireland when many thought that the Treaty was the
fate worse than death. Bessie and Mrs. Gogan almost come to
blows, but the barman throws them out. New combatants quickly
fill the vacuum, and The Covey begins arguing with Rosie and
Fluther. Fluther, in his inimitable grand manner, now plays the
rescuing knight to Rosie's damsel in distress. Again a fight threatens, but again the barman intervenes to throw The Covey out.
In the ensuing peace and quiet, Fluther effects his pick-up of Rosie,
and as he leads the whore off-stage, the Irish Tri-Color comes on.

And that was it. The sight of exit-whore, enter-flag, and flag
in a pub at that, was too much. With a good deal more provoca-
tion than they had had with *The Playboy,* the Irish began to rip
the seats from the floor.

After the police had thrown out the more vigorous protesters,
the play continued. Fluther and Rosie move out of sight and into
the snug to exchange words, and the soldiers come on stage to
recite the litany of the patriot.

LIEUT. LANGOON: Th' time is rotten ripe for revolution.

CLITHEROE: You have a mother, Langoon.

LIEUT. LANGOON: Ireland is greater than a mother.

CAPT. BRENNAN: You have a wife, Clitheroe.

CLITHEROE: Ireland is greater than a wife.

The figure of Pearse returns to the window, and in a final burst
of exultation, the men conclude their litany.

CAPT. BRENNAN: [*Catching up The Plough and the Stars.*] Imprisonment for th' Independence of Ireland!

LIEUT. LANGOON: [*Catching up the Tri-Colour.*] Wounds for th' Independence of Ireland!

CLITHEROE: Death for th' Independence of Ireland!

THE THREE: [*Together*] So help us God!

As the soldiers hurry off stage summoned by a bugle call, Fluther and Rosie come out of the snug on their way to Rosie's.

O'Casey's irony is ferocious, but, artistically, it is an irony that works by suggestive juxtapositions, and the manner in which these juxtapositions are placed in a context of comedy darkens the comedy in an almost expressionistic manner. The caricatured faces of the traditional stage-Irishmen become grotesque in the act's total configuration of meaning. The slapstick, burly, blustering, stage-Irishmen undergo a sea-change in the depths of our thoughts; their smiles become leers, and their seemingly innocuous patter becomes threatening. As tragicomedy Act Two is a masterpiece, and its greatness as a one-act play is not helped by its association with the melodramatic triteness of the other acts. Only an absolute master and genius knows when to stop, knows just how much is needed and has the courage to present a great one-act tragicomedy rather than a marred four-act tragedy with epic pretensions. Act Two stands by itself; its climax and resolution of action do not depend on the other acts; its allusions do not require the first act. It is a shame O'Casey felt it necessary to go on, but the fault is shared, for the common prejudice is that a one-act play is not "a major work." O'Casey went on to attempt a major work, a "Tragedy in Four Acts."

In Act Three the thematic use of dramatic space is less exciting than in Act Two, for in order to place an insurrection on stage, O'Casey had little choice but to use the traditional horizontal flow across the stage. As in Roman drama, the action takes place in a public street just outside a great house, but here, significantly, the great house, an old Georgian mansion, is a tenement with not a single pane of glass remaining in the once elegant tracery of the fanlight. Against this background of the past (and, one infers, of a past social order) gone to ruin, the slum dwellers come and go as the insurrection blazes and thunders off stage. The time of crisis has come, and, of course, in drama, crisis is the moment which reveals character entirely.

The time of crisis does not inspire any heroism for Ireland, but it does inspire the heroic behavior of one human being for another human being. Fluther, having played the clown, now plays the man. Nora has foolishly gone out to wrest her man from the clutches of the daughter of Houlihan, and it is Fluther who goes out to save her from death in the streets. And even Peter and The Covey have become friends in the frightening situation. But O'Casey is not moving toward any affirmation of Irish heroism, for the poor do not rally round the green flag but pour out of the slums to loot and pillage while the police and the army are distracted by the rebels. To the naturalistic imagery of prostitutes and brawling hags, O'Casey now adds the looters, and those who do not steal but stay home do so out of cowardice, not morality. O'Casey is remorselessly true to fact, but he is not a bleak naturalist, for having reached a nadir and sounded a bottom to humanity, he begins to reascend. O'Casey's ascent, however, is on his own terms: for him only the breath of life is worth carrying up; all the heavy abstractions of God and country are cut from the body and left to sink. The ascent involves a growth of character: Fluther attempts to become the hero he has always taken himself to be, and Nora, more unhappily, is pushed toward womanhood by the force of her suffering. Nora attempts to meet her crisis; she goes out to do battle with the mythic woman of black, but, unfortunately, Nora is armed with little more than tears and imploring tugs at the sleeve. Taunted by the slum women who have no husbands out in the Rising, Nora learns the futile emptiness of the abstractions and slogans with which Jack and his men have been distracted.

NORA: [*wearily*] I could find him nowhere, Mrs. Gogan. None o' them would tell me where he was. They told me I shamed my husband an' th' women of Ireland be carryin' on as I was. . . . They said th' women must learn to be brave an' cease to be cowardly. . . . Me who risked more for love than they would risk for hate. . . . [*Raising her voice in hysterical protest.*] My Jack will be killed, my Jack will be killed! He is to be butchered as a sacrifice to th' dead.

Unfortunately, little that Nora has accomplished on stage convinces us that she has risked more for love than the others have for hate. She has risked death to find Jack, but the gesture is a futile one of guilt and frustration; she is not saving Jack, she is imitating him. O'Casey is trying to lift Nora's laments into the realm of tragedy, but Nora is incapable of understanding her situation, and therefore she is incapable, as a dramatic figure, of generalizing her situation into anything resembling a tragic predicament. First Nora tries to assuage her pain with the thought that wherever Jack is he thinking of her and her body, forgetting entirely that it was disappointment with that body and the female emotional nature which inhabited it that drove Jack into the army in the first place. Nora, with instinctive awareness, associates sex with violence, but as a person of ordinary mind, she is incapable of resolving her suffering through intelligence. Her personal cry of suffering cannot echo with the anguished cry of mankind, and since she cannot lift her predicament into the dimension of tragedy, it falls into pathos. It is difficult to make a tragic heroine out of a pretty girl, and many respectable dramatists before O'Casey have encountered the same difficulty. The Ophelias, Cordelias, and Desdemonas are always the *means* of bringing suffering to others, but the tragedy takes place in Hamlet, Lear, and Othello. It is only when woman exults in destruction, when the womb of life becomes the organ of death, that we have the inversion of natural order that creates the terror necessary for tragedy. Medea, Clytemnestra, Lady Macbeth: these are tragic heroines, but poor Nora is

only an object of pity. Nora has her moment of insight; she sees
that all the men are afraid, that they are out, not because they are
brave, but because they are cowards who wish to prove themselves
brave in the eyes of others. Mrs. Gogan denies Nora's insight, and
thinks that the men are brave, but this sort of denial opens the
way to comedy, and, perhaps, the horrors of comedy are most
suited to O'Casey's view. Unfortunately, failing to achieve the
terror necessary for tragedy or the grotesque ironies necessary for
tragicomedy, O'Casey relies upon Boucicault melodrama.

Nora is led off stage in one direction; the looters go out in the
other direction. It only remains for Jack and Nora to confront one
another, and the confrontation is a predictable one. The Rising
fails; Jack, in retreat, stops momentarily at the tenement. Nora
pleads and pulls at Jack; Jack casts her to the floor. Nora sobs. The
scene is only too complete when we learn, at the curtain of Act
Three, that Nora was with child when her husband cast her to
the floor.

In the final act the three women of sorrow from Act One return
to the stage: little Mollser has died, in the midst of the gunfire,
from the consumption she feared, and Nora's baby has died under
the broken heart of her mother. The only energy remaining in the
play is that created by the reversal in character of Bessie Burgess,
a reversal that began at the end of Act Three when Bessie went
out to find a doctor in the midst of the bullets. O'Casey's indictment of the Rising is seen clearly in his creation of pro-British
Bessie as heroine, but, artistically, this inversion of villain into
heroine in a time of suffering is a revelation of humanity and compassion, and it is this humanity that becomes the central value of
the play. It is not Bessie's fight; therefore, her compassion is all
the more genuine. She cares for Nora more than her Irish husband
did. From her fellow Irishmen, Nora only receives more suffering.
Captain Brennan, once an old suitor, returns to tell Nora how
heroically her husband died. Bessie receives the news first, and
Bessie has nothing but contempt for the abstractions of the patriot.

BESSIE: [*with partly repressed vehemence*] Ay, you left him! You twined his Rosary beads round his fingers, an' then you run like a hare to get out o' danger.

CAPT. BRENNAN: I took me chance as well as him... He took it like a man. His last whisper was to "Tell Nora to be brave; that I'm ready to meet my God, an' that I'm proud to die for Ireland." An' when our General heard it he said that "Commandant Clitheroe's end was a gleam of glory." Mrs. Clitheroe's grief will be a joy when she realizes that she had a hero for a husband.

Such dry hot air is in need of a little spit, and although Bessie is quite up to punctuating Brennan's remarks in that manner, O'Casey prefers to pull out other stops with Nora.

[*Nora appears at door, Left. She is clad only in her nightdress; her hair, uncared for some days, is hanging in disorder over her shoulders. Her pale face looks paler still because of a vivid red spot on the tip of each cheek. Her eyes are glimmering with the light of incipient insanity; her hands are nervously fiddling with her nightgown.*]

It has been seen a hundred times before; the melodrama is nearing its end. Of the three women of Act One, only Bessie remains. Mrs. Gogan appears for the funeral of her little Mollser and tries to console Nora by telling her that if she had only been married a little longer, the death of her husband wouldn't bother her so much. The manner in which O'Casey portrays the alienation of the sexes in Catholic family life is, without a doubt, an indication of his religious bias; it is also a dominant theme in the play and it achieves its final realization in Mrs. Gogan's consoling remarks. Bessie feels sorry for Mrs. Gogan because she has lost a daughter, but Fluther, more Irish than Mrs. Burgess, is quick to rid her of that delusion.

BESSIE: Oh th' poor woman, o' course. God help her, it's a terrible blow to her.

FLUTHER: A terrible blow? Sure, she's in her element now, woman, mixin' earth to earth, an' ashes t' ashes an' dust to dust, an' revellin' in plumes an' hearses, last days an' judgements.

O'Casey's enraged indictment of the Irish cult of death in the
Autobiographies is well known, but one is in no danger of reading the play in terms of his other work, for the indictment could
not be plainer within the text: the funeral is the central celebration of Irish life.

The drama now moves to its close, and O'Casey resolves his
work with some skill. The symbolic use of space continues to the
end, and in a return to the confinement of the first act, O'Casey
crams all the characters into one room, and to intensify the pressure, the conquering soldiers enter to escort the coffin of little
Mollser out into the bullet-filled streets. There is no room to live
in the tenement; finally, the soldiers come in to evacuate it. At
the close of the play the tension of space is relaxed, and there is
room to take a few last breaths; but the momentary quiet exists
only to highlight and silhouette the death of Bessie. Nora in her
distraction runs to the window while the soldiers are busy trying
to root out whatever snipers remain in the block. Bessie pulls her
out of danger, and is shot herself. Her Christian act kills her.
Bessie's end, however, is no act of forgiveness, for she screams out
in full, human anger at the indignity of death.

> ... [to Nora] I've got this through ... through you, you bitch, you! O
> God, have mercy on me! [to Nora] You wouldn't stop quiet, no, you
> wouldn't, blast you!

Bessie's humanity is seen in her crudity and vulgarity; compassionate as she is, she is no embodiment of abstract goodness. A drunk-
ard and a foul-mouthed brawler, she is a celebration of basic
humanity, without pretension, without abstract virtues, without
lies. Bessie struggles to die with faith, but O'Casey breaks the
hymn upon her dying words; it is almost as if she were trying to
remember something but can't because it is so distant and irrelevant to her situation. Bessie dies, and Nora whimpers in the
corner. The inversion is complete; the sweet heroine of genteel
pretensions has become a useless object; the brawling, porter-
swilling hag has become, in death, a proletarian redeemer. As in

the case of another Marxist playwright, Brecht and his *Mother Courage,* the celebration of humanity takes place at the bottom, not the top.

It is curious, however, that even in his Marxism O'Casey requires a class system for symbolic purposes as much as Yeats does. Jack, though a proletarian, is just a little more refined and intelligent than the others; as a proletarian-hero, he is a hero by virtue of his middle-class characteristics. Appropriately enough for the tragic perspective in which a man's virtues are intimately related to, if not identical with, his tragic flaw, Jack is also a failure because of these middle-class characteristics. He does not sell out the revolution in favor of middle-class respectability, but he does march off to war for the baubles of a commandant's uniform. Nora is like Jack; she is more refined and considerate than the others, but she too fails because of her middle-class tendencies. Bessie has the proletarian value of energy; Nora values elegance, or at least as much elegance as her station in life permits. Energy and elegance are antithetical values, and O'Casey's work, in fact his whole career, was a celebration of energy and a scathing condemnation of elegance. Yet it is not creative, dynamic humanity that O'Casey praises but enduring, suffering humanity: its representatives include Juno in his best play, Bessie in *The Plough and the Stars,* and his own mother in the *Autobiographies.* The irony is that the suffering woman he presents is but one image of the Catholic archetype, Mary, Mother of us all. O'Casey's compassion is not for the soldiers who go out to fight for an illusion, but for the civilians who suffer because of these dreams of transcendental glory. The praise of the passive is the best defense the *status quo* could ask for, and, indeed, it is one traditionally used by the *status quo* to maintain itself. O'Casey is no conservative, to be sure; he is willing to fight, but only for his own cause. If the soldiers were going out to fight for the dictatorship of the proletariat, one wonders how O'Casey would celebrate the abstractions that cheered them on and the women who pleaded with them to suffer capitalism with dignity and resignation. Bessie becomes a heroine because she dies well, but so did the Christian martyrs, and so did the men of 1916, and O'Casey has, in the play, led us to believe that it is not enough to die well, that it is living which matters. No one is really left living at the end of the play. The English soldiers sing the war-song "Keep the home fires burning"; for a nostalgic Englishman it might bring tears, but for the Irish it is sung while their homes are burning. General Connolly accused the capitalists of using cheap myths to lead working men to death in the trenches of Flanders, but Connolly himself invokes the same deadly myth in calling Jack's end "a gleam of glory." No one wins; the play ends in a vision of futility. Perhaps if O'Casey had been able to cut away the heavy abstractions of pity and sentimentality, as he cut away the cheap lies that deluded his characters, the play might have risen over its ashes into tragedy.

Yeats claimed that pity was not a fit subject for art,[10] and it is precisely pity and sentimentality that clog up O'Casey's celebration of humanity. Perhaps tragedy is not a Marxist genre. Marxism has its anti-metaphysical attitude built into its system; evil is no universal force, no work of devil, original sin, or id; it is a malfunction of social structure. Denied the metaphysical, evil receives a local habitation and a name, not "chaos and old night," but the boss, not of the cosmos but of the sweatshop. Political conflict, seen by itself, is never as exciting as man's war against his divided self, his predicament, or his God, for these can generate the existential terror that is needed for tragedy. Political works of art, in their simplified psychology, fail to grasp complexity, and slip into the sentimentality of the working-class O'Casey or the clever topicality of the upper-class Auden of the 'thirties. Yeats quarreled with O'Casey's leveling philosophy,[11] as he quarreled with the socially urgent verse of the 'thirties. But perhaps one cannot be an artist of words and an artist of the state. The true Marxist

[10] See Yeats's Introduction to his *Oxford Book of Modern Verse* (Oxford, 1936), p. xxxivf.
[11] For the dialogue of Yeats and O'Casey, see Sean O'Casey, *Autobiographies*, *II*, p. 344.

artist is not a tragedian, but a builder of other wonders. As Trotsky said:

> Tragedy based on detached personal passions is too flat for our days. Why? Because we live in a period of social passions. The tragedy of our period lies in the conflict between the individual and the collectivity, or in the conflict between two hostile collectivities in the same individual. Our age is an age of great aims. This is what stamps it. But the grandeur of these aims lies in man's effort to free himself from mystic and from every other intellectual vagueness and in his effort to reconstruct society and himself in accord with his own plan. . . .

> Through the machine, man in Socialist society will command nature in its entirety, with its grouse and its sturgeons. He will point out places for mountains and passes. He will change the course of the rivers, and he will lay down rules for the oceans.[12]

O'Casey's *artistic* success with *The Plough and the Stars* comes at moments when he sees, beyond reform, into the comedy that underlies Marxist millenarian pretensions. In this comic view of human activity, communist O'Casey moves closer to so-called fascist Yeats. In choosing to make comedy out of his own political opinions by putting them into the mouth of The Covey, O'Casey reveals the dispassionate, aesthetic intellect of the true artist. Unfortunately, this was a level of genius that he could not sustain throughout his life. In the later plays dispassionate rage at man's existence is exchanged for impassioned ranting at caricatured ideas and institutions. In his best plays O'Casey made his opinions into fuel for his art; in the others he made art into fuel for his opinions. It was this change that brought about the famous clash between Yeats and O'Casey over the Abbey's rejection of *The Silver Tassie*.

> You are not interested in the Great War; you never stood on its battlefields, never walked its hospitals, and so write out of your opinions. You illustrate those opinions by a series of almost unrelated scenes, as you might in a leading article. . . . Dramatic action is a fire that must burn up everything but itself. . . .

> Among the things that dramatic action must burn up are the author's opinions. Do you suppose for one moment that Shakespeare educated

12 Leon Trotsky, *Literature and Revolution* (Ann Arbor, 1960), pp. 243, 252.

Hamlet and Lear by telling them what he thought and believed? As
I see it, Hamlet and Lear educated Shakespeare, and I have no doubt
that in the process of that education he found out that he was altogether a different man to what he thought himself, and had altogether
different beliefs.[13]

Yeats's criticism was brilliant (although his *action* in rejecting the
play was not); unfortunately, O'Casey's reaction to Yeats's ideas
only revealed the difference in intellect that separated the two men.

D'ye tell me that, now, Mr. Yeats? Well, I don't know; but one thing's
certain, and that is if Shakespeare became a more educated man while
writing *Hamlet,* then, it wasn't Hamlet who educated him, but Shakespeare who educated himself. But what proof—beyond an opinion—has
Yeats that what he says was so? [14]

The conflict between O'Casey and Yeats was probably inevitable,
for O'Casey had quarreled with everyone and everything all his
life. It was inevitable that a sensitive, lower-class playwright would
quarrel with the Establishment of Irish Art, for by 1928 Senator
Yeats, like Plato before him, had become as much an institution
as a man.

The real conflict between the two artists was the conflict between two wholly opposed world views. The opposition of the
tragic poet and the comic playwright was neither simply aesthetic
nor simply political; it was the clash between the Platonist and
the Marxist views of the nature of man, his society, and the universe. This clash was so pre-eminently the essential and irreconcilable conflict of human existence that neither Yeats nor O'Casey
could fight it out without profound respect for the other side. Only
the simple-minded partisans who push opinions in the street could
claim that one view was wrong while the other was right. History
is the place of encounter for these conflicting opposites; a mystic
like A.E. moves beyond history to some divine event, but Yeats
and O'Casey were men of civilization. The Marxist myth denies
inherent superiority, whether intellectual or spiritual; the Platonic

---

13 *Letters of W. B. Yeats,* ed. Allan Wade (London, 1954), p. 741.
14 Sean O'Casey, *Autobiographies, II,* p. 275.

myth claims that political power can be held under the aspect of eternity. The Church tried that experiment and failed, but the failure made a difference, and the difference is history. Now the State will try to do what Christendom could not. No doubt it too will fail, and once again the failure will probably make a difference, but that is not yet history.

CONCLUSION

IMAGINATION AND HISTORY

The first literary critic praised poetry above history because he thought poetry presented the universal truth of events and not merely the particular correctness of facts. Historians since Aristotle's time have avenged themselves on poets, and in our modern disenchantment with the visions and mythologies that led millions to die on the sacrificial altar of historicism, [1] few now would wish to exchange the discipline of historians for the divine madness of poets. And yet the Second World War which killed those millions in a burst of the irrational has made all merely academic schemes of history seem inadequate. The irrational, like a beast, seems to pursue us as soon as we turn and run, and if there seems to be little hope in taming the beast, perhaps we can at least come to terms with it. Poets have had long experience in coming to terms with the irrational, so there seems to be little reason in separating

[1] Karl R. Popper, *The Poverty of Historicism* (London, 1961). The dedication reads: "In memory of the countless men and women of all creeds or nations or races who fell victims to the fascist and communist belief in Inexorable Laws of Historical Destiny."

them from the study of history. If we wish to awaken from what Joyce called the nightmare of history, we shall have to stand still long enough to admit into our consciousness what would otherwise plague us in our dreams. We shall have to listen to those solitary inhabitants of the dark who have the visions and write the poems, if only for the very practical reason given by the economist Keynes: "The political fanatic who is hearing voices in the air has distilled his frenzy from the work of some academic scribbler of a few years back." [2] If we stand still long enough perhaps we shall see that the irrational is not only a beast, and that other legendary figures inhabit the obscure depths of imagination where no sociology is likely to reach. The individual alone in his study, or even transported in his vision, is not out of history, for history is the imagery of his vision as language is the expression of his thought. Imagination and history are separate and opposed only in the simple sociology that regards facts and values, social structure and ideology, as repetitive examples of objective truth and subjective falsehood. All facts, even scientific propositions, are immersed in values, but unfortunately we do not generally notice this until the elevated fact is dripping with blood. For the most part we have attempted to solve the old opposition between poetry and history through an academic administration which removes the study of history from the humanities. By permitting a managerial class to decide upon the real structure of human knowledge, the intellectuals have made it even more difficult to perceive reality. Our studies are too often forced to reflect little more than the structure of human experience *within* the university. Unfortunately, this fragmentation of knowledge cannot be helped, for, this side of divine illumination, there is simply no way to study "the whole of things" without a careful analysis of some distinct pieces. We can only hope that imagination will connect the dots, and that we will be able to see the integrity of the curve without spending a lifetime inking in a thousand points.

[2] As quoted in J. R. Talmon, *Political Messianism: Romantic Phase* (New York, 1960), p. 256.

If we are to create, beyond sociology, an anthropology that is truly a study of man, we shall have to begin with the awareness that the syncretic and reciprocal form of causality one encounters in the cultural process is far more complicated than the causality expressed in the mechanical models the social scientist still admires. To escape this complexity by proposing that what cannot be studied with a rigorous empiricism is not a fit subject of study at all, or by proposing that values can be regarded as secondary emotional reactions to more primary social structural functions, is simply to give up the search for knowledge in favor of university departmental "behavior routinized along highly specific professional norms." The American behavioral scientist makes an attractive whipping boy, but the humanist errs as often as the social scientist. To say, for example, with Senator Gogarty that "If it had not been for W. B. Yeats there would be no Irish Free State" is to concentrate, for rhetorical purposes, on one term in a causal set that had been overlooked by the other senator who questioned the nomination of a poet to a political office. The protesting senator was thinking, no doubt, of the creation of the Irish Free State in terms of the lock-out of 1913, Carson's gun-running, the Great War, etc., and was overlooking the literary movement which had intensified the nationalistic consciousness of a generation of Irishmen. *Cathleen ní Houlihan* did send out certain men to be shot, but many things had placed them in a frame of mind to be sent out, and these were the very things that had placed Yeats in a frame of mind to write the play. In the causality of the cultural process, A does not simply cause B: A affects B; B reaffects A; AB conditions the emergence of C, and before C is fully appeared, D is already coming forth with an effect that will entirely transform the completed ABCD. And even in such a grossly oversimplified four-term sequence, the greatest oversimplification is A, for the *alpha* that interests us may be the *omega* of a sequence that is absolutely necessary to the understanding of A. The statue of Cuchulain in the Post Office leads back to Macpherson, but if we were to continue the study, we would no doubt end up in the bosom of Abraham. The historian is thus forced to select, but since everything is related, he must be able to select the relevant from the relatedness of all things. In short, the historian must already possess the knowledge he is seeking to acquire. To understand history, one must stand outside history, not just to avoid bias, but to be able to perceive distinctness and relation. This separation of subject and object was a difficulty in classical theories of perception, but in modern philosophy, Whitehead's theory of *prehensions* would admit "the witness of the body" and permit us to think that, if we cannot stand outside history, we can at least comprehend it through the relevance of ourselves. Causal sets, syncretic and reciprocal causal relationships, will continue to be a problem until the physicist finds the mathematics to solve the many-body problem, but until such a time there is no need to think that history is worthless to the degree that it is not mathematically expressed. To pass over the merely social scientist, one can invoke the natural scientist, Werner Heisenberg:

In atomic physics the observations can no longer be objectified in such a simple manner; that is, they cannot be referred to something that takes place objectively or in a describable manner in space and time. Here it remains still to be added that the science of nature does not deal with nature itself but in fact with the *science* of nature as man thinks and describes it.

This does not introduce an element of subjectivity into natural science. We do not by any means pretend that occurrences in the universe depend on our observations, but we point out that natural science stands between nature and man and that we cannot renounce the use of man's intuition or innate conceptions.[5]

If intuition can be granted a place in natural science, imagination can be granted a place in the study of history. But really, whether we like it or not, there is no way to avoid imagination in the study of history: it takes imagination to frame a great question, but the syntax of that question structures the answer we will

5 Werner Heisenberg, "Planck's Discovery and the Philosophical Problems of Atomic Physics," *On Modern Physics* (New York, 1962), p. 20.

get even before we have begun the research. History is, in fact, a process by which a private imagination becomes a public event, but any study that restricted itself to public events would have to ignore the fact that history is also the process by which public events become private imaginations. It is unfair, of course, to expect the historian to do everything, when what he does is, most often, done well; consequently, the study of the transformation of public events into private imaginations has been left to art-historians and critics. But we must remember that this separation into two tasks is an administrative division, not an intellectual one. Easter 1916 is a public event which became a private imagination in the art of A.E., Yeats, and O'Casey. But to regard the historic event as the *known* with which we solve for the unknown of the work of art is to misunderstand history and art by distorting the relationship between them. The event of Easter 1916 is itself a work of imagination, and to understand the event we must take into account the manner in which private imaginations, like the writings of O'Grady, became part of the process of the public event.

A perception of a work of art involves experiencing the meaning of its aesthetic form, and not merely identifying the local allusions within the work. It is this aesthetic perception which will be significant when turned toward the event. It is not enough for the study of history to think of Yeats as a public man of affairs; that private part of the individual that we call the self is in many ways as relevant as the man who pays bills and signs documents. The self is the individual as a consciousness. Culture is a society as a consciousness. And the self is the theater of the cultural drama. The historian must therefore pay as much attention to Yeats's poetry as to his Senate speeches, for the psychological crisis of the self expresses the ideological crisis of the culture, or of the age at large. The individual works through culture to gain self-consciousness, but society also labors to become conscious of itself, and in this cultural labor, the individual as a fully realized self is one of its most important means: Ireland ignorant of Yeats is Ireland ignorant of Ireland. The self is individual, but it is not discrete;

what Whitehead said of "matter-of-fact entities" is true of persons, for the self

> ... is limited, obstructive, intolerant, infecting its environment with its own aspects. But it is not self-sufficient. The aspects of all things enter into its very nature. It is only itself as drawing together into its own limitation the larger whole in which it finds itself.[6]

G. H. Mead said that the consciousness of self arises from language, and that "it is the social process itself that is responsible for the appearance of the self."[7] Mead's point will serve as an analogy for the relation of art to society. As language is responsible for the growth of a consciousness of self by articulating the diffuse thought of the child,[8] art is responsible for the growth of society's consciousness of itself. As the self labors to find its proper relation to the other, to find its role, so society, in the creation of its own unique myth, labors to find its proper relation to the impinging force of other cultures. Overshadowed by imperial England, Ireland elaborated the Cuchulain myth; overshadowed by cosmopolitan France, Germany elaborated the Siegfried myth. An art of this mythic nature takes on the appearance of a religion, and in fact can become the surrogate of a religion. A religion like Christianity is not culturally endemic; it is catholic and international, and relates the individual to humanity, the soul to God. The messianic art of O'Grady, A.E., and Yeats, however, related Ireland in the fullness of a contemporary moment to destiny; it related the society in all its particularity to history in all its universality. Holy Mother Church could summon all children to her bosom, but only the messianic art of the Literary Revival could call out the name of Ireland for all the nations to hear in the reception line of time.

In the messianic idea of destiny, the underprivileged become transformed into the elect, and are filled with the consciousness

---

6 A. N. Whitehead, *Science and the Modern World* (New York, 1948), p. 96.
7 *The Social Psychology of G. H. Mead*, ed. A. Strauss (Chicago, 1952), p. 219.
8 I have in mind here the developmental theories of Jean Piaget and Heinz Werner.

that they alone have been chosen for some inscrutable end. In this inversion of values, the temples of Gizeh become as nothing when compared with the tents of the humble tribe; the libraries of Oxford and Cambridge as nothing when compared with the tales of the Gaeltacht peasant. Because an international religion is not endemic, the general atavism that rejects civilization tends to reject the religion of civilization; in the return to the primitive community, there is a return to the primitive religion. In Ireland's case this atavism did not involve, for the masses, a rejection of Christianity, but of Protestantism, for Catholicism was not the religion of the conqueror, but was instead its ancient opponent. The romantic atavism of Yeats and A.E., however, did involve a return to the pagan religion, and even Pearse who tried so desperately to reconcile Irish paganism and Catholicism, did so by praising the primitive shedding of blood in the language he had learned from Catholic martyrology. This close association of art and religion in the articulation of culture comes from the fact that art, in the primitive community, is not differentiated strongly from religious ritual; in many cases the two are one. Religion can create cultural consciousness, and in most messianic movements it is indeed a religion that carries the new myth. But if the movement is an artistic one, as in Ireland, or a political one, as in Nazi Germany, then one of its distinguishing features is its concern with experiences that are usually thought to be in the province of religion. Whether the movement is religious or artistic, its atavism distinguishes it as the movement now known as "nativistic." [9]

On the simplest level the nativistic movement seems to express the commonplace psychology of the underdog combined with the all too human desire to return to a simpler past. In sociological terms, the nativistic movement expresses the desire to exchange *Gesellschaft* (society) for *Gemeinschaft* (community). In times of crisis, when cultural identity seems to be on the verge of extinc-

[9] See Vittorio Lanternari, *The Religions of the Oppressed: A Study of Modern Messianic Cults* (New York, 1963); see also Anthony F. C. Wallace, "Revitalization Movements," *American Anthropologist*, LVIII (April 1956), 264-81.

tion, the desperate religion seems to explode. Toynbee has noticed
this phenomenon in the Hellenic age.

Undoubtedly both the Eleusinian Mysteries and the Orphic Church
did provide the Hellenic Society in the Classical Age with a spiritual
sustenance which it needed but could not find in the worship of the
Olympians, an other-worldly spirit such as we should expect to find in
a time of troubles, a spirit which we recognize as characteristic of the
universal churches created by internal proletariats in their decline.[10]

Whether it is the case of the Jews rejecting the Egyptian Empire,
the Irish rejecting the British Empire, the Black Muslims rejecting
America, or, as was evidenced at the United Nations General
Assembly debates on the Congo airlifts, the Africans rejecting the
entire civilization of the West, the pattern is similar. In the face
of overwhelming material evidence of the superiority of one culture over another, the inferior culture elaborates a new myth in
which it claims to possess the secret to a more holy, more moral,
or more beautiful way of life. And most often in the case of this
encounter of two cultures, the nativistic movement is led by a man
who has learned the ways of the overlords. The leader of the nativistic movement is a man who in himself is torn apart by the conflicting value-systems of Empire and Community. Pearse's father
was an Englishman, and Patrick Henry Pearse was not a cutter of
turf from Oughterard, but a barrister from Dublin. If the dominant civilization has reached that level of complexity where a sufficiently large number of its members are not caught up in the work
of Empire, then there appear the disaffected thinkers and the
symptom of revolution that Professor Brinton has called "the deser-
tion of the intellectuals." [11] Moses, the elegant man of Pharaoh's
court, leads the slaves out of bondage; the Marquis de Lafayette
becomes the champion of the Third Estate; Mahatma Gandhi, the
Oxford dandy, returns to the untouchables of India. And the list
could go on, including Sir Roger Casement, Lawrence of Arabia,

10 Arnold J. Toynbee, *A Study of History*, Somervell abridgement, Vol. I. (New
York, 1946), p. 26.
11 Crane Brinton, *The Anatomy of Revolution* (New York, 1952), p. 113.

and a whole generation of upper-middle-class Ivy-League under-
graduates of the Civil Rights Movement who have marched into
martyrdom in the tradition of the men of 1916. In each case the
leader is a solitary man seeking personal salvation in a public
event, seeking to overcome the crisis within himself that he sees
mirrored in the situation of history. The togetherness of the public event overcomes his alienation; the camaraderie of the revolutionary church provides a human community that did not exist
in the collective. The new ideology provides a system of values
that enables the individual to achieve a unity of being through the
medium of the newly created integral culture of the folk community. The explosive power of revolution comes from this encounter
of the intellectual trying to save his soul with the common man
trying to get even as well as equal. This revolutionary encounter
of the equivalents of Don Quixote and Sancho Panza creates a
situation in which each hopes to gain from the other what he lacks
in himself. The intellectual wants humanity; humanity wants intelligence to bring its masses to a lethal point. This burning up of a
personal crisis in a public event, this collective attempt at personal
transfiguration, is not merely the case of the intellectual's trying
to save his soul while the common man tries to save his skin, for
the common man is enchanted by a utopian vision as much as
the solitary knight. The old fiction that common men revolt only
when their skin is threatened does not seem to hold up under
scrutiny.

Poverty and degeneration have never ceased to be what they were
before Marx's time, and what he did not want to admit they were
despite all his observations: factors contributing to servitude not to
revolution.[12]

The revolution comes not when oppression is greatest, but when
oppression has been relieved somewhat; it comes when the revolutionary can glimpse his chance and has the energy to seize it. The
revolution came in Ireland when the farmers were profiting, as

[12] Albert Camus, *The Rebel: An Essay on Man in Revolt* (New York, 1956), p.
214. See also Crane Brinton, *The Anatomy of Revolution*, p. 29f.

agricultural countries always do, from the war; it came when the farm boys, who were not bothered by conscription, were jealous of the heroes of 1916 and were looking for trouble. And even our own American Negro Revolution did not come when oppression was greatest, when the slightest mumble of complaint would bring instantaneous murder; it came at a time of improvement, when prosperity dramatized what the Negroes did not have, and liberal whites were displaying the symptom that Professor Brinton calls the failure in confidence of the ruling elite. The appearance of conscience and a divided consciousness in the men at the top is a signal for the men at the bottom, who by force of adversity are not troubled by such problems, to strike for their rights. The most violent Negro riots did not come in the South, nor did they come in rat-infested Harlem; they came in Los Angeles, where postwar society is basically pleasure-directed and culture is primarily a matter of commonly shared patterns of consumption—automobiles, sport clothes, supermarkets, shopping-centers, swimming pools, etc. —a culture of consumption far more visible to a Negro in Watts than to a Negro in Mississippi. Economics has its part in the explanation of the riot in Los Angeles, but it is not the stale, trite economics of oppression; it is the economics of excitement and the everpresent irrational, for hate has its reasons which the reason can never know. Imagination as well as economics plays its role in revolution. Charismatic men are often possessed by mythic images of themselves, but all this can be taken account of, and there is no need to return to Carlyle's view of history as the biographies of heroes. The unhappy aspect of the intellectual revolutionary as tragic hero is not that he is ideologically motivated while the masses are economically inspired, but that when the lust for power is lacking in his own search for salvation he tends to ignore it in the revolutionary forces. Once the revolution is accomplished, and power has to be consolidated, the solitary rebel, and the intellectual values that have made him what he is, are often the first things to be cast aside. When the liberal aristocrats had served their purpose, they were led to the guillotine; once the

Anglo-Irish Protestants had served their purpose, they were swept out of office and Catholic legislation was enacted. The second *Senaed Eireann* was not like the first.[13] The beginnings of this shift are often seen in the middle of the revolutionary process, for in the Gaelic League, Catholic, violent Pearse was the successor to Protestant, nonviolent Douglas Hyde. Perhaps in a similar manner militant Stokely Carmichael will become the successor to nonviolent Martin Luther King.

The nativistic movement is thus not a rare occurrence, but almost a part of a cross-cultural metabolic process. The messianic cults are spots of fertile decay that have appeared throughout history when civilization and community clash. The nativistic movement is a rejection of complexity, a "simplification through intensity"; but this kind of simplification is the day-to-day substance of our politics, whether it is the African hysteria in the United Nations, or our own American hysteria at "the communist conspiracy." Civilization can content the man of Empire, the builder of wonders, from the entrepreneur to the astronaut who today flies "to a flashier bauble yet," and the elite of a scientific-industrial technocracy may find outlets sufficient for their energies and imaginations; but the men of artistic, religious, or humanistic sympathies seem to find the faceless imagery of the abstract too terrifying. The voiceless language of mathematics does not speak to them; they want a terminology of you and me, and not a remorseless algebra of a and b.

We are still living in the midst of the disaffection for civilization proclaimed by the nineteenth-century poets and writers like Matthew Arnold, William Morris, and John Ruskin. In the nineteenth century, Matthew Arnold reached out for the culture of the Celt in the same way that many thinkers now reach out for the energy and culture of the Negro. And the Negro Revolution, like the Irish, has its literary movement. The early Yeats, following the path of Morris and Arnold, screamed revolution, and was wel-

13 See *The Senate Speeches of W. B. Yeats*, ed. Donald R. Pearce (London, 1961), p. 25.

comed into the better salons of British power and was thus rendered harmless as a revolutionary. James Baldwin, shouting execrations and anathema, is welcomed into the best Manhattan penthouses, where his hands are politely tied by having an ash tray placed in one hand and a martini in the other. If history is always new in content and texture, it can repeat itself in form and structure.

What a Yeats or an Ellison learns in the camp of the enemy is, of course, complexity. This knowledge of complexity disqualifies him for revolutionary action, for the revolutionary agents are the great simplifiers; they unqualifiedly turn away from the terror of complexity. The agents must be great simplifiers if they are to rise to the purity of heart that is to hate one thing.

The moderates by definition are not great haters, are not endowed with the effective blindness which keeps men like Robespierre and Lenin undistracted in their rise to power.[14]

History often repeats itself, but imagination must always be more flexible than factual knowledge to see that history never repeats a pattern in the same way. Empire and Community have clashed all through history, but they have not always become involved in the internal politics of the Empire, as they were in the case with Ireland and England. The liberals attempted to give Ireland a revolution by due process of law, but Carson's hysterical violence on the Right brought on Pearse's sacrificial violence on the Left. The tragedy of history is that neither Left nor Right expresses a way out. For the conservative-romantic, liberalism with its emphasis on economics, philosophical positivism, and sociological behaviorism seems to be "a labor in a fury of abhorrence," an attempt to purify humanity out of consciousness, to pretend that the next social reform or the next scientific triumph will forever rid us of the inefficient ugliness of ourselves; but for him, Evil cannot be effaced by razing a slum or passing a bill. Whether he speaks in the terms of Yeats's *Will* and *Mask* or Freud's *id* and

14 Crane Brinton, *The Anatomy of Revolution*, p. 153.

ego, he merely elaborates original sin and sees Evil as an inescapable part of the dualistic structure of existence.

If existence is consistently dualistic, life is consistently muddling its given terms. Oppositions are neat, but as A.E. has shown, they never stay put. In the fury of any passionate conflict, the struggling bodies, like the fighting cats and dogs of the comic strips, spin into one another's place. One would hold man for God, the other would hold men for Man. We may choose between forms of tyranny, but we never can escape the tyranny of form. Of course *we* never choose; only individuals do. History never makes up its mind, but like a man climbing a ladder, reaches up to grasp the Left that it may pull itself up to the Right, and with each seizure, it imagines that it has ascended to the stars.

A SELECTED BIBLIOGRAPHY

Alvarez, A. "A Talk with Robert Lowell," *Encounter*, XXIV (1965), 40.

Arnold, Matthew. *On the Study of Celtic Literature*. London, 1867.

Barry, Tom. *Guerilla Days in Ireland*. Dublin, 1949.

Blair, Rev. Hugh. *A Critical Dissertation on the Poems of Ossian*. Dublin, 1765.

Boyd, Ernest. *Ireland's Literary Renaissance*. London, 1922.

————, ed. *Standish O'Grady: Selected Essays and Passages*. Dublin, 1918.

Brinton, Crane. *The Anatomy of Revolution*. New York, 1956.

Campbell, Joseph. *The Hero with a Thousand Faces*. New York, 1949.

Camus, Albert. *The Rebel: An Essay on Man in Revolt*. New York, 1956.

Carleton, William. *Six Irish Tales*, ed. Anthony Cronin. London, 1962.

Cassirer, Ernst. *The Myth of the State*. New Haven, 1961.

Caulfield, Max. *The Easter Rebellion*. London, 1963.

Clarke, Austin. See *The Irish Statesman*, V (February 20, 1926), 739-40; also March 6, 1926, 798.

Colum, Padraic. *Arthur Griffith*. Dublin, 1959. The American edition is entitled *Ourselves Alone* and contains an introduction by Crane Brinton.

————, and E. J. O'Brien, eds. *Poems of the Irish Republican Brotherhood*. Boston, 1916.

Connolly, James. *Labour and Easter Week: A Selection of the Writings of James Connolly*, ed. Desmond Ryan. Dublin, 1949.

"Craoibhin Aoibhin" [Douglas Hyde]. "A Plea for the Irish Language,"
    Dublin University Review, (August 1886), 666.
Crozier, Brigadier-General. *Ireland For Ever*. London, 1932.
Curtis, Edmund. *A History of Ireland*. London, 1964.
Daly, Martin. [Stephen MacKenna]. "Memories of the Dead," Dublin,
    n.d. Pamphlet in National Library of Ireland.
Davitt, Michael. "Irish Conservatism and Its Outlooks," *Dublin Uni-
    versity Review* (September 1885), 105.
de Grazia, Sebastian. *The Political Community: A Study of Anomie*.
    Chicago, 1948.
Duffy, Sir Charles Gavan. *The Revival of Irish Literature and Other
    Addresses*. London, 1894.
————. *The Voice of the Nation, A Manual of Nationality*. Dublin, 1899.
Eglinton, John. *A Memoir of A.E.* London, 1937.
————. "Philosophy of the Celtic Movement," in *Anglo-Irish Essays*.
    Dublin, 1917.
————, with others. *Literary Ideals in Ireland*. Dublin, 1899.
Ellmann, Richard. *James Joyce*. New York, 1958.
Ferguson, Sir Samuel. *Congal, A Poem*. Dublin, 1872.
Flanagan, Thomas. *The Irish Novelists*. New York, 1959.
Flower, Robin. *The Irish Tradition*. Oxford, 1948.
Freud, Sigmund. *Civilization and Its Discontents*, trans. James Strachey.
    New York, 1961.
Gibbon, Monk, ed. *The Living Torch*. London, 1938. (Prose collection
    of A.E.'s works.)
Gleeson, James. *Bloody Sunday*. London, 1963.
Gogarty, Oliver St. John. "An Angelic Anarchist," *Colby Library Quar-
    terly*, IV (1955), 27-9.
Gonne, Maud. *A Servant of the Queen*. Dublin, 1950.
Gregory, Isabella Augusta, Lady. *Cuchulain of Muirthemne*. London,
    1902.
————, ed. *Ideals in Ireland*. London, 1901.
————. *Lady Gregory's Journals 1916–1930*. London, 1946.
————. *Poets and Dreamers*. London, 1903.
Griffith, Arthur. *Sinn Fein*, February 2, 1907.
Heisenberg, Werner. "Planck's Discovery and the Philosophical Prob-
    lems of Atomic Physics," in *On Modern Physics*, New York, 1962.
Higgins, F. R. See *The Irish Statesman*, V (February 20, 1926), 739-40.
Hone, Joseph. *W. B. Yeats 1865-1939*. London, 1962.
Horgan, J. J. *From Parnell to Pearse*. Dublin, 1948.

Howarth, Herbert. *The Irish Writers: Literature Under Parnell's Star.* London, 1958.

Huizinga, Johan. *Homo Ludens.* New York, 1955.

Hume, David. *History of Great Britain.* 7 vols., London, 1767.

Joyce, James. "The Day of the Rabblement," in *The Critical Writings of James Joyce,* ed. Ellsworth Mason and Richard Ellman. New York, 1959.

————. Review of Lady Gregory's *Poets and Dreamers. Dublin Daily Express* (March 26, 1903).

Kelleher, John V. "Matthew Arnold and the Celtic Revival," in *Perspectives of Criticism,* ed. Harry Levin. Cambridge, 1950.

Langer, Susanne. "Expressive Language and the Expressive Function of Poetry," in *On Expressive Language,* ed. Heinz Werner. Worcester, 1955.

Lanternari, Vittorio. *The Religions of the Oppressed: A Study of Modern Messianic Cults.* New York, 1963.

Larkin, Emmet. *James Larkin: 1876-1947, Irish Labour Leader.* Cambridge, 1965.

————. "Socialism and Catholicism in Ireland," *Church History,* XXXIII, 462-83.

————. "The Roman Catholic Hierarchy and the Fall of Parnell," *Victorian Studies,* IV (1961), 315-36.

Lynch, Diarmuid. *The I.R.B. and the 1916 Insurrection.* Cork, 1957.

Macardle, Dorothy. *The Irish Republic.* New York, 1965.

MacDonagh, Thomas. *The 1916 Poets,* ed. Desmond Ryan. Dublin, 1963.

————. *Poems by Thomas MacDonagh.* Introduction by James Stephens. Dublin, 1916.

————. *Literature in Ireland.* Dublin, 1916.

Macpherson, James. *Temora, An Ancient Epic Poem.* Dublin, 1763.

MacSweeney, P. M. *A Group of Nation Builders: Petrie, O'Donovan, and O'Curry.* Dublin, 1913.

Malins, Edward. "Yeats and the Easter Rising," Dolmen Press Yeats Centenary Paper No. 1. Dublin, 1965.

Martin, F. X. "Eoin MacNeill on the 1916 Rising," *Irish Historical Studies,* XII, 226-71.

————, ed. *The Irish Volunteers 1913-1915.* Dublin, 1963.

————. *The Howth Gun-Running.* Dublin, 1964.

McBrien, Peter. "Poets of the Insurrection III," *Studies,* V (1916), 536-49.

Mead, G. H. *The Social Psychology of G. H. Mead,* ed. A. Strauss. Chicago, 1952.

Mercier, Vivian. "Standish O'Grady," *Colby Library Quarterly,* IV, 286-91.

Moore, George. *Hail and Farewell.* 3 vols., New York, 1912-14.

Mosse, George. *The Crisis of German Ideology: Intellectual Origins of the Third Reich.* New York, 1964.

Nevin, Donal, ed. *1913: Jim Larkin and the Dublin Lock-Out.* Dublin, 1964.

O'Brien, Conor Cruise. *Parnell and His Party, 1880-1890.* Oxford, 1957.

O'Broin, Leon. *Dublin Castle and the 1916 Rising.* Dublin, 1966.

O'Casey, Sean. *Autobiographies.* 2 vols., London, 1963.

———. *Collected Plays.* 4 vols., London, 1963.

O'Cathasaigh, P. [Sean O'Casey]. *Story of the Irish Citizen Army.* Dublin, 1919.

O'Flaherty, Liam. See *The Irish Statesman,* V (February 20, 1926), 739-40. Also March 6, 1926, 798.

O'Grady, Hugh Art. *Standish James O'Grady, The Man and Writer: A Memoir by His Son.* Dublin, 1929.

O'Grady, Standish James. Editorial in his *All-Ireland Review,* April 19, 1902.

———. *History of Ireland: Heroic Period.* 2 vols., London, 1878, 1880.

———. "Irish Conservatism and Its Outlooks," *Dublin University Review,* (August 1885), 4.

———. *Standish O'Grady: Selected Essays and Passages,* ed. Ernest Boyd. Dublin, 1918.

O'Halloran, Sylvester. *Insula Sacra, or The General Utilities Arising from Some Permanent Foundation for the Preservation of Our Antient Annals.* Limerick, 1770.

———. *An Introduction to the Study of the History and Antiquities of Ireland.* Dublin, 1772.

O'Hegarty, P. S. *A History of Ireland Under the Act of Union.* London, 1952.

O'Malley, Ernie. *On Another Man's Wound.* London, 1961.

Orwell, George. "The Art of Donald McGill," in *A Collection of Essays,* New York, 1954.

Pakenham, Frank. *Peace by Ordeal.* Cork, 1951.

Pearse, Padraic H. *Collected Works: Plays, Stories, Poems.* Dublin, 1924.

———. *Collected Works: Political Writings and Speeches.* Dublin, 1924.

———. *Collected Works: Songs of the Irish Rebels and Three Lectures on Gaelic Topics.* Dublin, 1924.

———. *Collected Works: The Story of a Success.* Dublin, 1924.

Plunkett, Geraldine. "Joseph Plunkett: Origins and Background," *University Review,* National University of Ireland, I, 11.

————. "Joseph Plunkett's Diary of His Journey to Germany," *University Review,* National University of Ireland, I, 11.

Plunkett, Joseph Mary. *The 1916 Poets,* ed. Desmond Ryan. Dublin, 1963.

Popper, Karl R. *The Poverty of Historicism.* London, 1961.

Prichard, James. *The Eastern Origin of the Celtic Nations.* Oxford, 1831.

Renan, Ernest. *The Poetry of the Celtic Races and Other Essays.* London, 1896.

Russell, George William (A.E.) *The Candle of Vision.* London, 1918.

————. "The Future of Ireland and the Awakening of the Fires," *Irish Theosophist,* V (1897), 66.

————. "The Inner and the Outer Ireland." Pamphlet, National Library of Ireland, Dublin, 1921.

————. *The Interpreters.* London, 1922.

————. *The Irish Homestead,* XXIII (May 20, 1916), 305.

————. *Letters from A.E.,* ed. Alan Denson. London, 1961.

————. Letter to Ernest Boyd, June 7, 1916, as quoted in *Colby Library Quarterly,* IV (1955), 42.

————. *The National Being.* Dublin and London, 1916.

————. *Song and Its Fountains.* New York, 1932.

————. "Twenty-five Years of Irish Nationality," *Foreign Affairs,* (January 1929).

Ryan, Desmond, ed. *The 1916 Poets.* Dublin, 1963.

————. *The Rising.* Dublin, 1949.

Shaw, Francis, S.J. "The Background to the *Grammatic Celtica,*" in *Celtica,* III Zeuss Memorial Volume, ed. Myles Dillon. Dublin, 1956.

Sorokin, Pitrim. *Society, Culture, and Personality.* New York, 1962.

Stephens, James. *The Insurrection in Dublin.* Dublin and London, 1919.

Synge, J. M. *The Aran Islands and Other Writings,* ed. Robert Tracy. New York, 1962.

Talmon, J. R. *Political Messianism: Romantic Phase.* New York, 1960.

Taylor, John F. "The Language of the Outlaw," Pamphlet, National Library of Ireland, n.d.

Taylor, Rex. *Michael Collins.* London, 1958.

Thurneysen, Rudolph. "Why Do Germans Study Celtic Philology," *Studies: An Irish Quarterly Review,* XIX (1930), 21-32.

Toynbee, Arnold J. *A Study of History,* Somervell abridgment, 2 vols., New York, 1946, 1957.

Trevelyan, G. M. *British History in the Nineteenth Century and After.* New York, 1966.

Trotsky, Leon. *Literature and Revolution.* Ann Arbor, 1960.

Viereck, Peter. *Metapolitics: The Roots of the Nazi Mind.* New York, 1961.

White, Terence de Vere. Book review in the *Irish Times* (November 14, 1964), 8.

Whitehead, A. N. *Science and the Modern World.* New York, 1948.

Wilson, F. A. C. *Yeats's Iconography.* New York, 1960.

Windisch, Ernst. *Tain Bo Cuailgne.* Leipzig, 1905.

Yeats, W. B. *Autobiographies.* London, 1961.

――――. *Collected Plays.* New York, 1962.

――――. *Collected Poems.* New York, 1957.

――――. *Essays and Introductions.* New York, 1961.

――――. *Explorations.* New York, 1962.

――――. *Letters of W. B. Yeats,* ed. Allan Wade. London, 1954.

――――. *Mythologies.* New York, 1959.

――――. Introduction to *Oxford Book of Modern Verse.* Oxford, 1936.

――――. "The Poetry of Sir Samuel Ferguson," *Dublin University Review,* II (1886), 941.

――――. *The Senate Speeches of W. B. Yeats,* ed. Donald R. Pearce. London, 1961.

――――. *A Vision.* New York, 1961.

――――, with others. *Literary Ideals in Ireland.* Dublin, 1899.

――――, with others. "Tribute to Thomas Davis." Oxford, 1947.

ACKNOWLEDGMENTS

Any book coming at the end of one's formal education, as this one does, is very much the result of the work of others. The Dedication expresses my overwhelming obligations, but there are others whom it is fitting to remember. To Pomona College I owe the kind of tutorial education that allowed me to avoid the routines of pre-graduate-school training and range beyond "the English major" in an Honors program in anthropology, philosophy, and litera-ture. To Cornell University I owe the training that helped me focus that education upon a single event. To my former colleague, Professor Emmet Larkin, now of the University of Chicago, I owe the elimination from the manuscript of many historically naïve generalizations and outright blunders. To Dr. and Mrs. Tony Cunningham of Dublin, who opened their home to me and my family and contributed so much to our stay in Ireland, I wish to express my deepest gratitude. To the Woodrow Wilson National Fellowship Foundation I owe my graduate study at Cornell as well as my fellowship to Ireland. Finally, to my wife

I wish to express my gratitude for help with the labor of galleys and index, but most importantly of all, for *listening* to the book at every stage of its progress: by listening and commenting she helped me discover that there is a kind of jargon that thrives in ink but cannot survive in spoken air.

WILLIAM I. THOMPSON

Cambridge, Massachusetts
February 1967

INDEX

A NOTE ON THE LINDISFARNE ASSOCIATION

The Lindisfarne Association is an educational and cultural organization preparing the ground for the resacralization of culture. Specifically it upholds, within the natural diversity of a planetary epoch, the following four goals: the transformation of individual consciousness; the understanding of the inner harmony of the world's great religious traditions; the illumination of the spiritual dimensions of world order; and the creation of an ecologically and spiritually appropriate meta-industrial culture. Within this context, the Lindisfarne Press seeks to disseminate and make available materials conducive to such a culture of true values and creative of a new harmony in and between humanity, nature, and the divine. Its range therefore includes: anthropology, politics, economics, biology, psychology, theology, philosophy, metaphysics, architecture, ecology, poetry, and art. For information on programs and publications, please write: The Lindisfarne Press, R.D. 2, West Stockbridge, Mass. 01266.